STU

Martin Rowson is an a cartoonist whose work   regularly in the *Guardian*, the *Independent on Sunday*, the *Daily Mirror*, the *Scotsman*, the *Spectator*, the *Morning Star*, *Tribune*, *Index on Censorship* and *The New Humanist*. His previous publications include comic-book adaptations of The *Waste Land* and *Tristram Shandy*, and with Cape and Vintage a novel, *Snatches*, and a memoir, *Stuff*. *Fuck: The Human Odyssey* will be published by Cape in October 2008. He lives with his wife and their two teenage children in south-east London.

ALSO BY MARTIN ROWSON

MARTIN ROWSON

Stuff

VINTAGE BOOKS
London

Published by Vintage 2008

2 4 6 8 10 9 7 5 3 1

First published in Great Britain by Jonathan Cape in 2007

Vintage
Random House, 20 Vauxhall Bridge Road,
London SW1V 2SA

www.vintage-books.co.uk

Addresses for companies within The Random House Group Limited
can be found at: www.randomhouse.co.uk/offices.htm

The Random House Group Limited Reg. No. 954009

A CIP catalogue record for this book
is available from the British Library

ISBN 9780099502654

The Random House Group Limited supports The Forest Stewardship
Council (FSC), the leading international forest certification
organisation. All our titles that are printed on Greenpeace approved
FSC certified paper carry the FSC logo. Our paper procurement
policy can be found at www.rbooks.co.uk/environment

Printed in the UK by CPI Bookmarque, Croydon, CR0 4TD

For my parents – all of them – and, as always,
for Anna, Fred and Rose

We are such stuff
As dreams are made on, and our little life
Is rounded with a sleep.

The Tempest, Act 4, Scene 1

CONTENTS

I didn't tell my sister that I was writing this book until after I'd finished it. This failure on my part was entirely down to cowardice, as I wasn't at all sure how she'd respond to me appropriating stuff — whether memories of our shared childhood, or our shared parents, their lives and their deaths — that more properly belong to both of us. Luckily for me, she doesn't seem to have minded too much, but she made an interesting comment on what I'd written. She told me that she felt rather detached from the whole thing, as if she'd just reread a novel she hadn't read since childhood.

I like that. It is, after all, almost exactly what I was trying to achieve in writing the thing in the first place. And while everything in this book is true, that doesn't mean that it contains the whole truth, or even most of it. Nor is it necessarily the kind of truth you can depend on. It's just the truth that I remember, or remember being told from the well of other people's memories. To be more precise, it's the truth as I remember it. But having put my hands up to the charge that I might be an unreliable witness, as far as I know it's still all true.

And anyway, corroboration at this stage is hardly practical. Most of my original informants are now either dead or beyond reach. Where possible, however, I've done my best, and I need to thank all the people who either reminded me of things I'd forgotten or told me stuff I didn't know in the first place; I also need to acknowledge those other people who were there at the time and to whom I showed the manuscript, for them to approve as a more or less accurate record; and also a third group who were kind enough to say they wanted to read more.

So, in no particular order, my thanks to Dawne and Douglas Waters, Anna Clarke, Fred Rowson, Rose Rowson, Jane Rowson, Jan Dendy, Charlie Adley, William and Jane Dorrell, Joyce Bridgeman, Ann Buttimore, Madeleine Marsh, Geoffrey Goodman, Clive Brazier, Andrew Bufka, Will Self and Patrick Wildgust. Thanks also, as usual, to my redoubtable agent David Miller (who, in addition to everything else, came up with the title), and to Dan Franklin and everyone else at Cape who helped with the production of this book.

I've been particularly careful with names, as in part they form a central theme to *Stuff*. To this end, I've only changed one name. If any of the named individuals in the following pages have issues with what I've remembered and how I've recorded it, that's what we have law courts for.

Martin Rowson
Lewisham

Dream

One afternoon in Palermo, nine months after my father died and five months after my stepmother had died too, I had a strange dream. In the dream I was in my late parents' house. In real life my sister and I had sold the house about a week previously to the property developer who lived next door, although for £300,000 less than my father had latterly dreamed that it was worth. Prior to selling it, we'd spent months procrastinating over how to clear it of the accumulated stuff of several lifetimes, my own included. Eventually, finally, we'd cleared the place, and the last time I'd been there, or would ever be there, the house was quite empty and unlike I'd ever known it.

Now, in the dream, I was standing in what had been my father's workroom. This, for the previous twenty years or so, had occupied the extension built on to the back of the house in the 1960s. In its time this room, about thirty feet long and fifteen feet wide, had served as a playroom, then a dining room, then a depository for all the things that couldn't, or shouldn't, find a place anywhere else in the house. Then, in retirement, my father had systemised the chaos into his workroom, even though he had another one upstairs, in addition to the garage, the shed, two greenhouses and all available space in the house or outside whenever he needed or wanted it.

Along the end wall of the room was a stack of about a hundred little plastic drawers containing washers, screws, nuts, bolts, nails and all the other bits and bobs he'd picked up, often literally off the pavement, over many years. Beneath this was a table that had once been the base for a model railway set, never completed. In its new incarnation it was covered in more bits and bobs, fragments of old clocks, tools, oily rags, reused margarine tubs, magnifying glasses, strips of wood, pencils, keys and a lot else besides. Further into the room, for ten years up to his death, had stood an enormous doll's house which my father had started making for my daughter when she was four, and which he finished three months before he died, by which time my daughter was thirteen. Next to that was what had once been our dining-room table, acquired from our dead dentist's widow after my father sold our previous, rather beautifully ornate dining table. The dentist's widow's table had been covered in clamps, lathes, milling machines and other stuff, while behind it, against the south wall, had stood a huge industrial drill, more plastic drawers, some steel cupboards, an old chest of drawers on to the top of which, decades before, my father had bolted a huge vice. On the wall itself was a chart on how to build a turret clock. Above this, on the high windowsills of the small windows in the south wall, were stored old balances, broken electric clocks, empty whisky bottles whose shape or design had captured my father's fancy, old milk bottles kept for similar reasons, various unidentifiable pieces of scientific equipment and, as we'd discovered when we came to clear the room, nine bottles of horse's blood.

Further in still, about two-thirds of the way to the kitchen, was a cupboard which was meant to mark the borders of the workroom. It was filled with cardboard box files of photocopied sheets on clock and tool maintenance, company prospectuses, catalogues and similar pieces of ephemeral literature, along with more tools, lengths of wood, strips of metal, sheets of wood and metal, more mysterious scientific instruments, cans and jars of powerful corrosives and other liquids, a shoebox filled with little tins of enamel paint of the kind used to paint model aeroplanes, paintbrushes, wire brushes, sticks, probes and much else. Leaning against the side of this cupboard were more sheets of wood and metal (there were also cardboard boxes overflowing with wood and metal beneath the various tables further back in the room), while on the kitchen side of the cupboard were more cupboards, containing Tupperware, Pyrex and crockery. On this side there was also a fridge, one of three in the area, which never contained anything except cans of fizzy drinks and boxes of chocolates. On top of the fridge were bottles of sherry, beer and wine, unopened. Straddling the border between the workroom and the kitchen stood my father's lathe, a monster of a machine, in which, with potentially fatal results, he'd once caught his tie and only just managed to turn the biggest lathe off before his face hit its moving parts.

Set into the north wall of the room were three large picture windows, looking out on to the garden and the mulberry tree my father had grown from a cutting he'd stolen from the fellows' garden in his old Cambridge college. Beneath the windowsill, running almost the length of the room, were more drawers, cardboard this time, containing yet more neatly sorted tools, lengths of wire, old plugs, carrier bags, sections of hosepipe and so on. Between the windows, in the little available wall space, hung several clocks, including two cuckoo clocks which I never remember working. On the windowsill itself stood my stepmother's single attempt to colonise the space, this half-hearted intrusion taking the form of pots and pots of orchids, mother-in-law's tongue and African violets, many of which she'd grown herself from cuttings she'd acquired, furtively with a thumbnail, from gardens round the world. Several decades previously she'd used the same space to breed guppies. To the

3

west, at the end of the room, was the door into the conservatory, the foundations of which, following my father's careful and exact instructions, I'd built when I was a student.

Everything that could be removed had now gone, and in my dream I surveyed the empty room, feeling just as sad as I'd done when I'd seen it in reality a few days before. In my dream I turned away from the window and the garden in the thin afternoon autumnal sunlight and then saw with dismay and growing alarm that the room hadn't been emptied after all. There, against the south wall, was the chest of drawers with the vice on top, and next to it was the vast drill. I was alone in the house and I started panicking. Everything was meant to go; the place was meant to be empty; my cousin Paul, who handily enough works in waste disposal, had dumped two tons of stuff nobody else could conceivably want, and yet somehow or other the fool had left all these things behind and I had no hope of moving them on my own.

Then, in my dream, I saw a dik-dik, a small African antelope, trot out from behind the chest of drawers. I stared at the creature in disbelief. My parents never told me they had a pet dik-dik. They'd never even given a hint that they were secretly keeping this animal. Why would they have kept such a thing from me? Worse, what was I meant to do with it now? Why had they left no *instructions* on its needs or welfare? For God's sake, what did it *eat*? Was I expected to take it *home* with me? What kind of *bedding* did it require? As the dik-dik snuffled round my feet I was gripped with a terrible, growing fear and I started twisting round where I stood in wide-eyed, lip-chewing desperation and horror.

Then a part of my mind, closer to consciousness or less anchored in dreams, started shouting in my head.

'Martin!' the other part of me cried. 'This is the stupidest fucking dream you've ever had! Now wake up!'

Earlier, on the morning of my stepmother's funeral, shortly before waking, I had another dream. It had been my parents' habit, whenever we arranged to meet either at my house, or somewhere between mine and theirs, to phone me to establish exactly which train they should catch and precisely when they should arrive. These details would then be repeated several times for purposes of clarification, and it used to annoy the hell out of me. Worse, they'd recently discovered conference mode on the phone, so my father would make the call and then switch to speakerphone so we could have a three-way conversation, most of which, inevitably, was inaudible.

In my dream my parents were asking me exactly what time they should arrive at the crematorium, and whether they should bring anything with them, and if they should what precisely should it be, while I kept on trying to get a word in edgeways. I finally managed to blurt out, 'I'm sorry! You can't come! You're both dead!' and instantly woke up in tears.

Just after my father died I dreamed he phoned me on a mobile phone (I didn't own one at the time) but it was a bad line and I couldn't hear him properly, and then the phone started to fall to pieces in my hand.

After my stepmother died, I dreamed my father phoned me again. I asked him where he was and if I could speak to my stepmother. He told me that she hadn't arrived yet because she was still too angry.

Some months after the dream in Palermo, I dreamed I was in Stanmore, where my parents had lived and where I grew up.

I loathe Stanmore, and tend to go into a mild kind of psychic shock whenever I go there. This is not because my parents lived there, although when my daughter was younger every time we neared the end of the A41, having driven across

London and swung round the roundabout to head into Stanmore, she'd be violently sick. In fairness, this can be put down to her chronic predisposition to carsickness and because we'd invariably started the day with a full cooked English breakfast. This was because we could never quite depend on the quality of the lunch we could expect from my parents.

But the fount of my loathing is that I can remember what Stanmore used to be like in the early sixties when I was very small, even though it had been subsumed into the expanding London suburbs decades before. That expansion had been stopped by the war. In a field next to the roundabout where Rose was always sick stood some ruined brick Piranesian arches, which hinted at the picturesque but which were, in fact, all that had been built of a viaduct for an extension to the Northern Line that never happened. Despite a small amount of post-war reconstruction, much of Stanmore was still retarded in the 1930s, and much more was still like it must have been in the early years of the century, so that it didn't seem ridiculous, then, to carry on calling it a village.

In the high street, the 'Broadway', the pavement reared up in steep, sloping banks, beyond which stood low rows of small shops, like the newsagent's whose frontage, painted customs shed green, concaved in from the street, its windows punctuated with hatches and kiosks, with papers and periodicals hung by pegs from its guttering. Next to it was a fish-and-chip shop in a single-storey shack, and next to that was another single-storey building containing a greengrocer's which sold its wares off the top of upturned orange crates, draped with artificial greengrocer's grass, an instance of innocent fraud which captivated me when I was a child. Further down the street was a petrol station of a kind unrecognisable even a few years later. Three pumps, looking like Futurist chess pawns, huddled on the pavement, each with an anaconda of rubber hose snaking from its flank up the side of the late-Georgian terraced house behind it up to a kind of gibbet hinged on to the front of the building just below the first-floor windows, allowing the hoses to swing out over the street below. The pumps also had little glass epaulettes on their shoulders which would fill up with petrol.

True, the coming consumerist apocalypse was hinted at by a desultory stab at a primitive kind of supermarket opposite one of the three pubs in the village, but we still had ditches on either side of our road, stinky, dank little creeks which seemed to justify the street's designation as a lane.

Then, when I was about six (shortly after I'd watched elephants walk down the high street to advertise a circus which had pitched its tents nearby in Edgware) the chip shop burned down, so the opportunity was seized to raze all the shops around it, including two of the pubs, and commence the ruination of the place.

If I seem to be painting a sentimental picture of this north London suburb, it's only because of what came next. My early childhood was no more idyllic than anyone else's, and my memories are almost certainly heavily subjective, but it remains objectively true that the buildings that replaced what had been there before seemed almost deliberately cavalier in their disregard for their surroundings. Where the chip shop, the newsagent's, the greengrocer's and one of the pubs once were now stands a fantastically ugly ten-storey-high late-sixties block out of all proportion to the buildings around it. Significantly, it once housed the regional headquarters of the Department of the Environment.

In 1964 I sat on my mother's shoulders to watch Sir Alec Douglas-Home on a soapbox campaigning in the general election that year. He held his hustings in front of the Automobile Association's headquarters, an inoffensive 1930s building which the AA abandoned about twenty-five years ago for an enormous dark brown New Brutalist monstrosity built close by on the site where a toyshop had once been. This, in its turn, had been abandoned to a series of retailing ventures none of which ever seem to last long. In place of the original AA building is a branch of Sainsbury's, built in poor man's postmodernist style, all glass and steel and stupid sculptures by the hissing automatic doors, although most people tend to drive to Hatch End or Wealdstone to shop at the Waitrose or Tesco superstores designed, like all the others, to look like a short-sighted and rather dim prep-school teacher's idea of a Roman villa (plus clock tower). Which in its turn means that Stanmore has become more and more like a nightmarish film set out of *The Stepford Wives*, the shops existing purely to disguise the car parks built behind them.

But if the new shops are repulsive, the recent housing developments are far worse. Property prices in Stanmore started rising exponentially years ago, and although my father's dream of selling his house for a million quid was a bit ambitious, the house opposite sold for over a million shortly after he died. This has led to a mild crisis of supply and demand, which was resolved by the simple expedience of pulling down existing houses and building blocks of apartments in their place. On the site of the old RAF base (the Battle of Britain was directed from Bentley Priory just north of Stanmore on the borders with Bushey) there are now vast blockhouses, with little twiddly bits around the edges as a sop to domesticity, standing as a bizarre tribute to Stalinist baroque in north London. I presume they've been designed by a clique of Romanian architects who prospered under Ceauşescu building ticky-tacky palaces, but have since fled their enraged and emancipated tenants for a better life in the West, and luckily for them they've found plenty of clients who admire both their vision and their relative cheapness. Or maybe they're the property developers' wives' second cousins.

A couple of years before my parents died, a row of fairly decent mock-Tudor semis round the corner from them was knocked down and another blockhouse built in its place, filled with tiny apartments (my parents went snooping round the show flats and said many of the dining rooms didn't have windows). In my dream I was walking past this new development when, again, my mobile phone (which I didn't own) rang, and it was my father, telling me that he and my step-mother were now inhabiting, if not exactly living in, one of these flats. I ran into the building and up a fire escape and there they were, wondering how to fit all the stuff from the old house into their new home. They gave me a cup of tea and a biscuit, and said how they'd been on holiday, but had then decided to move in here as it was more manageable. Otherwise they were just pottering around as usual. I didn't want to ask them if they were dead or not, but I didn't have to, as they told me that they were, and so in the circumstances they'd thought it sensible to move. I started hyperventilating. 'But why didn't you *tell* me?'

Then I woke up.

When I was fourteen or fifteen, I would regularly have terrifying, apocalyptic dreams from which I'd wake shaken but relieved to be awake. I've now forgotten them all.

When I was a very small child I used to have the same dream over and over again. I would be standing on the edge of a vast forest of enormous trees, something like sequoias, with brown-grey trunks. They stood before me in a perfectly straight rank, spreading left and right into infinity. There was no space between the tree trunks to enter the forest, and behind me a formless, smooth plain stretched away into distant gloom. In the dream the point of view was looking downwards from high up in the trees, but below the line of foliage so that all that could be seen were the trunks themselves and the small figure of myself, simply standing looking at the trees. Nothing

9

else happened, but the dream was truly horrible. I last had that dream in my early twenties.

Later, I'd have other recurring dreams, in one of which I'd find myself in a public place having forgotten to put my shoes on so I was only wearing my socks. In another, all would appear to be normal until I realised that the sun was shining high in the sky at midnight or one or two in the morning. Both dreams unsettled me.

When I was about eighteen or nineteen I was at home in Stanmore, lying in bed in the middle of night, when I woke up and felt one of my teeth fall out. I immediately panicked, then woke up. Relieved that it was just a dream, I felt my teeth begin to fall out. Then I woke up. Then my teeth began to fall out. I woke up, got out of bed and went to the mirror above the sink in my bedroom and felt my front teeth, which came away in my fingers. Then I woke up. This continued through nine or ten levels of dream until I finally really woke up. My teeth were fine.

Around the same time I spent a whole night semi-conscious lying on top of my duvet, aware that my body was being picked to pieces molecule by molecule, but I suspect that this is because someone had dropped some acid into my drink at the party I'd been to the night before.

At the end of the Michaelmas term of my second year in Cambridge, when I had a rather nice set of rooms above hall, I was sleeping one afternoon, as I tended to do, when my dreams were intruded on by loud, incessantly rhythmic music. The person I'd been speaking to in my dream suddenly pulled out a knife and stabbed me through the heart. I woke up gibbering, the room filled with the music someone was playing in their room down the corridor. It was dark outside, the courtyards of the college dimly lit close to the ground and in a state of lingering terror I slunk off in search of someone to have a drink with.

In another recurring dream I dream that I can ride a bicycle, which I can't when I'm awake.

And since my mother died during an operation for a brain haemorrhage when I was ten, I've had the same dream every couple of years. She turns up out of the blue, and admits that she's been *hiding*. I had the dream in the months after my father and stepmother died, and last had it about a year after the dik-dik dream, in Istanbul. In the dream my mother appeared in black and white, despite the rest of the dream being in full colour. I find these dreams oddly comforting.

For the record, all mammals dream. I'm told that someone's actually done the research and observed and noted that all mammals go through a period of rapid eye movement in their sleep, which is when we enter the realm of dreams. To be slightly more precise, all mammals dream except for monotremes, the order of egg-laying mammals whose only extant members are the duck-billed platypus and the echidna, or spiny anteater. They don't dream, and consequently have very poor short-term memories. This means that duck-billed platypuses often forget how to swim while they're swimming, and start sinking until they remember again. Again for the record, the duck-billed platypus is the only mammal, or proto-mammal, who is poisonous. The male has a spur on his back foot with which he can stab poison into an enemy, although with his bad memory he sometimes gets confused during lovemaking. The only other mammal with any toxic organ is the polar bear, whose liver, because of his diet of fish and blubber, contains poisonous levels of iodine. Most polar bears who die naturally die of liver cancer. The polar bear's poisonous liver cannot, however, be considered as an adequate defence against enemies, as it's only poisonous if you eat it, and the polar bear has no natural predators.

Given the fact that all mammals dream, I'm disinclined to read too much into dreams. If polar bears twitch in their sleep at terrible dreams about their livers, what conclusions can you reasonably draw? What do dik-diks dream of, and at the end of the day does it make any difference?

I once read of a theory about dreams. It posits the idea that mammals, who evolved contemporaneously with the dinosaurs, evolved the capacity to dream as a defence mechanism. For countless millions of years dinosaurs occupied nearly all the available ecological niches, leaving the mammals no evolutionary room for manoeuvre, so they remained fixed in their initial condition as small, shrewlike creatures who were, moreover, nocturnal. This was because the dinosaurs needed sunlight to rouse them from their nightly torpor, so the shrew creatures had to feed at night to avoid the dinosaurs. During the daytime, while the dinosaurs prowled around looking for food, the shrew creatures had to keep very still and very quiet, and the best way to achieve this was for them to sleep. But because mammals have larger brains than members of the other taxa, the parts of the brain that remain unsleeping in order to keep the animal alive need something more. Hence dreams. In other words we dream simply and purely to keep us amused while we sleep, which we do in order to stop us getting eaten.

I doubt that this theory is right, but it will do for now.

And although many of my dreams still tend to take place in my parents' old house, my father visits my dreams less often. When he does, we usually just have a chat about nothing in particular. I'm always pleased to see him. But I know he's just a dream.

Time, then, to breathe some flesh into the ether.

Bones

But before we deal with the flesh, we shouldn't forget the bones.

There was a box of bones in my parents' loft, hidden away near the chimney breast on one of the dozens of dexion shelf units, nestling between a clock kit, some board games from the 1930s, old textbooks, OXO tins full of lead soldiers, most of whom were missing most of their limbs, rolls of gaudy 1970s wallpaper, more strange bits of scientific kit, specimen jars, lawn sprinklers and a very beautiful model of a Blackpool tram made by my Great-Uncle Jak, which I'd coveted since I was seven.

It's impossible to say whose bones they are, but it's likely they belonged to an Egyptian who died centuries ago. The peculiar conditions of the Sahara are perfect for the preparation of bones. Tiny creatures having long since devoured the flesh, the sands of the desert preserve the bones from further decay, and Egypt, under British suzerainty, was the source of almost all human skeletons for the teaching hospitals of London from the late nineteenth century until Egyptian independence, and my father would have taken receipt of the bones when he was a medical student at St Bartholomew's Hospital in the 1940s. Like everything else, he kept them.

The skull, however, is missing. Although my father promised it to me a couple of years before he died, it was nowhere to be found anywhere in the house. I doubt that he buried it in the garden, though if he had it would have added to an existing, if scattered, ossuary. In addition to the skeletons of two dogs and countless guinea pigs and hamsters and mice and goldfish, there was also half a pig's skull, buried in the shrubbery about halfway down the garden, in the shade of one of the ancient oak trees. I know this because I buried it there myself, after a power cut had defrosted everything in the freezer, including the jointed parts of a half-pig, split longitudinally, which my parents had bought on an impulse driving back to London from Cambridge one afternoon. Having dumped all the other ruined food from the freezer, my father and I decided to bury the pig's half-head in order to confuse future generations of archaeologists.

Incidentally, throughout the latter half of the nineteenth century, several thousand tons of powdered mummified Egyptian cats were strewn over suburban English gardens as fertiliser.

Then there are my father's own bones. When he was four he fell victim to Perthes' disease, first described independently in 1910 by Doctors Legg, Calvé and Perthes. Up to that point this disorder of the hip in children from around four to twelve years of age was assumed to be a symptom of tuberculosis of the bone, except that in that latter case all the victims of the disease died. Anomalously, a small proportion of the children thus diagnosed didn't die, so a new diagnosis was required. I don't know why Dr Perthes pulled rank over Doctors Legg and Calvé and got his name on the disease which totally incapacitated my father for a decade and effectively stole his childhood from him.

If you contract Perthes' disease, for reasons still unknown, there is a temporary loss of the blood supply to the femoral head, or the ball section of the joint where the femur attaches to the socket in the hip. This section of the bone then dies. In the late 1920s the treatment for this condition was to encase the child in plaster of Paris from the lower abdomen to halfway down the thigh, and wait for the blood supply to return and the bones to reossify, effectively fusing the top of the femur with the hip bone. This meant my father was bedridden from the age of four until about fourteen, and was transported around in a large pram. It also meant that, as an only child, he was transformed into a kind of doll for his mother to play with, and it didn't occur to anyone to teach him to read or write until he was ten or eleven. He didn't go to school until he was sixteen, although this didn't stop him from getting a place at Cambridge when he was nineteen. One consequence of his neglected education was that his spelling remained terrible and he always moved his lips when he was reading.

Another consequence was that he had a pronounced limp, as one leg was shorter than the other, and that he couldn't bend his left leg at the hip. In order to sit down, he required enough cushions to position his body in such a way as to accommodate this restriction on his movement, unless his leg could poke straight down at the side of the chair, in a kind of half-genuflection. I don't remember ever hearing him complain much about this, although it also meant that he couldn't run, so we never played sports together when I was a child. This might be a factor in what I'd like to believe is my innate contempt for competitive sports, all of which I continue to insist are inherently fascistic. I've passed the legacy down to my own children, and when he was about seven my son Fred said, out of nowhere in particular, 'I'm glad I've got a real daddy, and not some fat bald man who forces his children to play football in the park on Saturday mornings.'

By the time he reached his mid-fifties, the state of my

father's hip was threatening to result in severe arthritis, so he underwent elective surgery to have one of the first hip replacements. They sawed away the socket part of his hip and the top of his femur and replaced them with a titanium simulacrum, and he took to pedalling for twenty minutes every day on an exercise bike. Nobody really knew in the late 1970s how long a replacement hip would last, although my father and his metal hip outlived and outlasted four of his consultants, who were taken off by a series of heart attacks, car crashes or skiing accidents. And his legs were now the same length, although he continued to walk with a limp, albeit a *different* limp.

When I visited him in hospital after his operation, I asked to see the operation scar and commented that the surgeons had done a pretty poor job as the scar was distinctly jagged. This is the kind of conversation you have if you grow up in a medical household. He replied that it was fine by him, because when he was on the beach people would naturally assume that he'd survived an attack by a great white shark. Despite his disability he was always a keen swimmer, and his father had won medals for swimming in Manchester before the First World War.

When my sister and I went to the Co-op Funeral Directors in Wembley to arrange my father's funeral and cremation two days after he'd died, we remembered simultaneously that the titanium hip might pose complications in his incineration, or at the very least make it difficult to get the lid on the urn. The funeral director was unfazed, having clearly come across this kind of thing before, although she did ask if we wanted to keep the prosthesis, as some people apparently like to do. We declined.

It was only months later, in clearing the house, that I found a photograph of my father before he became ill. In sepia and grey, bleaching out towards faded ochre at the edge of the picture, a small boy in shorts is shouting joyously at the camera. It's the only photograph I've seen of him from his childhood where he isn't lying flat on his back, wrapped in blankets on a kind of wickerwork gurney, staring sullenly into posterity.

My father's bones are now ash. He died of a pulmonary embolism three days short of his eightieth birthday. My step-mother's ash too. She died of cancer two months after her eighty-third birthday. My mother died, following her brain haemorrhage, aged thirty-nine. Jon, who'd been my best friend when we were seventeen and at school, died of a brain tumour a week before his forty-first birthday. My old schoolteacher Butti, who probably taught me more than anyone else I've ever known, although he never actually taught me in a class-room, died of a heart attack refereeing a rugby match in his mid-fifties. My wife Anna's father Russell died on Christmas morning 1999 in Charing Cross Hospital, of sepsis following elective surgery, two days after his eightieth birthday.

All of them are now ash, largely thanks to my great-grand-father, my father's grandfather Frederick Gittings Rowson, a prosperous plumber and builder from Lytham who got the contract to plumb the gas pipes into the first legal cremato-rium in England after the proselytisers and advocates of crema-tion finally overcame their opponents' religious objections, mostly centring round the Christian dogma of physical resurrection of the body during the Final Days. These well-intentioned people correctly saw cremation as a solution to the population explosion of corpses in the cemeteries of Victorian England, and I remember my father telling me that the principal apostle of cremation served time in prison after he illegally burned his late wife's body in his back garden. I've seen my great-grandfather's grave in Lytham churchyard, which also contains the remains of both his wives. Given the size of the tomb, they must all three have been cremated, although I don't know whether or not they were burned by flames fuelled by gas passing through my great-grandfather's own handiwork.

My great-grandfather married twice, but only had one child, my grandfather. He married once, but only had one child, my father. My father married twice but only had one child, and there the blood line ended.

My brother Christopher George Edmund Rowson, with whom I share my two middle names – George from my mother's father, Edmund from my father's father – was born prematurely in Hampstead Hospital on 30 May 1955 and died on 14 June 1955 of bronchopneumonia exacerbated by congenital oesophageal atresia. His blocked oesophagus had been operated on but, like our mother, he didn't survive the operation. As I was born four years later, I obviously never knew Christopher, what little there was to know of him. I do know that my mother had been hospitalised before his birth, suffering from high blood pressure, and that the ward sister, who eventually became my stepmother, tried to teach my mother to knit in order to make her sit still. My mother was never very good at knitting, which is one reason why we found a knitting machine in my parents' loft when we were emptying the house. But although Christopher only left tiny bones, he clearly left a huge void in my parents' life, which is why they adopted my sister only a few short months later.

You can speculate endlessly about Christopher, from his background, our parents, all the thousands of genetic and environmental circumstances that could have made him what he might have been, in order to fill the void he left.

I know nothing at all about Naomi, beyond her name and that she was nearly adopted by my parents a couple of years after they'd adopted my sister, that her birth mother had given her up for adoption and consequently could legally know nothing more about her, and that she had a brain tumour, and so was not adopted by my parents. I can only assume she ended her short life still in the Mother and Baby Home, doubly motherless. But without her death, without her tiny bones, my parents would not have been my parents, would not have adopted me in 1959 and I'd now be someone completely different. I don't know, but I can guess that her tiny bones soon became ashes, but what happened to them next is beyond speculation.

The ashes from Christopher's tiny bones lay in a little urn at my parents' home for a few years until my father deposited them in a bank vault. My sister was then around three and I was as yet unborn. My father once told me that as he was handing over the wrapped package containing his son, my sister was sat on the counter in the bank, and as the bank clerk took Christopher's remains to put into safe keeping, he said, smiling at my sister but unaware of what he was holding, 'Do you want us to put this one in the vault too?'

Christopher stayed in the vault until my mother died, a day before his fourteenth birthday. They were then buried together for another thirty-six years before my father and stepmother joined them.

Formaldehyde

You don't have to become ashes when you die.

In Palermo, the day after I dreamed about the dik-dik, we went to the catacombs beneath the Capuchin convent where, following a rudimentary mummification, the more prominent members of Palerman society have been hung up on the walls in their Sunday best to await the Day of Judgement, a practice that continued until about a hundred years ago.

When I was twelve, on a visit to Rome, we visited the Carmelite church with its cellars filled with beautiful geometric patterns made out of the bones of dead monks. Passing yahoos down the years had written their names on some of the skulls piled up within reach.

I was fourteen when we went on a package tour to Bulgaria, which included a few days in Sofia when our party was bussed off to file past the preserved corpse of Georgi Dimitrov, joint founder of the Bulgarian Communist Party, former secretary general of the Comintern and first prime minister of Sovietised Bulgaria. He was also accused of complicity in the Reichstag fire, but defended himself so skilfully that he was acquitted. My grandmother, my father's mother, was on the trip with us, and was in the process at the time of graduating from a lifelong airheadedness into a more terminal senile dementia. According to her, Dimitrov winked at her. This was twenty-five years after he'd died, in Moscow, while undergoing 'medical treatment'.

It was one of Stalinism's more sinisterly kitsch traits to preserve the bodies of dead old men in glass cases, like Snow White. I was seventeen by the time I finally got to see Lenin in Moscow (something I'd dreamed of doing for years), although I remember my father telling me he'd actually seen Lenin and Stalin together, very shortly before Stalin was removed in the dead of night and dumped in a grave next to the Kremlin wall during Khrushchev's de-Stalinisation. Later, my parents saw Mao Zedong in Beijing, although they said he didn't look that great. Geopolitical considerations at the time of Mao's death had precluded the option of handing his body over to the skill of Soviet morticians, so he was, instead, rather inexpertly preserved by the Vietnamese. Four years later Vietnam and China were at war, although that was a sideshow to Vietnam's overthrow of China's client necrocratic Khmer Rouge government in Kampuchea/Cambodia, where the remains of millions of corpses are now preserved in piles of bones in special museums.

As a child I always felt a strange affinity with Lenin and the Soviet Union. I suppose this was because my father frequently mentioned that he was born the day before Lenin died. When I was about five or six I remember standing next to my father towards the bottom of the garden as he was making a low and narrow concrete border around the flower bed next to the raspberry canes. Further towards the end of the garden, this bed contained the bones of Mandy Moo-moo, our Scottie dog who was run over when I was about four. I was there to help my father by imbedding pebbles in beautiful patterns in the wet concrete after he'd poured it into the ad-hoc mould he'd made out of bits of old fence. The last day I was in my dead parents' house, I walked through the garden one final time, smoking the cigarette I'd never have smoked there while they were alive, and when I came to the little wall by the raspberries I could just about read my own name, spelt out in a sprinkle of little stones nearly forty years earlier. Before I set the pebbles, while my father was still trowelling in the knobbly gruel of just-mixed concrete, kneeling on the knee of his leg that wouldn't bend at the hip and wearing, as he almost always did when gardening or doing anything else, a jacket and tie, we were clearly having a political conversation of some kind, although all I now remember him saying is, 'What do you mean, boy, you've never heard of Marx?', to which I replied, rather tremulously, 'I know who Lenin is.'

A few years ago in the *London Review of Books* I read that the food writer Elizabeth David's auntie played the harp at Lenin's funeral. The review gave no other details, although it's worth mentioning that one of Lenin's pall-bearers was Vyacheslav Molotov, described by Trotsky as a desiccated calculating machine, mediocrity incarnate and the best filing clerk in Russia. Trotsky wasn't a pall-bearer because the other members of the Politburo, led by Stalin, rushed forward the date of the funeral and didn't tell Trotsky until it was too late for him to get back to Moscow in time. In 1980, when they went on holiday to Mexico City, I suggested to my parents that they pay a visit to Trotsky's old home in Coyoacán, where he was murdered in exile by a Stalinist agent who, on release from prison in 1960, went to Moscow to pick up his Order of Lenin before setting up shop as a television repair man in Prague, where he died in 1978. My stepmother spoke Spanish, and my parents told me they spent a pleasant morning in the old Trotsky house and compound talking in Spanish to a nice old chap who was almost certainly Trotsky's grandson. My stepmother came from that generation of lower-middle-class ex-colonials who evinced a kind of congenital deferential Toryism, although the political opinion which dominated most of her thinking was that they were all as bad as each other, but for years I had a nice photo of her standing in the dappled shadows of lush tropical trees next to Trotsky's tomb, which is emblazoned with the logo of the Fourth International.

Molotov outlived Trotsky by forty-six years, finally dying aged ninety-six in 1986, so he would have been thirty-one when my stepmother was born, thirty-four when my father was born and thirty-nine when my mother was born. My mother predeceased him by seventeen years.

In the constellations of Venn diagrams that provide the geometry for everybody's life, my father and I intersected with Lenin because we both saw his corpse. My father and step-mother intersected with Trotsky when they spent a morning with Trotsky's grandson, who was living with his grandfather when Trotsky was murdered with the ice pick by Ramon Mercador, the Stalinist agent who ended up fixing Czech tellies. My mother, intersecting with me, my father and my stepmother, therefore intersected at one remove with Lenin and also with Trotsky, albeit posthumously for both of them. There appears to be no obvious intersection or connection between any of us and Molotov.

In his senescence, Stalin began to plan his last purge, an atavistic nod to his tsarist predecessors, a great Red pogrom against Soviet Jews to mark his final degradation into the status of chthonic Russian nationalist despot. The tsars would regularly unleash the Black Hundreds, gangs of Christian thugs, into the shtetls of the Jewish Pale as a matter of policy, to cleanse Holy Russia of 'foreigners' and unbelievers while simulta-neously sanguinarily soaking the podzol of the steppe in a repulsive sacrament propitiating the foul doctrine of Blood and Soil. Stalin's earlier purges had been expedient, to exterminate his party rivals and thereafter terrorise the population into a cowed compliance to the inevitability of the triumph of his Historical Will. His valedictory purge, or the one he planned, was an intentional evocation of darker and even more cynical expedients, and didn't happen only because Stalin himself died in March 1953.

But his death came too late for some. Stalin had already forced his daughter Svetlana to divorce her Jewish husband, and Molotov to divorce his Jewish wife, who was thereafter arrested, although she was released and reunited with her husband after Stalin's death. But in addition to the institutionalised paranoia as policy Stalin had been operating since the early 1930s, as he grew older he became more personally paranoid. Marshal Zhukov, the victor of the Great Patriotic War and conqueror of Berlin, had been marginalised after the war in part because of the way he rode his horse during the victory parade in Red Square, with Stalin, horseless, looking on thin-eyed from the top of Lenin's mausoleum. Moreover, Stalin was increasingly suspicious of Molotov ever since he'd heard how Molotov, visiting the United Nations in New York, had then travelled to Washington in a train. Stalin imagined that, in the capitalist West, this would only have been possible if Molotov had bought his own train, which he could only afford to do if he'd been an American agent. There are persistent rumours that Stalin, after suffering a stroke at his dacha at Kuntsevo, was finally poisoned by Molotov.

Molotov, unlike many of his old comrades, succeeded in outliving Stalin, as did Lavrenti Beria, the head of Stalin's secret police. Beria didn't last for long though, as Molotov, Malenkov, Khrushchev, Bulganin and the rest of Stalin's gang moved quickly to prevent him from seizing power. He was accused of being an English spy and leading an anti-party faction and was summarily shot. One of the consequences of this was that the latest edition of the *Encyclopaedia Sovieticus*, almost ready for the printers, had to be revised at short notice and the lengthy entry on Beria replaced with a curiously long article on the Bering Straits.

After Khrushchev replaced Malenkov as General Secretary of the Communist Party, he cleared out most of the rest of the Stalinist Old Guard, although more benignly than Stalin would have done. Molotov was sent off as Soviet ambassador to Mongolia, departing on the same train as Malenkov, who'd been sent off to manage a power station in Siberia, and he repined in Ulan Bator until purged a few years later when the latest anti-party plot was uncovered. This time he was expelled from the Communist Party, although he was rehabilitated and his party card returned to him a couple of years before his death during Gorbachev's season in power.

In 1976 I went on a school trip to Moscow, Leningrad and Novgorod. We were meant to go to Kiev, but Sputnik, the youth division of Intourist, screwed up, so instead we spent three nights in Novgorod, which boasted several medieval churches (transported there from around Russia), in some of which Alexander Nevsky had once prayed, plus an elevator factory and a population who were all permanently drunk. This was during the great Brezhnev stagnation, although I'm told you can still step over comatose drunks lying on the pavements of Moscow in mid-morning, as I suppose you've always been able to. In Leningrad we were put up in a hotel normally reserved for the exclusive use of pissed Finns on weekend booze cruises to escape the prohibitive price of alcohol in their gloomy homeland of lakes and forests. I was in our room drinking vodka with about three or four other members of our party, plus our Komsomol guide Vadim, when a pissed middle-aged Finn burst into our room brandishing a half-empty bottle and shouting 'Viva Stalin!' I got unsteadily to my feet and shouted 'Viva Trotsky!' back at him, and we continued this dialogue in the corridor for a few minutes until other hands guided us back to our respective rooms. In central Moscow, wandering round on our own one evening we fell in with some Eritrean students from Lumumba University. A year or so later, after Mengistu had seized power from Haile Selassie in Ethiopia, the Soviet Union switched sides in Eritrea's long struggle for independence, and I can only suppose that my Eritrean friends didn't last much longer at Lumumba or, for that matter, anywhere else.

I returned from Leningrad with my guts teeming with a microscopic internal parasite called *gardia lamblia*, which I initially tried to poison with whisky. My father got very excited about this, compelled me to produce stool samples (I gagged over the toilet bowl as I collected them) and took them off for analysis at his laboratory in Gray's Inn Road. Forty per cent of Western tourists would return from Leningrad infested with these creatures, as a result of eating unwashed cucumbers. The same percentage now return in the same condition from St Petersburg.

When I was about nine my father got just as excited when I contracted Coxsackie virus, which causes a severe inflammation in the throat. It was only decades later that I discovered that this exotic-sounding disease is, in fact, named after a small town in upstate New York where the first outbreak occurred. Throughout my childhood my father was constantly taking throat swabs and blood samples from me. By and large, the throat swabs were worse than the bloodletting: I'd open my mouth, my father would tetchily tell me to open it wider, hold my tongue down with a spoon and poke a cotton bud down my throat, withdrawing it just before I either choked or threw up. For years and years, every time I had a slight respiratory infection he'd dose me up with a particular brand of a mild antibiotic which he must have received free and in bulk, so that by my mid-twenties, following each dose, I'd have a reaction which took the form of severe photosensitive conjunctivitis. When I was twelve, before we went to Rome and saw the skulls of the Carmelites, my father had heard that there was cholera in southern Italy, so inoculated the whole family. Unfortunately he gave me an adult dose. Soon I was bedridden with the dose of cholera he'd given me, and also with a raging temperature, delirium and strange, wakeful visions. When I was twenty-three, shortly after graduating from university and back at home marking time, I contracted chickenpox, which my father decided it would be wisest to sweat out of my system. When my temperature peaked at 104, I had wakeful visions then too, at which point my parents caved in to my repeated pleas that they call the GP, who pointed out that while my father's method of treatment was sound in itself, these days doctors tended to factor in patient comfort as well.

Not that my father ever claimed to have much of a bedside manner. He once told me how he still regretted being bullied into signing the Hippocratic oath. This was one reason why, soon after qualifying as a doctor, he moved into pathology, then virology. Once safely sequestered in medical research, he became part of an international scientific fraternity whose higher calling enfranchised its members beyond the hard political realities of the times. Which is how he came to be in the Soviet Union in 1958, 1962 and 1965.

When I was clearing my parents' house I found an old cardboard box in the loft containing postcards sent home from the Soviet Union. My father wasn't a great letter writer, but he'd send postcards to my mother, my sister and me from wherever he went on his international scientific jaunts. He sent me (I was three at the time) a picture postcard of Yuri

Gagarin and someone else, smiling as they read a newspaper. On the back he wrote: 'These two men are the causmanaughts.' As I've said, his spelling was never very good. The postcard finishes with 'We are having very good weather but I miss you all'.

I still have the Collins Russian phrasebook he bought for his first Soviet trip. I took it with me when I went to the Soviet Union, although the only phrases I succeeded in mastering were the Russian for 'hello', 'goodbye', 'please', 'thank you' and 'I don't speak Russian'. While I was there I discovered purely by accident that 'yob' is the Russian for 'fuck', and went through a stage, whenever I did a cartoon on a Russian or post-Soviet subject, of writing 'Fuck the Pope' in Cyrillic script on a building somewhere in the background of the cartoon. Only one of my employers, a Sunday paper in Dublin, ever noticed.

The phrase 'I don't speak Russian' came in useful during my trip, as the Moscow telephone exchange was so unreliable that I was constantly receiving phone calls from unknown Russians in my hotel room. My father told me that on his trips to the Soviet Union he would be frequently stopped by Muscovites in the street and asked directions. He assumed this was because the Western cut of his suit marked him down as a very senior apparatchik who was bound to know everything.

Among the other useful phrases in the book are 'May I offer you an English cigarette?', 'World Congress', 'Not a drop', 'Please let me have a hundred good-quality Russian cigarettes; one with mouthpieces and the other without', 'Russian tobacco is very good quality', 'I propose to take you to a shoe factory', 'Can we avail ourselves of the services of persons familiar with ironworks, tanneries, sawmills, machine-building plants, metallurgical works, oil refineries, sugar refineries, glassworks, iron foundries, chemical factories?', 'I am interested in farm machinery' and 'What fertilisers do you use on the collective farm?' I don't know if my father ever used any of these.

My childhood fascination with the Soviet Union must initially have been inspired by my father's trips there, which were strangely frequent given the circumstances of the times, and because of their strangeness tantalisingly exotic. The place itself, as I discovered later, was far from being exotic in a way most people, debauched by stranger, gaudier, further-away places, would now understand, but in the early 1960s the almost entirely unattainable and unbreachable otherness of the Soviet Union obsessed me. I had Soviet posters (of Moscow landmarks rather than Workers and Peasants) on my bedroom wall; I played with two ceramic-headed muzhik rag dolls brought back from the Soviet Union; in *The Man From U.N.C.L.E.* I always favoured Illya Kuryakin over Napoleon Solo, not (like my sister) because David McCallum was cuter than Robert Vaughn, but because Kuryakin was Russian; when I was about eight one of my school friends had a birthday party which entailed twenty-five small boys swarming over a golf course in Ruislip shooting cap guns at each other, dressed as spies, so I went as a Russian spy. But I wasn't simply a Russophile. I've met the type often since – usually slightly mad women who fall for the whole moody Russian soul number, and as they grow older and lonelier and madder spend more and more time holding thin, frail candles in dark and smelly Orthodox churches in Kensington. I was a *Sovietophile*, even though, as I got older, I became increasingly aware of the Soviet Union's many shortcomings. That was why, aged around twelve and after reading *Animal Farm* and *1984*, I switched my allegiance from Lenin to Trotsky, and painted one wall of my bedroom dark red over which I then painted an eight-foot-high silhouette of Trotsky's head in black gloss paint. I told someone I was a Trotskyite when I first arrived at my suburban public school, which was an insane thing to do in 1972 in Northwood given the political development, class background and general ignorance of my contemporaries. Then again, they also took the piss out of me because my voice had broken, so I could soon comfort myself with the realisation that what tormentors I had were just a bunch of boneheaded fascist retards.

But politics was only a small part of my Sovietophilia, just like it played only a small part in my decision, travelling on trains around Western Europe when I was nineteen and often discovering, too late in the circumstances, that there was no toilet paper, to wipe my arse with pages torn from Solzhenitsyn's *The First Circle*. The attraction of the Soviet Union was its otherness, its difference, its enticing obscurity and its power to emancipate little boys from the middle-class suburbs where they were growing up in a pastel-coloured 1960s dream of decent respectability against a backdrop of even more suffocatingly decent and respectable suburban villas from the 1930s. There was also its dangerous hints of treachery, anti-patriotism and the offer of an alternative to the system the grown-ups (or most of them) admired, endorsed and supported. In short, the main point about the Soviet Union was that it wasn't America.

My father had a fierce love for the films of Humphrey Bogart and the Marx Brothers, but had a curious dislike of America. The only part of sovereign United States territory he ever trod on was during a brief stopover in Alaska on his way to Japan in 1966. On virological business, or for pleasure in retirement, he went to Israel, India, Czechoslovakia, Hungary, Albania, Australia, China, the Norwegian Arctic Circle, Cuba, Finland, Holland, Hong Kong, Mexico, Latvia, the Soviet Union, Iceland, Greenland,

Italy, France, Turkey and many other places, but apart from Alaska the closest he ever got to the United States was visiting the Canadian side of the Niagara Falls. Something in this physical repulsion must have influenced me, and although I've been to the United States several times and loved the place, I remember being furiously anti-American as a child. I suspect that this was in part because I consumed a large amount of American TV, like a lot of other people of my generation, and unlike many of them, but like many others, I took an instinctive dislike to the vision of blond-haired, freckle-faced cutesy spunky childhood it peddled. I specifically remember watching an old movie on TV one afternoon when I was about eight, although I can't remember what it was called. The story was simple, about an American boy in Tokyo in the 1950s who somehow or other gets separated from his parents and is befriended by a little Japanese boy. The film's polemical purpose must have been to cement US-Japanese friendship in the aftermath of the Americans carbonising hundreds of thousands of Japanese citizens and then occupying their country, but even that didn't excuse one exchange when the nauseating Yank brat says to his Japanese buddy, 'You speak good English,' and gets the reply, 'No, I speak American.' I remember this enraging me at the time, for a mixture of reasons, including pedantry, a vague sense of English nationalism, a precocious distrust of banal propaganda and wanting to throw up at the fatuous sentimentalisation of such obvious and irredeemable lickspittling little shits.

So during the 1972 Olympic Games I cheered when the Soviet basketball team beat the American basketball team. I always gunned for Spassky against Fischer. In the film *The Billion Dollar Brain* the clever Russians beat the mad, maverick anti-communist Christian Americans in a beautiful reworking of the battle on the ice from Eisenstein's *Alexander Nevsky*, and I cheered again.

When I was nine we went to Helsinki for another international scientific meeting, and in my father's spare time visited a fortress island in the Gulf of Finland, about two miles offshore. On the island we wandered into an old art gallery, which was curated by a very old woman decked in pearls who started talking to us in heavily accented English. When my father mentioned Leningrad (I think he was asking if you could see it from the island), she sighed, clutched her breast and cried, 'I can never call it that. For me it will always be St Petersburg!' I remember finding this performance mannered, gauche and deeply irritating all at the same time.

When I was seven or eight, I was exploring a large old wardrobe in my parents' bedroom. It was a wonderful wardrobe, originally built for a colonial clientele as it was easily dismantled and then put back together again, and had delightful little secret compartments for everything you could imagine, including one drawer labelled 'Requisites'. On one of the shelves on the inside of the door I found a wad of roubles. Ever since then a very small part of me liked to pretend that my father was really and truly a Russian spy, and the same small part of me was ever so slightly disappointed that there wasn't a thickset stranger standing at the back of the crematorium at my father's funeral, in a fur cap and with snow on his boots, who'd leave without saying a word after dropping a small floral tribute, with no message, on the steps outside. It did, at least, start snowing heavily an hour or so after my father was cremated.

In 1983 I asked my father what he was going to do to mark the centenary of Karl Marx's death. We were standing in the back garden in Stanmore at the time, and I think we were pruning the mulberry tree he'd grown from the stolen cutting. He told me he was thinking of going to Highgate Cemetery so that Special Branch would take his photograph as they snapped the throng of commies. 'Then,' he continued, 'when the dear Russians invade they'll find my photograph on the Special Branch files, marked down as a dangerous Soviet sympathiser, make me Minister of Health and then I'll be able to lock up all the people I hate in mental hospitals.' It was the perfect answer.

And when our son Fred was born, as Anna was being cleaned up by the midwives and medical students, I was given the baby to hold and he started mewling quietly. To calm him I stuck my nose up against his fontanelle and started humming the first tune that came into my head, which happened to be the Soviet national anthem.

Three weeks or so later, back home, Anna was having a bath when Fred woke up crying. I didn't want to disturb Anna as she needed rest and relaxation more than Fred needed feeding, so I rocked him in one arm while, with some difficulty, using my free hand to shake my LP of the Red Army Choir singing the Soviet national anthem out of its sleeve on to the record-player turntable and then plonk the stylus into the grooves of the first track. As soon as the opening chords struck up Fred stopped crying and started smiling the most serene and beatific smile, his eyes glinting with fathomless joy as he stared over my shoulder into some distant, magical place.

Given half a chance I could have brainwashed him into being the perfect Manchurian Candidate for Gorbachev's reformed Soviet Union, except they closed the fucking place down when Fred was three.

As to Molotov, I never met him and nor did my father, although both of us could have done if we'd tried, I suppose, as he lived on and on in obscure retirement in Moscow. Still, by concluding the Molotov–Ribbentrop pact Molotov made possible the Nazi invasion of western Poland and Britain and France's subsequent declaration of war on Germany, an event which significantly affected the lives of my father, my mother and my stepmother, as we'll see, as well as adding exponentially to the volume of human ashes throughout Europe and the world.

By the way, the name given to the fabricated conspiracy which Stalin hoped to use as a pretext to unleash his valedictory progrom was 'The Doctors Plot'.

Distance

Distance lends enchantment to the view. I wrote this line in Gothic script, along with the next part of the couplet ('and robes the mountains with its azure hue', as it happens), above the window in our dining room, which looks out over Lewisham, and in particular on to the Citibank Building, a tall and slender office block abutting the multi-storey car park on top of Lewisham shopping centre. My purpose, obviously, was ironic, although on clear if windy days you can just glimpse kites flying in the distance on Blackheath.

Nonetheless, it's a truism. The allure of the Soviet Union was its distance, geographically, politically and culturally. Strangely, its growing historical distance seems to have detracted from its enchantment, and the current view is that Communist Russia, along with all its satellite or buffer states, was an unremitting hellhole, one vast and brutal gulag with absolutely no redeeming features whatsoever. In this view of history, the final liberation of the countries that made up the Soviet Union and the Eastern Bloc (and that 'k'-less geo-political formulation seems to have died along with the place itself) justifies all the hot parts of the Cold War – the neurotic obsession with security, the carnivalesque iconography of spies, the fetish of the Bomb and all those dead people who died in making the world safe from the threat of communism. We all know about Vietnam, and probably know something about Chile, where people were thrown from helicopters and musicians had their fingers broken in sports stadiums before being murdered; we probably remember something about Central America, the Contras, the Death Squads, the 'disappeared' in South American dictatorships, the torture chambers throughout the Free World which, for some reason or other, were an essential component in all those 'bulwarks against communism'. Nobody in what used to be called the 'Free World', I suspect, now remembers much about the million or so people killed in Indonesia in the 1960s as a result of the suppression of a communist insurrection. Instead, we remember all the people Pol Pot killed, while forgetting that most of them (like most of the victims of Stalin's early purges) were actually supporters of the regime who fell victim to the twisted, paranoid matrices thrown up by failed utopianism.

I'm not trying to get you to forgive the barbarity with which Stalin and his various heirs sought to create what Trotsky called 'the first truly human society'. But you can only look into the distance if you get some sense or other of perspective.

So I remember, when I was in my mid-twenties, having a drink with someone I'd been at university with, in a pub opposite the Earls Court Exhibition Centre where we'd just met for the first time in several years at a musical instrument fair (he was then, briefly, a member of a rather plummy New Romantic band called the Roaring Boys, manufactured by clever A & R men at CBS, and who shortly thereafter sank without trace). At the time it was a badge of Western journalistic machismo, almost a kind of initiation rite, for ambitious young reporters to sneak into Afghanistan and join up with the mujahideen, then fighting against the Russians and with the military and financial support of the West. A mutual acquaintance of ours had recently been the latest person to go off on this Richard Hannay jaunt on behalf of the *Sunday Times*, and my old university friend was recounting, second-hand, our friend's various hair-raising adventures. I listened politely, and then said that, all in all, I was probably on the side of the Red Army on this one. At least they allowed Afghani girls to go to school, and by and large didn't, when coming across a girls' school, rape and then murder its occupants. My university friend looked at me with a startlingly pure loathing and said he wanted to smash my face in, and I haven't seen him since. I do wonder, though, whether he now ever reflects how the Soviet Union was an effective bulwark against the murderous kinds of nationalism and theocratic extremism that have beset the world since its collapse. Probably not.

The distance works in other ways. In Berlin, next to the museum near the old Checkpoint Charlie, you can buy Soviet-era kitsch, in the form of little badges that, you're meant to imagine, once adorned the front of the furry hats worn by Russian soldiers patrolling the Berlin Wall. These, I suspect, are all freshly made by Kosovars and Uzbeks working illegally in sweatshops in blockhouse apartments in what used to be East Berlin, scratching a precarious living supplying the heritage industry.

Although when Anna and I stopped off in West Berlin on our honeymoon in April 1987, en route by train to Budapest, Vienna and then Venice, and we were walking in the Tiergarten one morning, we saw a jeep straight out of *The Third Man*, containing a British, French, Russian and American soldier patrolling the different zones of Berlin, still divided up and occupied by the former Allies forty-two years after the end of the Second World War. I remember thinking how ludicrous that jeep was, a little, slightly scuffed symbol of the absurdities of the stasis of the Cold War. I also remember saying to Anna how, even so, it was teetering on a kind of cultural brink, just about to tip from being evidence of the burden of History into being Heritage, with the horrors of the past neatly sanitised for day trippers and schoolchildren. There was no reason at the time to imagine that these patrols by representatives of the Four Powers wouldn't continue for another fifty years, by which time the antique uniforms and quaint old car would be as chilling as Changing the Guard at Buckingham Palace. The soldiers in the jeep would probably sell tea towels and clotted-cream fudge each time they stopped to pose for photographs with the tourists.

Later, we edged sideways through passport control into East Berlin and caught our train to Budapest. Luckily a Hungarian lutanist joined our carriage at Dresden and bought us both a sandwich and a cup of coffee, as earlier I'd been unable to exchange any Western currency with the sleeping car attendant in our carriage because (as he made clear in a subtle little mime) the colleague sitting next to him was a Stasi nark. Just as bad, for my purposes, his colleague in the next carriage along from ours didn't have enough East German marks to cover the smallest of my Western banknotes. We arrived in Budapest the next morning tired and dirty and hungry, and after I'd finally succeeded in exchanging some dollars for forints, while Anna was propositioned several times by the kind of person you'll generally find at any railway station anywhere in the world, we caught a taxi to our hotel.

The rain was falling like stair rods, and I've seldom seen a simile, or even a cliché, come up so fully to expectations. Through the grey murk we could just make out tall, grim and suitably totalitarian-looking buildings, as trams sloshed and roared at us out of the occluding downpour in our tinny little car. Then, on the car radio, Prokofiev's 'Dance of the Capulets' started booming out. Its 'Bom de bom de bom de bom, de bom de bom de bom bom!' provided an instant and perfect soundtrack to the grainy, grey-on-grey Cold War Le Carré movie we found ourselves in: familiar, and therefore suddenly safe and, in a strange way, cosy. It was, if you like, instant nostalgia for something which was still happening.

None of which detracts from the reality of life under communism. My father and I both laughed at the advice we received, on our separate trips to the Soviet Union, that the reason bathroom sinks in Russian hotels had no plugs was that the peoples of the Soviet Union prefer to wash in running water. I also laughed when I was a student and used to listen to Radio Moscow in the middle of the night, sitting up reading or writing an essay or drinking. I laughed specifically at the programme for Youth. Like most over-optimistic and small-minded ideologies, Soviet Communism placed a great faith in Youth, although in my experience once you get past the ranks of Horst Wessels, swots, Boy Scouts, sports stars, smiling Christians, collaborators and creeps who'd shop their parents for thought crimes just to get another badge and a sticky gold star on the big board at the end of the barracks, you'll find a mother-lode of resentment, rage and embarrassment. When I was on my school trip to Moscow in 1976, it was arranged that we meet some Soviet Youth in a restaurant. Most of them, like most of us, sat hunched up, mute and surly, having no more to say to us than we had to say to them. However, I clearly remember the unacknowledged but obvious leader of their group, a well-dressed young man with a neat haircut that would do its business just as well in the Pentagon, a Mormon college in Utah, at a Young Conservatives' dinner dance in

Guildford, a Rotarian's charity disco in Ruislip or, latterly, in a New Labour think tank. He, unlike most of the others, spoke English, but with the curious sing-song American twang that seems to have been a specifically Soviet phenomenon. I asked him if he was a member of Komsomol, the Communist Youth Organisation, to which he replied, 'Of course.' I then tried to pick a fight with him about Trotsky, but before we could get very far we had to sing folk songs to each other. I have a truly horrible feeling that our teacher made us sing 'Kumbaya'.

When, three years later, I was listening to the Youth programme on Radio Moscow, a similar, although female, sing-song Soviet-American voice was reading letters from 'the young people of Greyed Bridden' asking about life among the young people of the 'Serviette Yunyun', including one from Gary, in Hull, who had written to ask what the young people of the Soviet Union thought of punk music. 'Well, Gary,' I remember the announcer saying, 'to tell you the honest truth, they've never heard of it.'

At the same time, in England, it was fashionable among punky young people with a fondness for the Clash and similar bands to affect to wear kitsch Soviet badges. I gained a small amount of credibility by having some I'd actually been given in Moscow. Meanwhile, our Russian and Eastern European contemporaries were furtively listening to the Beatles on reel-to-reel tape recorders.

And of course I grew up, like everyone born between the end of the Second World War and 1990, under the shadow of the Bomb. I never really thought of it as much of a shadow, although I was an enthusiastic supporter of CND, but that was because it was a counter to all those young Tories with haircuts like my friend in Komsomol. I remember a huge CND march and rally in 1983, and the group behind us, marching in a neat rank (me and my friends were slouching, and nipping in and out of pubs along the route). They were clearly members of some lefty groupuscule, and had an interesting chant, slightly at variance to everyone else's. The first part was the same: 'One! Two! Three! Four! We Don't Want No Nuclear War!' but thereafter it changed to 'Five! Six! Seven! Eight! Protect the Soviet Workers' State!' Their policy, I suppose, was to get rid of Britain's nuclear weapons, leave NATO, join the Warsaw Pact and get them back again.

In the resurgence of CND most people, I suspect, were far more concerned with not dying, and other people not dying too at the instigation of their government, and were (and remain) profoundly irritated by abstract geopolitical principles that couldn't be bothered with body counts. That was, and still is, the abiding mindset of both the political elites and their doppelgängers among the equally sinister fantasists who sought and seek to replace them, like the groupuscule marching behind me in 1983 or their more pious successors. Although I personally never thought they'd Drop the Bomb, I recognised that it was essential that as many people as possible should shout very loudly that they shouldn't, particularly when countered with fatuous insults accusing us of being 'Unwitting Dupes of Moscow' (as opposed to Witting Dupes of Washington) or instructing us, in the infamous government pamphlet 'Protect and Survive', on how to place our dead loved ones in bin bags after a nuclear attack, and where to leave them. Faced with this, on top of riots, mass unemployment, an obsession with national security, the hounding and jailing of civil servants and the rest of the vile zeitgeist of the early 1980s, I could even just about stand hearing Susan Hampshire or Julie Christie singing 'Where Have All the Flowers Gone' at every single CND event I ever went to.

I was in my early twenties at this time. My father was in his late fifties, so maybe he didn't feel the same youthful thrill of the chase at ragging the Power as I did. Then again, I still do, and a few months after my father died in 2004 I received a letter from CND telling me that his subscription was due for renewal.

I was in my early thirties when the Soviet Union collapsed, so for my entire life up until then seeing a Russian was really rather exciting, although White Russians didn't count. Later exiles and refugees counted to a certain extent, like the artist another university friend married who said on her application form seeking permission to leave the Soviet Union that she couldn't possibly live in a country where you couldn't easily buy tampons. Another Russian friend left the Soviet Union to go to Israel, but left there for London as soon as he could. During Gorbachev's period of reform, his family kept writing to him to say that now things were relaxing he should visit them. He replied that, as he regularly broadcast on the BBC Russian Service, he'd obviously be arrested immediately he arrived on Russian soil. Things relaxed more, but still he insisted it was too dangerous for him to visit, until finally the Communist State collapsed and his family came to London to visit him, driving him crazy as they dragged him on endless shopping trips down Tottenham Court Road buying electrical goods. This suggests that geopolitical and ideological considerations were not perhaps the only factors in play.

These days most of the distance has gone. I never seem to be able to board a train from Charing Cross to Lewisham without there being at least two or three Russians on board, either yelling at the tops of their voices and laden with bags of shopping, none of it food, or sullen skinheads who, I always assume, are either gangsters' gunsels, neo-Nazis or gay. By and large I'm pleased, if hardly excited, to see them. But they've lost something of their exotic potency, something of that magical difference which, despite my selfish subjectivity, they're probably better off without, even though losing the Cold War and winning their freedom meant a decade of penury governed by gangsters before Russia started its return to a kind of twenty-first century, semi-democratic tsarism.

Then I look again at the postcards my father sent home from Moscow in 1962, and the distance starts to work its enchantment again. It's not just his handwriting or his untrustworthy spelling, or the instructions he wrote to me, aged three, on the postcard of the cosmonauts. 'Remind [my mother] to keep all the stamps & to water my vine.' Now that he's dead I can't help but find a deeply affecting poignancy in the banality of his messages: 'This morning I went to the Exhibition of Economic Achievements which is most interesting. This evening it is raining & I have had dinner in the Hotel'; 'I have just returned from an evening trip on the Moscow Canal. They have some very nice boats. You can have dinner and watch the doings on the way.' But the postcards enchant me from their distance in time and place for more reasons than just personal or emotional ones. Partly it's the stamps, special editions marking the forty-fifth anniversary of the October Revolution, with pictures of the triumph of Soviet Sport, with cyclists and ski-jumpers on the two-kopek stamps, people playing volleyball on the four-kopek stamps, and the ten- and twelve-kopek stamps showing a rowing eight and a goalkeeper leaping diagonally across the stamp to save a goal, a stylised Soviet sun shining brilliantly out of the top right-hand corner.

My enchantment is nothing to do with sport. As I've said, I abominate sport, particularly in its totalitarian kit, with all that Youth smiling and smiling with clean, blank, idiotic faces as they march round the stadium waving flowers at the crowd at the latest Spartakiad. It's to do with the colours.

They haven't faded, as these cards were stored away from sunlight in an envelope for decades. But the colours aren't quite right, and nor are they in the pictures on the obverse side of the postcards. The flesh tints on the cosmonauts' faces are a fraction too pink and sienna to be quite believable, the sky behind them too blue; in the postcard of Red Square the sky, conversely, isn't blue enough, while the red brick of the GUM department store (where they were still using abacuses when I went there in 1976) is just that wrong shade of terracotta and the shadows on the Kremlin wall are too deep, too dark and too crisp to be precisely of this world. And the pale cream of the Hotel Ukraine, where my father stayed and had his dinner, has a blurred yet uniform quality which gives it a strangely ethereal quality. The last postcard is of an Aeroflot twin propeller airliner, CCCP-M960 painted on its flanks, hanging in front of a blotchy, botched cloud-scape of a grey, white and cerulean that's never quite existed, or at least ever been truly seen. My father must have been in a rush when he sent this to my sister, as all he's written on the back is her name and address, the words 'Hotel Ukraine, Moscow, 22.7.62' and 'Love . . .' and then his signature.

Since its collapse, it's been generally accepted that the Soviet Union was such a disaster of malevolence and incompetence that these colours, skewed minutely but perceptibly into their different if parallel spectrum, must be as they are because of the pitiful shortcomings of Soviet photography and photo-graphic reproduction, even though my sister and I now possess several Soviet cameras my father returned home with in the early 1960s which put his Western cameras, of the same vintage, to shame. Or maybe their apparent artificiality mirrors the entire artifice of the face the Soviet Union presented to the rest of the world, the shiny if increasingly tatty façade disguising the wretchedness and bankruptcy behind.

Maybe.

Maybe a truer picture, albeit an aural one, is painted by a recording we have of Sviatoslav Richter playing Moussorgsky's *Pictures at an Exhibition* in Sofia in February 1959. I love this recording, partly for the music, but mostly for what it evokes. Each chord of the Great Gate of Kiev plinks and then thunders round the dimly yet overlit Great Hall of the People I can see in my mind's eye. Beyond the music you can hear coughs and snuffles of an audience, grubby and underfed, wrapped up against the cold and the Cold War, while the front row is filled with cabbage-faced, melon-headed party stooges in their baggy suits, shifting with boredom and impatience and constantly sneaking a look at their wristwatches, which don't really work. In a grand antechamber, later, there'll be a reception of smoked meat and vodka for the stooges while the rest of the audience blow their noses waiting for a tram home in a blizzard, and Richter will be whisked away in a party car through streets emptied by the fraying imperatives of history.

The concert was recorded in the month I was born.

But I still remember with a kind of contrarian pleasure how, when I was eleven or twelve, I'd take a diversion on the way home from school in Harrow to the corner of the high street where, opposite a bank, was an unmanned and unguarded box containing free copies of *Soviet Weekly*, a propaganda sheet in full colour, filled with photographs of Soviet achievements in industry, art, sport, agriculture and space exploration. The colour in the photographs was similar, if not identical, to that on the postcards; the blue, again, was slightly too blue; the green of the steppe a hint too blue too, the flesh tint also a hint too pink and sienna to be precisely human.

45

However, the shots of interiors – of ministries, arts complexes, factories, canteens and Soviet show homes – were, as I discovered a few years later, entirely accurate. Even into the mid-nineties, after it was all over, there were hotel rooms in what had been Eastern but was now Central Europe where the corporate style of the German hotel chains that had bought them up had yet to rip out the retarded sixties Soviet chic that shrieked out of *Soviet Weekly* and, in an earlier style, out from my father's postcards; that odd amalgam of veneer, Formica, plastic and steel, the overall colour a mauvish brown with redemptive rectangles of pastel blue or brownish yellow, with a low black ceiling, frosted glass in the lowly set wall lamps, the whole thing suggestive of a distinctly Scandinavian modernity that had lost its vital spark as it moved, too slowly, eastwards. There was usually a plastic chandelier not far away.

The thing is, that's the aesthetic that, at several removes, informed my parents' house from the 1970s until they died. The places I visited in the Soviet Union when I was seventeen weren't that much different from Harrow a few years previously, where the interior decor lingered, as it always does, for a few years more.

Those colours, not quite right, a little off-kilter from how we normally think we see reality, too pale or too brash, are how I remember the colours of my childhood.

And I'd catch the bus home from Harrow to travel the short distance of a few miles to Stanmore reading *Soviet Weekly*, holding it conspicuously and provocatively in front of my face to annoy the housewives.

Colours

The colours changed. There's a pale, pale speckled blue that I associate with my early childhood, along with a pale, yellowish off-white. This, by and large, was the colour of the kitchen in my parents' house in Stanmore. There was a kitchen unit of an early utilitarian kind, with a cupboard for saucepans and drawers for cutlery and gingham or white tea towels, with a blue stripe at either end. Its top was blue, as were its plastic door and drawer handles, but of a deeper hue. This piece of furniture survived all my parents, having been exiled to the garage to house yet more tools when the new kitchen was installed in 1984, for more money than my father had originally spent on buying the whole house twenty-six years earlier. My cousin finally smashed it up and dumped it with all the other rubbish.

The stove was also off-white. It had an eye-level grill, which I remember catching fire one evening when my mother and I were out picking up my father from Stanmore Station. Its four gas hobs would light, with the aid of a match, with a satisfying woof. At its side was an odd kind of flame-thrower attachment, attached by a flexible pipe, wrapped in fabric, to the body of the stove. You'd squeeze the trigger on the thing to light it from one of the hobs (which you'd already lit with a match), so you could then light the eye-level grill. Above the grill was a useful rack to dry or warm your plates on, unless the grill was on. In that case they'd get red hot, and if you left something inflammable up there it would catch fire, as my parents found out. The whole thing, in retrospect, seems to have been both highly functional and singularly stupid in design. I remember it as symbolising the unambitious prosperity of the times.

There was also a Hoover twin-tub washing machine and spin dryer, also off-white. That spin dryer was a wonderful thing, triggered by closing the blue metal lid embossed with the Hoover logo. The drum beneath would then start spinning faster and faster until you opened the lid again, when it would slowly slow down in great whooshing loops of noise. I clearly remember lying in my bedroom above the kitchen one afternoon, having been sent to bed by my mother for some now forgotten crime, and hearing the spin dryer: it went 'Voooom-vooom-voom-vom-vom-vomvom-vomvomvomvomvomvmvmvmvmvmvm-vmvmvmvmvm-vmvmvomvomvoomvooom-vooom-voooom-vooooooooom-vooooooooooom-vump', a sound I found enormously comforting.

I'd hear other noises in bed. At night, in summer, I could never quite tell if the slurred susurrations I could hear from the sitting room were the sound of one or other of my parents drawing the curtains (although I now remember that it must have been my mother – my father didn't believe in closing curtains, saying he had nothing to hide) or the sound of distant applause on the television set.

Later, if I was awake, I'd hear my parents going to the bathroom or the separate lavatory, which was next to my room, and one brick's thickness from my head. My night-times were filled with the sounds of pipes flowing and cisterns filling and emptying with a soft roaring. Usually I'd awake to hear the same reassuring symphony of sounds.

When we got central heating, which was about the time the extension was built on the back of the house where my father ended up keeping all his tools and where I dreamed I saw the dik-dik, there was a new noise that terrified me for years. Just outside my room, beneath the floorboards, there was a pipe going to the airing cupboard which heated up and cooled down as the central heating came on and went off. In so doing it also expanded the wooden board above it, which would start to click, slowly at first, and then at closer but still irregular intervals, until it started to contract in the same way. It was, I suppose, something like the Chinese water torture, or the tactic of the North Vietnamese Army who realised they could completely demoralise American troops by firing blank artillery shells at irregular intervals all night long, stopping their enemies from getting a good night's sleep. Later, the particular floorboard had got so warped it always creaked and squeaked in a particular way whenever anyone stood on it. I could tell who was stepping on it anyway, lying awake, listening for the footfalls.

Because of his leg and his limp, my father's footfall was the most recognisable, and was usually the first I'd hear in the morning as he came down the landing to have a shit in the upstairs lavatory. Like Tristram Shandy said of his father, Walter, he was the most regular man in everything that he ever did that Tristram ever knew, and this was certainly true of my father and his bowels. Years later, when I was in my late teens, my father would boil up saucepans full of porridge every Sunday morning and bring a bowl of it to me in bed at around eight thirty, the better to get some roughage inside me. By the time I woke up properly some hours later, it would have congealed into a cold, solid, rubbery lump, which I'd eat anyway so as not to hurt his feelings. It took me about eighteen months to build up sufficient callousness and ingratitude to tell him that I didn't want his porridge, at which point my stepmother admitted that her porridge gave her crippling indigestion all day long. My father switched to eating bran instead, for what good it ultimately did him.

The central heating changed the kitchen. I can't remember what was there before, but dominating it throughout my childhood was a massive oil-fired boiler, again off-white with a blue top. In front of it stood an old metal fireguard with a strip of brass running along the top of its plaited mesh. I last saw it, still rusting behind the shed, the last day I walked round my parents' garden.

But the central heating introduced a smell into my life I still find irresistibly seductive. I don't remember the central heating ever being turned on much before Christmas, though I suppose it must have been, but I always associate the smell of dust gently burning off the freshly hot metal of recently heated-up radiators with Christmas, darkness outside, a protectively comforting warmth inside, and all of it summons up and summarises my childhood up to the age of ten.

There were other colours from this period which I can see quite clearly in the kaleidoscope of my memory. Some of them are bright, primary colours, others are a softish beige, like the curtains, or the old television we were given by our next-door neighbour, Edie, which I watched Kennedy's funeral on when I must have been about four and three-quarters. Then there was the equally soft, dull, dark grass-green carpet in the sitting room, the Indian yellow of the checkered fabric on the three-piece suite, which was old then but managed to survive several more upholsterings for another three decades. There was the grey to black slush, churned, frozen and refrozen on the side of the road during the winter of early 1963, which I remember as being, oxymoronically, both hard and soft, crunchy and smooth, like cold halva. There were other browns, in the panelling in the downstairs hall running up the outside of the stairwell, or brass or gilt tarnished to umber on the metal light switches, or the deeper brownness of all the doors in the house, except for the ones painted white in the kitchen, which were, of course, off-white.

I can remember the colour of sheets and blankets, or great big cream-yellow Bakelite wirelesses, the colour of the insides of the old smoking carriages you used to get on the Underground, with plastic dials and knobs with serrated rims so you could get a better grip tuning from Radio Luxembourg to the Light Programme to the Home Service and onwards to Hilversum, once the thing had warmed up. There was also an early transistor radio, sheathed in a spongy, faux-leather light blue plastic case, with the same tooth-edged dial, which we listened to in the bath, something else which was off-white. My memory of listening to *Music While You Work* in the bath must come from when I was very small, as they broadcast that in the middle of the morning. A clearer memory is of *Sing Something Simple* on a Sunday evening, and an attached memory that even then I recognised there was something infinitely creepy about the Mike Sammes Singers singing 'Michael, Row the Boat Ashore' accompanied by an accordion. I preferred the precise colour of the light cast in the bathroom by the electric bulb, encased in a glass bowl through which, opaquely, you could see the dead bodies of what I always thought must have been bees, although they were almost certainly dead bluebottles. The frosted glass lent the corpses a charmingly fuzzy dark incoherence, as they did to the other dead insects in the light fitting in the downstairs loo.

Then there was the old gas fire in my parents' bedroom, which I remember back then as being a room filled with speckled light rushing out through the holes in the translucent, yellowy-white lampshades hanging from the ceiling and on the bedside tables, next to and thus intensifying the ivory glow from another great big cream-yellow Bakelite wireless. The gas fire was nearly as wonderful as the Hoover twin-tub washing machine. Its gas jets would heat up the ceramic griddles behind the wire mesh into pools of glowing heat, but best of all was a truly weird accessory above the fire itself, but integral to it, where two little doors would open with a clunk and some strange bit of kit, for holding a kettle or heating a samovar and stacking toast folded out with another clunk. I remember being enchanted by those little doors and what could possibly lie behind them, once you'd shrunk yourself down and negotiated the tea/samovar/toast rack-thing portcullis.

But I think my favourite colour from my early childhood, which I still find almost overwhelmingly evocative of that time, is that transient, palish cerise of neon street lights just as they come on, but before they've properly warmed up into their mature orangey yellow. For whatever reason, I associate this colour with sitting in the back of the car (which was a maroon Austin A40: maroon is another colour I associate with the early 1960s; our later Austin A40s were always pale blue). My mother is driving, though who knows where, and behind her, between her and the driver's seat, are the thick square cushions my father was compelled to sit on when he drove in order to accommodate his leg. Outside, the leafless, spindly outer branches of nearby trees are lit sideways or from beneath in the early-evening gloom, and everything everywhere is basically all right.

As I said, the colours changed. After I went to school, I remember the colours being harsher, but also everything being grey, that particular dappled mix of Payne's grey, Prussian blue and lamp black and titanium white, thinned to a smear, that typifies the pavements of Victorian London's outer suburbs after rain. Another grey was the grey of the asphalt in the playground, an amalgam of tar and little pebbles, which always seemed to me to have been designed specifically to rip the skin and flesh off small children's knees and palms. My short trousers were grey, my shirt was a soft cotton grey thing which no schoolchild appears to have worn since 1966. The sky was grey, as I remember it. The books were grey, the food was grey too, and the only point of colour was a vast, rather bad painting in the annexe dining room where the smallest children ate their grey lunch. It was brown and dirty orange, and depicted a man raking up fallen leaves for a slowly burning, smoky bonfire. I remember its details clearly, so it obviously did its business as 'Art', successfully conjuring up, with its broad, bad brushstrokes, the wistful melancholy of autumn and, beyond that, a general air of transience, decay, ageing and a mawkish suggestion of final mortality. Whether or not these are emotions which should be engendered in five-year-old boys is another question entirely.

The other colours I can see are ones that I never saw myself, or saw second-hand, filtered through other people's perception, or ones that I've imagined, or transposed from elsewhere on to scenes I never witnessed. These are the colours of my parents' childhoods: mahogany, gold, dirty blue-grey, dirtier blue-brown, feeble yellow, black, charcoal black, coal black, umber tinged with deep yellow, bright blue, pink, deep sky blue, blinding scarlet, vivid, lush green, chocolate brown, violet tinging towards a deeper, darker purple and then, once more, into black. And white against cream against grey and then into an unfocused sepia blur. When I imagine their childhoods, that's what I see, though I'm not entirely sure why.

Childhood

My mother was born in Mitcham, in the southerly reaches of the London sprawl, on 7 October 1929. She was the third of five daughters, and was born at 5 Mortimer Road, the home of her parents, Eva Jessie Bovill (née Stapel) and George Raphael Buick Bovill, and her older sisters, Charm and Jean. Her younger sisters, Dawne and Penny, were born later. My father always referred to them as the Bovrils.

I've stated these facts so boldly because I have nothing else to work on beyond her birth certificate. I never visited Mortimer Road, which the family had moved on from years before I was born. Nor did I ever visit any of her other various homes, except the one I grew up in with her. After Mitcham, the Bovill family lived variously in Carshalton, a guest house they ran in Westcliff in Whitstable and a further house in Whitstable called 'Beggar's Roost', where her parents were living when they died, years after my mother's death. I never saw any of these places. I'm only aware of ever seeing my grandfather, George, once, and that was in the garden at Stanmore, next to the old white wooden greenhouse, after my mother's funeral. I have no memory at all of ever seeing my grandmother.

My father was born in Blackpool, a mile or so inland from the North Shore and on the way to Fleetwood, on 20 January 1924. He was the first and only child of Gwendoline May Rowson (née Knight) and Edmund Rowson. He, too, was born at home, at 'Linwood', which was another name for 16 Gosforth Road. I got to know this house far, far too well, first when I was seven, and then, frequently, after my mother died when I was ten.

So, obviously, after an initial period of never seeing my paternal grandmother, I saw a great deal of her. Although I never saw the inside of my grandmother's house again after I was aged about twelve, in the next five years I felt that I saw far too much of her.

My paternal grandfather died suddenly in 1951, of a heart attack, in his early sixties, so I never met him at all, and my father seemed disinclined to fill in the gaps I might, had I thought about it, recognised that I had in my knowledge.

My stepmother was born in Buenos Aires, Argentina, on 4 March 1921. She was the second of three daughters born to Edith Marion Smith (née Charlton) and Charles William Smith. She was born at home as well, in the Villa Ballester, Boulevard Lacroze. I've never seen this place, and nor did my stepmother after 1938, when her family returned to England.

As I'm writing this I have on the desk in front of me a folded, foxed and yellowing piece of paper written on in faded ink, in Spanish, in copperplate script, and stamped twice, in violet ink, with the official seal of the Civil Registrar of Buenos Aires. Despite trying for more than forty years, my stepmother never managed to teach me more than the Spanish for 'a small piece of cheese, please', which I can say but couldn't begin to be able to spell. So although I don't really know what it says, I can work out enough of it, and whether

I can or not, it remains a wonderfully exotic document, fizzing with magical realism.

I never consciously met my stepmother's father, who died in 1963, even though I first met my stepmother when I about six days old, and may even have met her before I met my mother and father. I knew my stepmother's mother well, and liked her a lot.

Because I was never in the company of my mother's parents, I never had direct sight of the other end of all those taut and indestructible wires and threads that trail behind all of us to our past, though I remember that I was half consciously aware of the barbed hooks with which they'd attached themselves to my mother, or at least of the scars they'd left behind.

I can, therefore, only guess what her childhood must have been like, augmented by information given to me by my Aunt Dawne, my mother's younger sister. Of the five Bovill daughters, only Dawne and Penny are still alive. My mother and her eldest sister Charm both died of brain haemorrhages, although Charm died when she was eleven years older than my mother was when she died. What Jean died of is something of a mystery, but that's a story for someone else to tell, if it should be told at all.

But my guess is that my mother's childhood was pretty bleak. When she was four the family moved to a two-bedroomed house (plus box room) in Carshalton, where three of the girls shared one bed, nightly swapping places so no one would always be stuck in the middle. I remember, when I was small, my mother would play the 'three-in-a-bed' game, where we'd sing along with the words 'There were three in the bed and the little one said "Roll over! Roll over!" So they all rolled over and one fell out. There were two in the bed and the little one said . . .' And on it went, and we'd fall out of my parents' double bed laughing ourselves stupid. It was only after I visited Dawne on her farm in Kent and she told me about their sleeping arrangements that it occurred to me that this game might have had any significance beyond the pure joy of it. Maybe it didn't, and all in all I prefer not to delve too deeply.

Still, my mother's early childhood seems, from what I've heard and from what I remember hearing, to have been difficult, although I suspect that her parents' childhoods weren't much better. Her father, George, got his exotic middle names, Raphael Buick, from his father, who was French, and may or may not have been married to his mother when he was born, but who certainly abandoned his family when his son was very small. My mother's mother was half-German, and she and my mother never seem to have got on together very well. My Aunt Dawne thinks this is because they were too similar in temperament, which often explains things like that without quite justifying them.

Either way, the family's circumstances in general were not prosperous. George was a Hoover salesman, although on the copy of my mother's birth certificate dated 29 September 1954, which must have replaced the original, either lost or destroyed, he seems to have been promoted to being a 'Packing Factory Manager' from the Hoover salesman he's described as being on my parents' wedding certificate from a year previously. Dawne suspects that this was her mother's doing, because it wasn't true.

He was certainly still a Hoover salesman when the Second World War broke out, partly, as we've seen, because of the actions of Vyacheslav Molotov far away in Moscow. My mother was nine when war was declared, and I remember her telling me that she was always getting her mother in trouble with the wardens by pulling open the blackout curtains. I seem to remember this anecdote being told to me quite affectionately, another funny story from your childhood to tell your children in your turn. But now I think about it I can't remember my mother telling me any other stories about her life before the age of ten, so maybe the anecdote wasn't quite as affectionate as I thought it was.

Later, when my mother was in her late teens, Dawne remembers seeing her throw a bowl full of washing-up water over their mother, and I'm certain I remember my mother referring to her mother as a 'bitch' within my hearing, although I don't think she talked about her directly to me in terms like that, although she never baulked at talking about other people, often her friends, in similar or worse terms when I was within earshot. In fact, I don't think she ever really talked to me about her mother at all, or her father. But even if she did, they would have been conversations between a woman in her thirties and a child under ten.

However, when she was ten, my mother's childhood was quite transformed.

My father's childhood was far, far worse than my mother's could have been, yet it's hers that I think of as dirty blue-grey, blue-brown and charcoal and coal black, and then black. There's no real reason for this I can pinpoint, apart from what little I've heard or can guess at. My father's childhood I see as mahogany, dirty green, violet to purple, silver and gold.

His Perthes' disease ripped his childhood away from when he was a little boy aged four, and left him immobilised and effectively bedridden for the next ten years. But he'd been born into burgeoning prosperity. His grandfather, Frederick Gittings Rowson, had done extremely well for himself, rising up from being a plumber to being a property developer and then becoming a member of the boards of directors of various concerns around Manchester, Liverpool and Lytham St Anne's.

So my father's father was born already made and had no need to make himself like his father had done. He entered Lincoln's Inn to read for the Bar, and then entered chambers in Manchester where he had an imposing grandfather clock which now stands in our downstairs hall, near to the stuffed wolf. He eventually became a King's Counsel, bestowed on him by George VI, and the first Recorder of Blackpool. Acting in the former capacity, he once appeared for Blackpool Corporation when they tried to prevent the Communist Party holding meetings on the sands. He also became a Freemason, which was then, and may still be now, a prerequisite of becoming a Pillar of the Community.

In the exact Kremlinology needed to define the fluctuations between and within the strata of the British social classes, he was probably a couple of pegs above his wife, my father's mother. Her father, Arthur Knight, was a commercial traveller in late-nineteenth-century Lancashire who decamped to America with his wife, where his children, my grandmother, her younger sister Audrey and little brother Jak (the name he preferred to his given names, Jonas Arthur Knight), were all born, in Fall River, Massachusetts. I remember my grandmother telling me they had a sweep carriageway in front of their grand house, but it seems my great-grandfather didn't find his fortune, or enough of it, and so returned to England, richer only by three children. I don't know how he prospered back home, although he found enough money to send his eldest daughter to a finishing school in Switzerland. Later, as my father would often tell me with glee, his father and his father's father-in-law would often see each other on the platform at Blackpool Station, waiting for the train to Manchester, my grandfather off to his chambers or to court, while my great-grandfather was off to hawk his wares round the streets. My father told me they'd nod politely to each other, and pretend my great-grandfather was carrying a large suitcase because he was off on holiday or on a jaunt to the Pennines or a sea cruise to take the cure or anywhere except trudging from door to door, hawking.

The house in Gosforth Road was built by my father's grandfather as a wedding present for his son and new daughter-in-law. More correctly, I suppose, he had it built for them, and it was an imposing building of smooth, red Lancashire brick. When I knew it it was still, I imagine, much like it had been when my father was confined there in the 1920s and 30s, although there was an accretion of stuff which had built up over the years, slowly but inexorably filling every available space.

My father never made a big thing about his childhood, but would make amused references to it now and again. He often used to say he did things 'in my pram', and I was quite old before I worked out that he was in his pram until he was a teenager. I remember him telling me about how the next-door neighbour, a prosperous butcher, would amuse him by demonstrating how to poleaxe a cow, explaining the precise mechanism of the operation, and how the hollow tube of the poleaxe, its business end sharpened to aid dispatch, would smash down through the beast's forehead, while bits of the brain, thus pressurised, would squirt out of a little hole halfway up the tube.

He also told me how he learned to knit in his pram, presumably to pass the time, and he was also bought part-work magazines many of which I now own, subsequently bound together in vellum covers with beautiful illustrations of their subject matter embossed on to the front and spines. *Wonders of the World*, *Railway Wonders of the World*, *Shipping Wonders of the World*, *Countries of the World*, *Wonders of World Engineering* and *Wonders of the Air*, each collated into two thick volumes, all display a hearteningly optimistic and progressive, if slightly imperialist, view of the world beyond Gosforth

Road. I think they must have had some influence on my father, who maintained an interest in, enthusiasm for and optimism about technology all his life. He filled his time in other ways. In the back garden in Blackpool, still there in the 1960s but increasingly dilapidated, was a greenhouse with wire mesh instead of glass windows. In this, he told me, were kept flocks of songbirds, and as a boy he and his tutor would plant the birdseed to see what grew. He told me that as often as not they ended up growing cannabis plants.

And he would have gone on little outings. I found a photograph in my father's desk of him being wheeled along Blackpool Pier on a kind of flat trolley, pushed by his uncle and mother, with his father striding ahead. My father looks bored and embarrassed.

I know his father read him *Just William* and *Winnie-the-Pooh*, and I read my children the William stories from the same books. Being published before the Second World War, one of these pale red volumes contains the chapter about William and the Outlaws becoming Nazis in order to torment a local Jewish shopkeeper, a story missing from later editions.

His father read to him because he wasn't taught to read or write until he was about ten. I suppose, although again I'm just speculating, that when he became ill when he was four he got stuck in a kind of rut. Illness tends to infantilise everyone, but if you're little more than an infant anyway the effects must be worse: the relative helplessness and vulnerability of infancy have the terrible potential to become permanent and never-ending, a plight which was almost certainly compounded by my father's domestic circumstances.

My father's father was clearly ambitious. I never knew him, and my father rarely talked about him, except, in passing references, as a 'little round man'. However, at my father's funeral

I met a friend of my father's from university, someone he'd often mentioned by name, who'd been his best man at his first wedding, but whom he'd never sought out for me to meet over the previous forty-five years. I think, on the whole, my father liked to compartmentalise things. After the funeral, at what wasn't quite a wake (although it could hardly be called a reception either) in a mock-Tudor hotel in Ruislip, I said to my father's friend that he was the only person I knew who was still alive and might have met my grandfather. My father's friend said that he had indeed met him, as my father's father would often come down to Cambridge from Blackpool and set himself up in a hotel, from whence he'd issue an invitation to my father to bring along a friend for dinner.

'I never met two people less like each other in my life,' my father's friend said.

He went on to describe my grandfather as a typical Northern lawyer, loud and fairly brash, of the hail-fellow-well-met variety who are exactly the type of person you'd expect to be rolling up a trouser leg in a provincial Masonic lodge, then standing his round of drinks with the aldermen, the cigar ash falling to the thin, plain carpet, with maybe a speck or two settling for a second on a mayorial chain of office.

For some reason or other I always associate that particular milieu from between the wars with crazy golf.

Then my father's friend said that he once had dinner with my grandfather when he was in Cambridge, holding court in the Blue Boar, and he was the friend my father dragged along. My father's friend described how my grandfather lengthily and noisily laid out exactly what my father was going to do next, and my father's friend would sneak a look at my father, who sat quietly, smiling benignly, with clearly no intention of doing a single thing his father proposed. That sounds just like my father.

Among the plans my father's father had for his son were

that he would be a lawyer, so my father joined Gray's Inn, like his father before him, and ate his three dinners, but became a doctor. He also planned for my father to become a Mason, and of the two letters I found in my father's desk from his father, one is a lengthy catechism of bullshit about what a Mason is and how he should behave. My father wasn't a Mason, although he told me several times that he'd been to a couple of lodge meetings and had never seen such a lot of bollocks in his life, with fat municipal worthies in aprons building imaginary walls. Nonetheless, he kept his father's Masonic accessories, the dark pinafore and the scrolls and the medals, which now sit in an old leather briefcase in my studio. This might mean that there's a possibility that I'm now likely to have my liver ripped out with silver trowels and buried between high and low tide to the light of a full moon, but I doubt it.

In the other letter my father kept his father trusts that his studies at Bart's are going well, promises to send a thin volume recently published by a local doctor, an old friend of his, also promises to send more cigarettes and alcohol, and hopes that my father isn't finding the fog too tiresome.

I have some other letters written by my grandfather, to my grandmother. They're full of phrases like 'thank you for your ripping letter' and how things are absolutely 'topping', and date the undated letters like the rings in a felled tree.

And so I wonder how my father and his father got on. Part of me suspects that the ambitious young barrister was secretly deeply disappointed that his only child turned out to be a cripple, but I'm probably doing his memory a great disservice. And anyway, my father's problem wasn't so much his father as his mother.

When I was staying in Blackpool with my grandmother for the first time when I was seven, not having really known her at all before then, I remember her telling me that her husband had said, after their son was born, that that was it and they weren't having any more. She also told me about my father's birth. To be exact, she said she was lying in bed one morning when suddenly she felt this dear little baby wriggling in the bed beside her. Even at the age of seven I knew that this was nonsense, and I remember that I wondered why she was being so coy about the nature of childbirth.

I later realised that she would have been quite incapable of talking about it in any other way. I think that she spent her entire life pretending that nothing more untoward than a little china ornament being in the wrong place on a doily ever happened to anyone. I also suspect that her finishing school finished off what was her natural predisposition to smile enchantingly at the world and never allow a thought of any kind to enter your head, in case it delayed tea. In her favour it has to be said that she was completely without malice, probably because that would have involved levels of calculation it would have been impossible for her to accommodate. But she wasn't by any stretch of the imagination a bad person. In many ways she was positively good. She drove an ambulance in the war, for a start, and I'm sure she was a perfect and ornamental partner for her husband, engaging in small talk with all those aldermen and smiling for the cameraman from the *Blackpool Echo* at another municipal beanfeast. She was also kind, and very generous in her own way, and rather adventurously active for her generation, learning to drive, flying in aeroplanes, and playing golf with the best of them. So it's unfortunate, and probably not her fault, that neither I, nor my sister, nor my mother or my stepmother, could stand her.

It's just that her terms of reference were so stultifyingly narrow. I remember, when I was seven, complaining one day of having a slight headache, and thereafter being compelled to lie on a couch all day in a darkened room with a damp handkerchief over my face. The handkerchief may be a later elaboration, but I remember the crushing, deadening boredom lying in that room, unchanged since the abdication crisis, the thin light seeping miserably through chinks in the thick curtains, and later trying to read something, but being told kindly but firmly that I mustn't do that as it would strain my eyes.

Well, she may have been right, but I suspect that she didn't really approve of reading anyway. You might find out something you really didn't want to know that hinted at a world which featured anything more worrying than a round of golf and wafting round the house occasionally rearranging another ornament, while (after her husband's death and the disappearance of the servant classes) her sister and brother did all the housework and the cooking. And I suppose thinking everything's lovely is an admirable way to get through life, so long as you can keep it up and ignore everything going on around you. But this wasn't genetic. I remember my father telling me that his mother's mother, a woman he clearly liked, was always offering the sensible if cynical advice: 'Never believe anything you hear, and only half of what you see.' And it's slightly odd that my grandmother should have sustained her defining blitheness while her husband was appearing, either for the defendant or the Crown, in some of the grislier murder cases in the history of the North-East, and in the late 1940s her son was busy chopping up cadavers down in London.

Then again, the workings of the human body were something else best not thought about, and I remember her getting quite angry when I was seven and I used the word 'bladder' in a little song I'd made up about adders.

I think it was actually my father who said that his mother had treated him like a doll, and in a way she never stopped.

I remember going into a local newsagent's in Blackpool with them both when I was seven, my grandmother was seventy and my father was forty-two, and she introduced him to the shopkeeper as 'my little baby'. I remember my father grinding his teeth with rage and shaking his hand free from hers. So it's not surprising that for six years they thought it was fine just to wheel him along the prom, read to him and, without doubt, love him very much, but with a cloying thoughtlessness that, knowing him as I did later, must have driven my father mad. God only knows what was happening inside his head throughout this time.

Then, when he was ten, my father's parents employed a retired schoolmistress whose name, to my shame, I can't remember. I remember he told me that she'd had some kind of nervous breakdown, and was facing retirement with despair. But instead she was set to work again teaching my father to read and write, and carried on teaching him until he went to Rossall School in Fleetwood when he was sixteen. In different ways this coming together saved them both.

My stepmother's childhood was, in comparison to my mother's and father's, blissful.

Between the wars Argentina was a *de facto*, if not *de jure*, part of the British Empire, and her father was Chief Accountant at the Anglo-Argentine Railway Company. Among my step-mother's thousands of photographs I found a group portrait of what I assume to be the executive officers and directors of the Anglo-Argentine Railway Company. My stepmother's father is there, four along from the left in the second row from the front, holding a cigar, flanked by Englishmen and Argentines, the two groups differentiated only by the magnif-icent moustaches of the latter, and most of them are also holding cigars. It's an interior shot, and shows an enormous and ornate round arched window with lace curtains, several

66

display cabinets filled with cut glass and some exotic, spiky tropical plants, probably in pots, although these are hidden from view by all those prosperous-looking men, smoking away in their wing collars and waistcoats. The photograph has faded to sepia with age, but must have been taken around 1920.

Again it reeks, in retrospect, of what would later be called magical realism, that specifically South American sensibility encapsulating the fractured history of colonialism, jungles and weird whimsicality. And although their lives can't have seemed at all out of the ordinary to my stepmother's family at the time, even within the context of their neocolonialist circumstances, the stories she told about her childhood (which were very good stories, by the way) are definitely strange.

For example, on one of the sea voyages back to England which the family took every few years, from the rail of the liner she saw two hammerhead sharks fighting in the ocean. Another time, she said that flying fish landed on the deck of the ship.

And of course their lives were extraordinary, compared to how people were living back in grey old England, and extraordinarily comfortable as well. They lived in a villa, but something almost unrecognisably different from the suburban villas being built back home, with their damp crazy paving and trim hedges. They had (by their lights) foreign servants. The little Anglican girls were educated by Catholic nuns in a foreign language they weren't allowed, by their father, to speak at home. There were wild parrots living in the garden, perching on the lush and exotic vegetation. It must have been both strange and, as everything in your childhood is once you've lived it, entirely familiar, but still wonderful.

There were, of course, slightly sinister undercurrents which the little girls wouldn't have thought much about at the time. Apart from the British expat community in Buenos Aires, there was also a large German community. Thirty years or so before my stepmother's childhood, Elisabeth Nietzsche, the sister of the philosopher, had tried to establish a kind of Nietzschean, ur-Nazi commune up over the border in Paraguay, and Argentina itself was a strange place even by the strange standards of South America.

An instigating genocide, soon after the Europeans arrived, had emptied the land of its original aboriginal people, so it was (unlike Australia or North America) almost literally an 'empty place', fantastically wealthy in land and resources, waiting to be filled up with ambitious Europeans. So there were Italians (some of whom ended up siring President Galtieri, who lost the Falklands War) and Lebanese (who sired President Menem, the first democratic president after the fall of the discredited junta following Mrs Thatcher's reconquest of the Falklands) and all those Welsh down in Patagonia, who speak only Welsh and Spanish, whose presence there meant that the only British political party in Parliament to oppose Thatcher's campaign to retake the Falklands was Plaid Cymru, the Welsh Nationalists, who could not countenance the possibility of Welshmen fighting against and probably killing Welshmen.

There was also, and still is, a large British community, and between the wars the British, including my stepmother's father, more or less ran the place. There's even a scaled-down copy of Big Ben in downtown Buenos Aires. The name Buenos Aires, incidentally, as is often the case among British expatriates, was shortened into the slightly slangy, cosy BA, as in 'back in Beeyay', just like Britons who've spent time doing whatever they do in Saudi Arabia always call it Saudi. This not only suggests a familiarity with the extended family of tribal despots who, adjectivising their country with their own name, redefined Arabia as their personal property, but also, on the part of the expats, is another instance of how we name and rename things in order to control them, like we do with our pets and our children.

Despite having written to them several times to tell them that my stepmother is now dead, every couple of months I still receive, forwarded from my parents' old house, a copy of the Anglo-Argentine Friendship Society's newsletter. I also sent them a copy of the photograph of my stepmother's father smoking a cigar with his colleagues in the Anglo-Argentine Railway Company, but I got no reply. The newsletter is filled with nostalgic memories of the good old days between the wars, interspersed with information about who's alive and who's dead, and appeals to help support the by now very elderly remnants of the British community in their various nursing homes in Argentina. It's a curious publication, and the readership it serves is also curious. You'd best describe them as colonials, but they don't quite fit the template, and not just because Argentina was never a British colony. Despite those old, old people staring out of the windows of their rooms in the suburbs of Buenos Aires at the jacaranda trees, I get the impression that there was no real spirit of colonisation, no serious intention to settle permanently in the place and make it their own, no desire to stay on, and those who did only did so as a kind of mistake, relics of a different time, human flotsam left behind by the ebbing tide of history. I can't quite think of any comparable community: they weren't or aren't like the miserable crofters of the Falkland Islands, or the white farmers of Rhodesia/Zimbabwe, or the British in India who 'stayed on' after independence, or even like those bankers and oil men and arms salesmen and advisers who offer their advice on God knows what and furtively sip a beer in their arid compounds in Saudi or other parts of the Middle East.

There's a feeling of permanent impermanence about these non-colonising neocolonialists, who nonetheless gave every appearance of being something which they weren't and so ended up caught somewhere between imperialists and guest workers, half exploiters and half exploited, recreating a patch of England, with its little Big Ben and church socials and no Spanish in the house, in somewhere deeply un-English, the bright tropical glare from the garden fading the catalogue from the Home & Colonial.

So there are the photographs of my stepmother as a little girl, laughing at the camera aged about four as she scrambles out of a creek in the pampas, looking almost feral, and a few years later, there she is again, dressed as a harlequin standing among bright-eyed young men made up as nigger minstrels for what appears to be a concert party at the local Anglican church hall in the suburb of Buenos Aires near where they lived, in a photograph which looks as though it should have been taken in Worthing or Reigate or any other 1930s English dormitory town, reeking of unambitious municipal pride, floral clocks, cream teas and model villages, and not a gaucho within ten thousand miles.

If you think about all those expat communities living in close proximity, the settlers and the non-settlers, it retrospectively compounds the sense of oddness about Argentina. With the ten feet of topsoil out on the pampas, where the gauchos were said, when hungry, to kill a steer and eat only its tongue, throwing away the rest of the carcass in a display of casual but studied profligacy, this was clearly a land of opportunity and wealth: I suspect there was probably an unspoken assumption that this place could almost become a South American USA, the mirrored Rorschach blot when you fold the Western world in half along a line somewhere between the equator and the tropic of Cancer. As we know, that never happened. You can blame Perón, or the military who 'disappeared' all those communists and socialists and trade unionists, or rampant inflation and endemic economic incompetence. Or you could just blame a frame of mind that produced both Borges and Eva Perón, who would raise her arms in exultation before vast crowds of adoring Peronistas, the gold bangles and bracelets clumping down from her wrists to her armpits as she shouted, without a hint of irony, 'We shirtless ones!'

My stepmother was spared the post-war history of Argentina, although she had many friends who stayed on and presumably suffered along with everyone else, irrespective of whether they viewed their neighbours as hosts or natives, people who considered themselves unquestionably English but had names like Tito or Perula, people caught halfway between two places, neither of which, perhaps, was ultimately home.

Looking back to between the wars, the juxtaposition between the English and German communities now seems the strangest, in the light of what had happened already, and with the hindsight of what happened later. My stepmother's father had served in the First World War, and she told me a story about how he once captured a German soldier whom, according to him, he was meant to shoot, but instead he turned his back after telling his captive to scarper. But first, my stepmother told me, he'd taken the German's watch, which now belongs to my stepcousin, his grandson. She also told me that her father really, truly hated Germans, and that presumably included the ones in Argentina. Nonetheless, once a year he would go to a grand dinner, organised to promote good relations between expat Germans and Englishmen. The *placement* would alternate German and Englishman, so they'd be forced to speak to each other, even if a few years previously they'd been trying to kill each other, or at least each other's compatriots, and each diner would have a little flag of his respective nation at his place. My stepmother said her father would never let his daughters ask him or even talk about these dinners, but she remembered that he'd always come home from them very late and apparently very drunk, even though he seldom drank heavily and appears to have been, from what I've heard, a man consumed with a sense of self-control and, for that matter, control over his family.

(Later, in the post-Second World War world into which I was born, the attempts at reconciliation seem altogether less convivial: town-twinning and singing 'The Happy Wanderer' instead of eating steak and getting pissed serenaded by the cicadas in the hot night outside, but there you go.)

My stepmother herself, with her two sisters, had a stranger encounter with Germans than their father's annual descent into bibulous bridge-building and fence-mending. When she was about ten, her family went on holiday to a seaside resort to the north of Buenos Aires. Her parents were staying with some friends in a hotel in town, and on these friends' recommendation had dispatched their daughters to a children's holiday camp which turned out to be run, literally, by Nazis. This would have been in around 1931, so these were Nazis *avant la lettre*, true believers in the manifest destiny of the Fatherland and the Aryan race, the legatees to Elisabeth Nietzsche's failed commune in the jungle, even though they were far, far away from the pine forests and the Rhine and all the other symbols of Germanness that got the Nazis so murderously misty-eyed.

Each morning, my stepmother told me, the children would be woken by women with whistles. Each action of the day would be dictated by adults with whistles: a whistle told them when to start washing, and when to stop; a whistle indicated when they were to start eating, and when to stop. After breakfast, a swastika flag would be hoisted up the flagpole which they then had to salute, presumably again to whistles, and then they'd be loaded on open-backed trucks and driven down to the sea. Wearing only swimming trunks, the children would then sunbathe, lying on their backs for a strictly observed

72

period of time until, with another blast of the whistle, they rolled over on to their reddened little tummies. Seventy years later, when she told me this story, my stepmother said she'd never seen such appalling sunburn in her life.

Then one of her sisters got ill, and was being treated both harshly and negligently by the Nazis, rather unsurprisingly. Back at the beach a few days later, braising in the harsh tropical sun, my stepmother saw her mother in the distance walking by the sea, so she made a break for it. She told me she was chased for several hundred yards along the beach by three great blond beasts until she reached her mother, salvation and escape.

Strangely enough, although my stepmother told me many stories about her childhood in Argentina, she didn't tell me this one until about three years before she died, when I visited her at the Royal Marsden Hospital, three hours after she'd come round from a general anaesthetic after she'd had an emergency mastectomy. She seemed in remarkably good spirits in the circumstances, and the story amazed me and made us both laugh.

It was Germans who made my stepmother's family finally leave Argentina altogether, in 1938. Although they'd returned on home leave periodically throughout her childhood – and seen flying fish and fighting hammerhead sharks, and been dunked in soapsuds by sea cooks dressed at King Neptune as they crossed the equator – England must have been a strange and alien place, grim and grimy and cold and half ready for war. It was her father's precognisance of the coming war which, she said, meant they had to go 'home'.

A few years after my father married my stepmother, I found some stuff her father had received at the time of the Munich crisis. As a member of the British Legion, he'd volunteered to act as part of a peacekeeping police presence in the Sudetenland, the German-speaking part of Czechoslovakia, what Hitler said was his last territorial claim on Europe, and was ready at a moment's notice to go to one of several embarkation points in preparation to be sent to what Neville Chamberlain called 'a faraway country of which we know little'. I don't know why, but I have this very strong impression that British Legionnaires were going to keep the Czechs and the Germans apart armed only with bowler hats and umbrellas, but I must have made that up myself. Among the stuff he'd been sent were a British Legion armband, details of the command centre in Brighton he was to report to, and a photograph of Field Marshal Earl Haig, the butcher of the Western Front, with a form letter from Marchioness Haig telling the recipients that she was sure the photograph would comfort and inspire them as they went about their difficult task. Then Chamberlain sold the Czechs down the river at Munich, the Nazis scored another triumph of their twisted will, and so my stepmother's father never went to Czechoslovakia. The Nazis back in Argentina, meanwhile, were presumably biding their time and polishing their whistles.

Years later, my father also had a trip to Czechoslovakia disrupted, when the scientific symposium he was due to attend in Bratislava was postponed due to Russian tanks crushing the Prague Spring, that brief interlude in the Cold War when reform-minded communists under Alexander Dubček attempted to loosen the grip of the kind of senile Stalinism Brezhnev was determined to maintain throughout Eastern Europe. Dubček was duly purged, although like Molotov and Malenkov and unlike Beria or Nagy in Hungary twelve years previously, he wasn't forced to pay the ultimate compliment to Stalinist realpolitik with his life. He spent the next two decades overseeing the boilers beneath a building in, I think, Bratislava. My father finally made it to Bratislava in 1970, after my mother had died.

Czechoslovakia no longer exists.

On a much tinier scale, my stepmother and her family's fortunes changed as dramatically as Dubček's. Her father's pension from the Anglo-Argentine Railway was never paid. Rather than living in a villa with servants in South America, going to parties or upcountry on amazing trips to fabulous waterfalls, driving through jungles, crossing and recrossing oceans and, she often told me, spending her childhood eating olives instead of sweets, they all ended up in a small bungalow in Angmering, a village two miles from the English Channel in West Sussex, four miles east of Littlehampton. Her mother returned to nursing, becoming the local district nurse. Her father, a linguist fluent in several languages, soon got slightly shadowy employment in a branch of the government, and subsequently spent most of the coming war in Canada. My stepmother, aged seventeen, was sent to work in a department store in Worthing, selling things she'd never previously imagined existed.

My stepmother was eight years older than my mother, who was five years younger than my father, so my stepmother reached seventeen in 1938, my father in 1941 and my mother in 1946. Their seventeenth birthdays are thus staggered across the years which saw the most terrible war in human history and which resulted in the deaths of at least 60 million people, a lot of them deliberately murdered by the Nazis, a few of them reduced to sticky ashes by the explosion of two atomic bombs in Japan. For my mother, however, the war was a godsend, although all the advantages she won from it had completely disappeared by the time of her seventeenth birthday in October 1946.

In the summer of 1940, after the evacuation from Dunkirk, the invasion of England seemed almost inevitable, and so the Hoover Corporation, with its headquarters in North Canton,

Ohio, offered some of its English employees the opportunity to have their children evacuated to the United States. My mother's father, being a Hoover salesman (despite his wife's attempts, like various of Stalin's henchmen, retrospectively to change history in subsequent documents) was thus in a position to send his three middle daughters across the Atlantic to America and safety, travelling many degrees of latitude further north, and in the opposite direction, to my stepmother coming to England two years before.

So Jean, my mother and Dawne travelled to London, said goodbye to their parents at Euston Station, went up to Liverpool, boarded a ship, arrived in New York and caught a train to North Canton. Jean was then sent somewhere else, and my mother, aged ten, and Dawne, aged eight, didn't hear from her, or a single word from their parents, for the next five years. Apparently the farewell with their parents was brief, although Dawne tells me that her father told her years later that he then went with their mother to a park in London where she howled with grief for about a quarter of an hour.

The two little girls were placed with a family called Kohr, a German family. The father was a local school superintendent, in charge of seven schools. The girls had their own bedrooms, which meant they also had their own beds. They had a large garden. They went to school, where my mother played the trumpet and was in the school band. They had friends. I found my mother's old address book in my father's desk after he died, and it's filled with the names of people with addresses in Ohio. They also had, or found, a loving and supportive if alternative family, along with a wider sense of community, which gladly welcomed my mother into the local Pentecostal church, and in my father's desk I also found the little pamphlet my mother received from the church when she was baptised there in 1943. But most of all they had Space, wide open spaces in the mythological but also actual

American sense, along with all sorts of other, different kinds of space.

The story of my mother and Dawne's time in America now belongs more properly to Dawne than to me, so I'm not going to usurp it. But the way she described it makes me imagine their lives as like something out of Norman Rockwell or the good bits in *It's a Wonderful Life*, an amalgam of all those aspects of America in the middle of the twentieth century that makes it appear so attractive in retrospect: part New Deal optimism, part homestead, white-picket-fence and warm-apple-pie decency and security, part Hollywood myth-making, but with the myths, like most myths, rooted in an underlying truth.

The mythology, or aspects of it, spun itself enduringly round my mother. Dawne tells me that throughout her early adulthood my mother was always talking about earning enough money to buy a one-way ticket back to America, and although she never did that, there were smaller, but perhaps more telling things as well, like what she drank and the way she ate. As a child, I can't ever remember my mother drinking tea, but I remember, though I can't remember being told this, that she only drank coffee – strong, black coffee – because it was, in a way, more American. Likewise, she ate in a partic- ular and rather peculiar way, always cutting her food into smallish pieces with her knife and fork, and then discarding the knife and transferring the fork into her right hand and using it alone to eat with, and this, I remember knowing, was a distinctly American way of doing things. And when I was small I remember we'd go to Selfridges twice a year, once at Christmas, to see both Father Christmas and Uncle Holly, a specifically American avatar who was there as part of the department store's never-ending homage to its American founder, Sir Gordon Selfridge. The other time we'd go would be on the Fourth of July, American Independence Day and, quite coincidentally (or maybe not), my sister's birthday.

I once met one of Dawne and my mother's American family, 'Auntie' Coila, Mr Kohr's sister. I was at home with my mother during the day, so this must have been before I went to school when I was four and a half, but maybe it was later. I don't remember my sister being there, although she tells me that she was. I remember we went to the Alpine, a restaurant a mile or so up the road from my parents' house, in Bushey. I can just about remember what Coila looked like, but not well enough to describe her here, but I can remember her and my mother looking at each other with affection, sizing each other up after twenty years, and Coila saying something about how my mother had lost her accent, and I distinctly remember butting in to say that I'd had an accent a week or so previously, when I'd shat myself. I remember my mother quickly and curtly silencing me.

Whatever my mother's life was like in America, and whatever lasting legacy it left her, it ended abruptly in May 1945. According to Dawne, almost as soon as the war in Europe ended the authorities made it clear that English evacuees, having no further reason to stay in America, now had to return to what they'd once called home. They left in short order, chaperoned on the train from Ohio to New York, thence on the ship returning to Liverpool and on to another train which took them back to London. Once they arrived at Euston Station, the girls and their parents both walked straight past each other, each failing to recognise the other.

And then they went back to Carshalton, back to the two rooms, the one bed for three of the sisters, and according to Dawne the only one who seemed pleased to see them was the dog, by now twelve, who had no problem recognising the little girls from five years previously and followed them everywhere.

My mother was now fifteen. In Ohio she was just on the point of entering high school, of starting her real education. That would now never happen; once she was back in England she was now above the school-leaving age, so her education stopped dead. Instead, she went to work on a production line in the 'Bourgeois' Perfume Factory.

Years later, after their mother died, Dawne found a letter in the back of a drawer from Mr Kohr in Ohio. He'd written to my mother's parents to say that he understood that my mother might have problems in England in continuing her education, given the disparities between the American and British education systems. In the letter he offered to pay for my mother's further education, or help in any other way. My mother's parents never replied.

Ten or so years previously, but belatedly, my father's education started. Although he never told me much about it, I got the impression that my father and the retired schoolmistress developed a kind of mutual dependency through learning, him helping her just as much as she was helping him. Whatever she did, in that dark, quiet house, she succeeded in either creating or catalysing a sense of wonder and enquiry that characterised my father for the rest of his life, while I suppose he restored to her her sense of usefulness. Where my father's inextinguishable scepticism, towards whatever orthodoxy he found in his way and towards authority in general, came from is another question, but she planted something in him, just like the old woman and the little crippled boy would plant the birdseed in the back garden, just to see what grew.

By the time he was seventeen, my father had been out of the plaster cast for about five years. He could walk unaided, but

79

with the distinct gait he continued to have until his hip replacement thirty years or so later. He was now at school, but he never told me anything about his schooldays, except that he played golf instead of rugby, and he never spoke with affection or anything else about either friends or contemporaries or teachers. I imagine that he was keeping himself to himself, lying doggo, but, as he must have been doing all his life, quietly observing and analysing everything that was going on around him, and just as quietly judging it.

So, aged seventeen, although several years apart, each of my parents probably viewed their prospects with something close to despair.

Both my mother and my stepmother, either screwing the lids on to scent bottles or selling stays to the stout wives of stockbrokers, must have been frequently haunted by thoughts of those childhood idylls, their own personal Americas, which had been snatched away from them by the vicissitudes of history, both post- and antebellum, bequeathing them instead the grinding grey humdrummery of post-war austerity or pre-war Worthing. I imagine they must often have thought that, although they'd hardly started, the best part of their lives was over.

And my father, denied a childhood and now in a milieu of unfamiliar sporty schoolboy brutality punctuated by Lancashire respectability, might have wondered when his life was due to begin.

Smells

The editor of a magazine I used to work for once told me that our sense of smell, because it was the first to evolve, has evocative powers far greater than the other senses. This is rather odd, not because it's not true, but because the magazine he ran was about the technology of rock music and part of me thinks he should have talked up hearing and, therefore, the potency of cheap music (I managed to keep going there for six years, despite my one joke on the subject – constant references to a Lee Harvey Oswald Fender Strat – soon beginning to pall).

They say that hearing is the last sense to leave you when you're dying. I hope so, as I've said goodbye to at least two people who were within hours of dying.

About ten days before my friend Jon, who'd been my best friend when we were seventeen and who'd worked for and later edited the same rock-music magazine, died of a brain tumour, I read him Nick Kent's essay on the Rolling Stones, originally written for the *NME*, later anthologised in *The Dark Stuff*. I hope he could hear me, although while I was reading to him he just stared at his hands, moving them around in front of his face examining the lines and whorls and cross-hatchings on his palms. By this stage he was in a hospice in Hammersmith, near where he lived, near where my wife grew up and next to the hospital where I was born. The hospice, with its quiet corridors, thick carpets, pastel shades and pale sub-Georgian wallpaper tastefully covering the walls up to the equally tasteful plywood dado rail, seemed more like a provincial motel, but I suppose someone must have thought that this would make a house of death more congenial for the patients and their visitors. It didn't quite work.

Another friend of mine from school once told me that when his mother was dying, again of cancer, his brother insisted on singing her his own folk-rock compositions. My friend said these were not only appalling, but only served to compound the appalling circumstances they all found them-selves in, and he was sure his mother hated every second of it. But you can't be sure. Maya Angelou sang to Jessica Mitford when she was dying, and Peggy Seeger sang to her ex-husband Ewan MacColl when he was dying too. They probably enjoyed it, and anyway, it's the thought that counts.

I don't sing particularly well, although I enjoy singing a lot, so with Jon I did the next best thing and read to him about singing instead. He'd always liked the Rolling Stones, much more than I did, so I suppose I was trying to fill some last moments together where conversation was no longer an option by combining two of the great enthusiasms of his life, rock music and journalism. Mostly, though, I reckoned that he was probably as bored and embarrassed as I was with my attempts at that particular kind of one-sided conversation you only have with the very ill or the dying, always spoken slightly too loudly, with an entirely false bonhomie and optimism, and probably exclusively conducted for the benefit of the speaker rather than his or her mute interlocutor.

I was going to read him another Nick Kent essay, about Iggy Pop, when I went to see him the following week. I tried to ring his wife several times in the previous day or so, to find out when it would be convenient or appropriate to call round, but her phone seemed to be out of order. When I arrived at the hospice, Jon's room was filled with members of his family, and I instantly recognised that I'd intruded on to something final and far more personal than I had a right to witness. He was on his deathbed, and although that phrase has been used as a cheap metaphor too often to have any real meaning, when you see it the power of that one word is suddenly restored.

It now seems horribly inappropriate, but I was mortified with embarrassment at my bad timing. I shouldn't have been there: we had been best friends, but we weren't any more, and although I'd been visiting him in hospital throughout his illness out of much more than merely a sense of duty, I was very conscious that a large part of it was because I knew I needed to do the right thing, to behave in that obvious but still slightly indefinable way that nonetheless was clearly more for my benefit than Jon's. Put bluntly, it meant I hadn't acted like a schmuck. To put it more pompously, I knew I had to act honourably, to cling on to whatever flotsam of normality or good behaviour or even just plain decency was to hand amid the wreckage.

It's a good thing most of us do behave this way, however you choose to analyse the underlying motives. But in his room in that awful bloody hospice I still felt that suddenly I'd stopped acting decently and I tried to leave, but Jon's wife, then almost his widow, is considerably less feeble than I am, and told me to give him a kiss and say goodbye. He died the next day.

At his funeral, on what seems to have been the only decent sunny day that spring, they played Iggy Pop's 'Lust for Life' and songs by the Kinks, the Monkees and the Byrds, and I gave one of the addresses. This was the third funeral I'd spoken at in two years, and by now I knew the drill, which is to make them laugh and make them cry. In many ways funerals are a subset of showbiz, a ritualistic spectacle the purpose of which should be to make you end up feeling magnificently sad and therefore, somehow, better. So I said that having been his best friend when we were at school, I'd always been struck, over the next twenty-five years, how youthful – literally, full of youth – Jon remained, and how, in the days since his death I'd never felt so old. I also said that when we were at school – and I included in the pronoun many people I'd been at school with who were now in the crematorium – Jon, unlike the rest of us, was having regular sex with someone else. We then all got slightly drunk, and I went mad for about two months, deluding myself that Jon's death somehow or other marked the end of my childhood.

It snowed heavily after my father's funeral, but this was nothing out of the ordinary as it was late January, and it took two of my cousins, separately and going in different directions, about eight hours to get home. He would have liked that. It took Anna, Fred, Rose and me two hours to crawl across London through dreadful traffic, and then Anna and I watched *Casablanca*, my father's favourite film.

It snowed after Charles I's execution, around the same time of year. Lord Clarendon wrote that the blanket of white settling on the dead king's coffin proved his innocence. My father was ash by the time his blizzard started.

It was lovely and sunny on the day of my stepmother's funeral, but sunny in that oddly urban way, where the spring flowers and the trees, freshly in leaf, make you feel wonderful, and then your eye gets caught by a patch of dusty pavement or a slightly dented street lamp, and you're suddenly filled with dismay and disgust.

My father-in-law's funeral was also in January, and it was cold and wet, but we still let off the firework I'd bought for Millennium Eve, but hadn't used after he'd died on Christmas Day. Anyway, my father-in-law was of a generation and a frame of mind absolutely to insist that the next millennium wouldn't start until 1 January 2001. The firework was Chinese, and consisted of a box containing a hundred little tubes, each containing a mortar, which, once my brothers-in-law had lit the blue touchpaper, went off serially, each with a blinding flash of white light and a thunderous explosion, rattling the windows at the back of our house. I'm told you could hear it miles away, and it terrified some of our neighbours' children. It's what my father-in-law would have wanted.

Years earlier, my father-in-law had given a favourite cat a Viking funeral, pushing the burning little boat he'd made for the event into the Thames just by Hammersmith Bridge, at midnight.

And my old schoolteacher, Butti, had his funeral on Halloween, 1998, in Kensal Green Cemetery, in the freezing cold, semi-derelict Victorian chapel of rest. Although it might seem tautologous to say it, there are few places more instantly funereal than a Victorian cemetery, specially in autumn, especially in the pouring rain, particularly one of those enormous necropolises skirting London, created to accommodate the exploding population of corpses as London seethed ever outwards. Our son Fred, then ten, had said the night before that he didn't want to go to the funeral, because, I suspect, he thought it would be too upsetting, too beyond his experience to be bearable, but I said that he had to go, not out of duty or decency, but because, I promised him, it would make him feel better. The next day, as we walked through the deluge and the mud and mulching fallen leaves between the leaning graves, following the hearse and the single Irish fiddler just behind it, as we processed in a long, bedraggled column from the chapel of rest to the crematorium, Fred and I cried our eyes out. Later, he conceded that he did, indeed, feel better.

Butti also had African drummers. I think Jon had some Vaughan Williams on top of the rock 'n' roll. My father-in-law had some Schumann, and we left the crematorium at my stepmother's funeral to the sound of Doris Day singing 'Che Sera Sera'. Some of her old friends, old people I hardly knew, looked a bit disapproving at that, but I explained that it was one of the tunes she'd often whistle as she pottered around, and anyway it summed up not only her approach to life, but also the particular way she approached her own death. At my father's funeral we played 'As Time Goes By', sung by Dooley Wilson, from *Casablanca*. My sister and I finally picked on that song because my father loved *Casablanca* and collected clocks, so it seemed appropriate. But we'd had a lot of trouble thinking of any music for the funeral, as my father always insisted that he was tone deaf.

I spoke at all of those funerals, and in each case I tried to make them laugh as well as making them cry. Our children went to all the funerals except Jon's, and cried so loudly at all of them that I toyed with the idea of hiring them out as professional, fittingly demonstrative mourners to grieving families who didn't really like their loved ones but wanted to keep up appearances.

I didn't speak at my mother's funeral. I was only ten. And anyway, I didn't go.

I can never quite decide what I want played at my own funeral, and for that matter I can never decide what kind of funeral I really want. Part of me would like to go like the late Ayatollah Khomeini, pulled from his coffin by four million grief-stricken and hysterical Iranians. Stalin's funeral wasn't bad either, with hundreds of people trampled to death in Red Square as they took the old monster off to be pickled. I remember watching Leonid Brezhnev's funeral on TV, just like I remember watching John F. Kennedy's, when I was about four and half. In the early sixties, primitive satellite transmissions from America always had a widish black border to left and right of the image, so what I remember is grainy, monochrome and slightly squashed. Brezhnev's funeral, in contrast, was in the vaguely washed-out but simultaneously weirdly garish colours of satellite transmissions of the early 1980s. They were playing Chopin's funeral march, very slowly and ponderously, and then the pall-bearers dropped the coffin as they lowered it into the grave at the foot of the Kremlin wall.

Actually, you don't even need to have a funeral. Another part of me is attracted to Jeremy Bentham's idea of having yourself made into an auto-icon, wax moulded round your bones before you're dressed in your best suit and sat on a seat in the hall ready to greet visitors as they come in through the front door.

In that case, I presume the question of music at my funeral wouldn't arise, although a selection of my favourite songs and tunes could be burned on to a CD and played continuously from somewhere hidden about my person. Better still, someone could hide a little speaker in my waxen mouth, which would hang slightly open so that I'd appear to be singing whatever track was currently playing as you skirted round me with a frisson of disgust.

Assuming my family don't go down that route, I still can't decide what should be played at my ultimate gig. For a long time I wanted to trundle towards the flames to the sound of the overture from Wagner's *Tannhäuser*, partly because it's deeply stirring music, and partly because it provided the basis for most of the songs sung by Elmer Fudd and Bugs Bunny in the cartoon *What's Opera, Doc?*. Then I decided that that was all a bit grand, and many people might not get the joke by that stage, so I thought 'I Can See For Miles (And Miles)' by the Who might fit the bill, but now I've gone off that idea too. But I definitely want the (strictly non-religious) service to end with 'Telstar'. It's relatively short, so won't carry on playing interminably to an empty room if hardly anyone turns up, and it's also guaranteed to cheer up the most miserable occasion, so the mourners would be sent on their way with a spring in their steps and, I hope, a smile on their lips.

But none of it will make any difference to me, because I'll be dead.

Whether it's played at funerals or not, you can't deny the potency of cheap music, or its evocative power. After Jon died, I brooded away listening to any old pompous garbage I could find from the 1970s, because of its tremendous power to conjure up when I'd been at school. I got over it. But, like everyone else, a snatch, or even the opening chord, of any particular song can transport me to a certain time and a particular place. Any ska record immediately makes me think about a street quite close to the north end of Ladbroke Grove, just south of the Westway flyover, in 1983, and I'm surrounded by scummy concrete, post-punk haircuts and a kind of muddle-headed, cross but ultimately optimistic youthfulness. *Dark Side of the Moon* by Pink Floyd makes me think of carpets and curtains and other upholstery made of a thick, corrugated material, probably in Letchworth in the early to mid-1970s, and then it makes me think about the nursing home run by nuns where my stepmother's mother lived. More precisely, it makes me think of the driveway, tall trees in full leaf but dripping with water in heavy rain. There's a defining muddiness in the air, but the hint somewhere close by of an open log fire. Really early Beatles' songs make me think of the car park behind British Home Stores in Watford, me in the car aged four or five, glancing nervously out of the back window at the pale buildings and wasteland beyond the car-park entrance. Mid-period Beatles, for reasons I can't under-stand at all, makes me think of cheese-and-pickle sandwiches. Late Beatles is too overlaid with accrued crust upon crust of associations to work so precisely, and too many last smoochy dances at adolescent discos have diluted any magic 'The Long and Winding Road' might ever have had. Not that I used to go to discos much.

Other songs from my early childhood, by bands – or possibly groups – like Dave Dee, Dozy, Beaky, Mick and Titch or early Manfred Mann remind me instinctively of the old, cream Bakelite wireless next to my parents' bed, and then I'm reminded of Battersea Fun Fair, the entrance terrifyingly besieged and blocked by mods or rockers.

I think I was fortunate that my childhood and adolescence coincided with that intense, six- or seven-year period which arced from flower power to glam rock to prog rock to pomp rock to punk, so all I have to do is think of a particular song and it can pinpoint a particular time more accurately than carbon dating. For instance, while I was sitting my Maths O level the song 'January' by Pilot ran through my head over and over again, so I only have to hear or even remember the song's opening chord and I can conjure up the mood and the smell and whole zeitgeist of the mid-seventies in an instant and then focus in closer and closer until I'm sitting at the desk in the enormous exam hall, wondering what the hell to do with the quadratic equation in front of me, though why anything by the Human League takes my mind to a petrol station halfway up a hill in St Albans is anyone's guess.

Meanwhile, almost everything recorded between 1983 and around 1990 makes me cringe and think of shopping centres.

But my editor was right. The sense of smell is more powerful, has more potency, and often works, in evocative terms, in reverse. I could easily walk down that street near the top of Ladbroke Grove without being reminded for a second of some song by the Beat or the Specials, but all I have to do is think for a fleeting instant about some place or time, and I can almost always instantly smell it too.

If I think about Alan and Beryl Grover, family friends from my childhood who lived up towards Bushey, I can see their 1930s semi, but far more tellingly I can smell, or I'm aware of the memory of the smell of, their spaniel Sherry, which then makes me think about their cat Sandy and then remember a late afternoon in the spring of 1966, as Alan brought in a box of bottles and packets of snacks which they were intending to party on as they watched the results come in from that day's general election, and I remember contemplating the crisps greedily and imagining what a wonderful thing an election must be, even if it was then unattainable for me.

Bob and Beth Gamble's house, meanwhile, always smelled of Sunday lunch.

And my grandmother's house smelled of furniture polish, fried bread, mould and TCP, while my parents' house, up till the last day I was there, smelled mostly of Hoover bags and radiograms.

You can play this game for ever. There's been a smell, not the slightest bit unpleasant, that's lingered round the entrance to the food hall in Selfridges for at least the last forty-three years, or since I first remember smelling it. When I was a student, the staircases I lived on in my college both smelled, similarly but not identically, of a certain kind of rubber flooring material and lentils, and on the occasions when I've gone back there, they still do. Other enduring smells are more obvious, like the same smells you get round different parts of London Zoo, but there's also a smell that I remember from when I was very small that's stayed around in bits of the Natural History Museum, which seems to have nothing to do with taxidermy or formaldehyde and is, in fact, indescribable although quite pleasant. There's another smell, again difficult to describe but precisely linked to its location, that's been wafting round the Science Museum just round the corner, likewise for decades.

There are other smells I imagine I'll never smell directly again, like the famous smell of Gitanes and disinfectant that would greet you as you climbed down off your train once it had arrived at the Gare du Nord. That's now completely gone, although I caught a tiny hint of it, halfway up one of the platforms, as I got off the Eurostar a few months ago. There are larger clouds of this miasma still to be sniffed at the Gare de Lyon. The smell of routemaster buses is now almost entirely lost, along with the deeply comforting, throaty staccato made by the bus conductor's ticket machine. The smell of old London Underground carriages has gone too, along with the carriages themselves and their slotted wooden floors and the padded seats you could whack with your satchel until the place was filled with thick clouds of years' worth of dust, some of it originating from before the Second World War. The smell of the cardboard boxes you'd get round toffees in from vending machines on the station platforms isn't there any more, although if you keep your eyes open and your nose twitching, you can still find Penguin paperbacks of a certain vintage that smell of chocolate. And there was the smell of the coarse papier mâché they once made Guy Fawkes masks out of, or the smell of old comic annuals, or the sour sickly smell of developer in my father's darkroom, or the plasticky smell of Dymo tape, weird sticky stuff that extruded from a machine cunningly designed to punch letters in relief into the tape. We had one of these gizmos at home when I was about eight or nine, and at the time I'm sure everyone thought it had revolutionised labelling, bringing it into the space age and killing off paper labels written on in copperplate stone dead. Then it was killed off in its turn by Post-it notes. To be honest, punching the word 'fuck' into little raised letters on a strip of red plastic eventually lost its appeal, although there was stuff in my parents' house, after they died, still labelled with Dymo tape. Age had faded the labels, deprived them of their stickiness, and stolen their smell.

The two strongest smells from my childhood, or the smells I remember best and strongest, are of Watford and my school, respectively.

I hated Watford, partly because of the smell, mostly because my mother seemed to be addicted to going there to shop or, worse still, to think about shopping. She did this in the most irritating way imaginable, which involved me and my sister walking in front of her so she could keep an eye on us, but she'd always stop to look at something in some shop window or other and neglect to stop us too, so my sister and I would continue walking down the street until we'd turn round and our mother would be nowhere in sight. I remember this happening all the time, though it couldn't have happened that often, but I do remember several times being held in the arms of a policeman, and my mother rushing up, apologising to the rozzer and accusing me of running away. We both knew that this was monstrously unjust, and if anyone had run away, it had been her. Then, on top of the very real risk of abandonment once you got there, we'd drive into Watford along a road bordered, on the edge of town, by a vast gasometer filled with coal gas, or town gas as it used to be known, which leaked the most revolting smell in the world, of farts and rotten eggs and cheesy socks moulied up with shit, piss and sick. Having got that out of the way, if we ever got into a shop, it would be either British Home Stores, which even now has the same thin custardy smell seeping out of the cafeteria, or Marks & Spencer's, where we'd wander like the dead in interminable circles of Shopping Hell, little Dantes glumly observing an eternity of utter, balls-aching, mind-crushing, soul-destroying boredom, while my mother held up different cardigans in front of herself, seemingly incapable of ever deciding which one she wanted, even though they were all only 39/11d, with sometimes maybe a tantalising final ha'penny added on as a further insult to the credulous.

To give her her due, my mother did try to ameliorate our circumstances. Sometimes she'd pretend that we were the parents and she was the child as we walked round hand in hand trying to get her to stop being naughty. There was possibly more truth to this than I appreciated at the time. But there was still always the chance of a redemptive bribe in the form of a Wimpy at the Wimpy Bar, before hamburgers were debauched by the smirking Fordist corporatism of McDonald's, and you could watch a fat, greasy bloke in a stained apron flip your burger while he fried your onions and toasted your bun as plastic oranges circled slothfully in a glass tank full of orange-coloured water and, hours before, he'd have watered down the ketchup in the red plastic tomatoes. Even better, outside the air was filled with the smell of roasting coffee from the coffee house further along the street.

This was a treat, a genuine treat, much better than going to the Kardoma or the Golden Egg or even somewhere where there might be a chance I'd get a rum baba wearing a flimsy hat of artificial cream, and incomparably better than the Lyons

Corner House, just about still going, but dark and dingy and reeking, I later recognised, of the Blitz.

When I was about five, my mother and I went to the Lyons in Watford, and I suppose as yet another bribe she bought me some ice cream, little crenellated pale yellow vanilla spheres topped with chocolate sauce. I remember eating the chocolate sauce with pleasure, but couldn't get my spoon into the ice cream because it was made of wood. Looking back on it, I blame them for putting their display models within reach of the public, particularly gullible five-year-old members of it, although it's just possible that in that dark, ochre and brown interior, already so antiquated it had nearly completed the process of metamorphosing from a catering outlet to a film set of a catering outlet, they'd given up any pretence of serving real food any more, and were just doling out prop food. We'd rumbled them, so I got some real ice cream to keep us quiet before the staff sneaked off to carve some more pork chops out of balsa wood.

Wooden ice cream, Marks & Spencer's, the gas works and the boredom led me to develop an almost neurotic aversion to Watford, to the extent that I'd often nag my mother to leave me on my own at home, aged about five or six, any consequent danger I might thus have been in far outweighed by the horror of the alternative, Wimpy or no Wimpy. It also nurtured in me an abiding hatred of shopping, and an odd kind of visual dyslexia, which I still can't quite shake off, about gasometers. I must have been over thirty by the time Anna explained to me that gasometers operate telescopically, and that there isn't a pit beneath them, equal in volume to what you see above ground, into which the gas tanks sink when empty. I still don't quite believe that this isn't the case, just like I can never see someone playing the trombone without secretly being astonished that, when the trombonist pulls in that sliding handle, the mouthpiece doesn't shoot gorily through the back of their head.

My aversion to shopping is easier to explain. Shopping is basically boring, up there with double physics or church services or the Royal Tournament or tea with a distant and ancient relative in the pantheon of boringness. Part of my fundamental philosophical objection to Thatcherism was that, at heart, it was all about shopping. By the time of the high summer of Thatcherism, in the late eighties, there was a general mood that everyone could have whatever they wanted whenever they wanted it, mostly based on being able to queue up for hours to get into the car park outside Ikea on a Sunday morning.

I managed to avoid Watford for years, although I did occasionally venture there in my late teens, and I remember around 1976 or 1977 my friend Jon lending me his copy of *The Naked Lunch* at a bus stop near the swimming pool, another place I associate with a distinct smell from when I used to be taken there as a small boy for swimming lessons. The lessons didn't really work, although I can still smell that unique cocktail of chlorine, Wagon Wheels and bags of potato crisps with their little blue patch of waxed paper, twisted round a tiny deposit of salt.

After my father died, I spent much longer round the parts of north-west London I'd prowled in my late childhood than I'd done for about twenty-five years. If I had to drive somewhere, from Stanmore, I found that I could still find my way almost by a kind of autopilot, and much was as it had been, certainly for thirty years, probably for sixty. The rows of suburban semis stayed the same, with maybe a satellite dish here or there, but most of those had been superseded, I suppose, by cable. The little oases of blocks of 1930s shops hadn't changed much either, with the same dry-cleaners or newsagents or travel agents or Indian restaurants or greengrocers, with maybe a larger, flashier pane of glass here, or an ironmonger's transmuted into a wine bar there. But what I did notice, driving through Harrow to register my father's death or driving from Stanmore to my sister's house in Hanwell, west of Ealing, through Greenford, was what had happened to the wasteland. These were those occasional places throughout the suburbs, either near railway lines or behind gasworks or abutting old, abandoned and dilapidated small factories, snatches of no-man's-land that no one had ever thought to develop because they were too inaccessible or remote or poisonous or just ugly, or because someone, somewhere, recognised their role as wildernesses of nettles and tetanus specially preserved as somewhere where small children could risk their lives, or at least their knees. And now every single one had a superstore built on it.

Later, I went to order my parents' gravestone, to replace the one that had covered my mother and Christopher's ashes for the previous thirty-five years. I had to do this in Bushey, as the church in Stanmore would only deal with one particular and specified monumental mason, so I drove across London, taking an early turning before Stanmore so I'd avoid driving past my parents' house which we'd sold six months before.

Bushey was pretty much unchanged. The old timber yard was still there, where my father would frequently take me to buy more wood for whatever DIY project he was currently engaged in, or to beg a bag of sawdust as bedding for our guinea pigs. I imagine it still smells exactly the same, of hot wood being sawn up by enormous circular saws, their teeth biting into the timber with a Doppler roar I can still hear now.

Having ordered the stone, along with a smaller stone for

our dead cat who'd been put down eight days after my step-mother died, I then set off for Whipsnade Wild Animal Park for reasons which needn't detain us here. In order to join the M1 I had to drive through Watford, so I followed the road up through Bushey, under the railway viaduct, to where the gasometer should have been, standing like a stinking guardian of the town beyond.

It was no longer there. Nor were any of the old roads. They'd been replaced with a massive new ring road circling the centre of the town, which was now occupied by a truly enormous, almost cubic building, like a massively oversized Zeppelin hangar. It must have covered acres and acres of ground where the streets were once filled with the smell of roasting coffee. Occasionally glancing sideways as I circum-navigated this monstrosity, now and again I'd glimpse clumps of ducts snaking down the sides of the building, or grating concealing enormous fans and coolers and heaters and all the other stuff you need to stop a modern building freezing or cooking or suffocating its transient occupants. I didn't stop. I had no wish to explore its rows and rows of shoe shops and tacky boutiques or even to discover what its filtered, artificial air smelled like.

My school, incidentally, smelled of boiled mince and incense.

Mould

Viewed from the present, the past is refracted through too many prisms and lenses picked up on the journey ever to be seen quite clearly. Apart from the universal tendency towards sentimentalising, or at least sanitising, the past, and cocooning it in what's usually a false nostalgia, if you think back to a specific time and imagine you can, in memory, capture its general zeitgeist just from the date, you'll inevitably end up getting it slightly wrong. It's just the way humans cope with the passage of time and the constant accretion of the new; most of them are hopelessly tardy, and people in the past were anchored in their past too, so when we look back and think we can see how things changed and developed on their way up to now, too often we're looking just at the avant-garde, and we ignore the garde itself, the vast majority still stagnating in the swamp of ten or twenty or thirty years previously.

Take the 1960s. I was ten and five-sixths on New Year's Eve, 1969, a night I don't remember at all, so it's hardly surprising that I have neither any memory nor did I experience what most people now imagine they mean when they speak of 'the sixties', and though I have clear memories of things that happened to me then, none of it had even a whiff of Woodstock. Instead, although leavened with a bit more prosperity and a slightly less stifling stiffness, for most people it was probably still pretty much like the 1950s had been. My 'sixties' came later, soaking into the mid-1970s like spilt milk spreading through a rug.

And more than that, I suspect that for many people the way they experience history endlessly unfolding all around them means that they reach a kind of supersaturation at a certain point, and get stuck there. This doesn't necessarily mean that these people live in the past, and anyway that's just a crude insult hurled by the impatient and callous. It means that many people find a point of subjective comfort and security, the place where, culturally and maybe even spiritually, they reached the imago stage of their personal metamorphoses. Nor is this just personal. Whole swathes of society seem to choose to be marooned on little islands of past time while the tsunami of history surges inexorably onwards into the future.

To put it another way, the past is not just another country, but actually a penal settlement, from which most people only get a few days' furlough.

And that's why my parents' house, when they died in 2004, seemed still to be firmly yet happily stuck in about 1976; why my grandmother's house, in 1966 or 1969, when I spent a long time there, was still stuck around 1936, though parts of it went back a lot further than that; why, throughout the 1960s, my school stank of 1947; why the suburbs I grew up in in the 1960s were actually still living almost exclusively in the 1950s or, occasionally, the 1930s. Then, as often as not, everything suddenly jolts forward in an attempt to catch up.

As I've said, my mother didn't like my father's mother at all. I think that this was mostly about ownership, and partly another aspect of my mother's lifelong game of emotional musical chairs. She was always falling out with her friends and then making up with them again, and she treated her family in the same way, although she ultimately fell out with her parents completely, though not for the reason I'd always believed. I think this was the way she kept things under control, or more precisely under her own control, although I hope, if she'd lived, she'd never have fallen out with me.

As a result I don't remember meeting my grandmother, my father's mother, until I was seven, although I think I must have met her sister Audrey, and maybe I'd met my grandmother too, because I distinctly remember Audrey's husband Teddy, an immensely tall man wearing a bowler hat (although I can't remember his face), leaning against the birdbath in our garden in Stanmore and telling me stories. Teddy died in 1964, and my father dumped the birdbath soon afterwards as another part of his forty-year-long mission to turn a suburban rose garden into a rhododendron-filled wilderness. Teddy had married Audrey in the 1920s, when he was in his late forties and she was in her twenties. He'd been some kind of intelligence officer in the Middle East during the First World War, and I now have the shell case inlaid with gold and silver he bought as a 'Souvenir de Damasque' (it says so on the case) in 1917. This is an artillery shell, and was presumably gathered from a former battlefield where it had been shat out of the breach of a big gun and was later taken away to be converted into a tourists' trinket. Later, still in the army, Teddy was deemed sufficiently tall to be part of the Prince of Wales' Guard of Honour on his Imperial Tour in the early twenties, although the future Edward VIII, a short man like all the Hanoverians, must have looked ridiculous waving to the natives flanked by men twice his height.

My father used to write to his mother once a week, after lunch on Sunday, with *Semprini Serenade* playing on the wireless in its sinisterly saccharine way. I'd often then walk down the road to the postbox with him. I imagine his letters were as bland as the postcards he'd sent from the Soviet Union. But this was about as close as I ever got to my grandmother, all that way away up in Blackpool, until my mother's first illness.

She had some kind of heart attack, I think, which Dawne now puts down to all the coffee and cigarettes she consumed, to look American and stay thin. Whatever happened to her, it changed her life in various ways. For a start she stopped smoking, and in another little self-conscious Americanism started chewing gum instead, which she'd snap loudly in her mouth, between her tongue and soft palate. She also had to stop fostering children, which she'd done for as long as I could remember.

There were always babies around when I was a small child, which I don't remember objecting to at all because they were a familiar part of my surroundings. I remember she used to change their nappies in the kitchen on a table next to the cooker, and I was just the right height to get an eye-level view of the process, the safety pin holding the terrycloth together being undone and the nappy then folding out to reveal the solid little yellow turd inside. Her foster-babies' turds seem in my memory to have been much more solid than my own children's, but that was probably the result of the Cow & Gate formula babies' milk she fed them. I still have some of those Cow & Gate tins, as my parents kept sugar in them for the next forty years. The only foster-baby I can really remember was called Ringo by my mother, because he hadn't been given a name by his birth mother, although I remember my stepmother repeating a story about another of the babies who was black, and was turned over to lie on his stomach in his carrycot by a friend of my mother's when they were out together one day in Stanmore. When I was clearing out my parents' house I found an album of photos of all the babies she'd fostered, along with their names and whether or not they'd been successfully placed with new families after they left my mother's care. A depressingly large number hadn't been, and I can only begin to guess at whatever might have happened to them subsequently.

Her illness also meant she was put on a course of daily tablets, including what my parents jokingly called 'Tinkle tablets', all of which were kept in little glass bottles in the kitchen, each one labelled with a day of the week. After my mother died my father flushed all the tablets down the downstairs toilet. The stain they left in the U-bend, a smeary rainbow of different bright colours, stayed there for years.

Another consequence of her illness was that my parents decided they needed a month's holiday for her to convalesce, which they spent in Majorca, without me or my sister. For reasons I still don't understand, my sister went to stay with our friends Bob and Beth Gamble and their daughters Julie and Catherine in Oxshott in Surrey, people I knew and liked who lived in a place, with its huge, wooded, boggy garden, which I really rather loved, while it was decided that I should travel two hundred miles north to somewhere I'd never been before to stay with three old people I wasn't even sure I'd ever met.

I remember that journey north. My father drove us up there in our new sky-blue Austin A40, although I don't remember going on any motorways, but maybe that's because there weren't any. I remember sitting in the front passenger seat with my feet resting on a big cardboard box full of Lego, which I suppose was meant to keep me amused for the next month.

Somewhere near Preston we stopped at a level crossing, and a steam locomotive went past. My father told me to remember it, because soon there wouldn't be any steam trains left, and so

I have. I remember the wet, dark trees, the black, grey engine, and red lights shining out against a general lowering murk.

I don't remember arriving in Blackpool, or meeting the three old people I was going to spend the next month with. I do remember that I had to share a bed with my father. It was an old and enormously tall bed that I couldn't get into without standing on something else, in a room with thick, dark curtains and darker, thicker, monumental furniture, wardrobes and dressing tables of a massive imperialist brown solidity, mostly covered in little bits of kitsch. It was completely unlike my bed at home, which was low, with a sprung mattress and no head- or footboards, and I can still remember the intense sense of loss and betrayal I felt when I found I could no longer fit my head underneath it.

The first night of my stay I hardly slept at all. The bedsprings in the monstrous bed had sagged with age, and try as I might I kept slipping into the middle where I'd get squashed by my father, who seemed to be sleeping like a log. So I ended up clinging to the side, while my father continued being a log, but a log being endlessly sawn up, like the timber in Bushey, with roaring snores. The next night we put the musty and immensely heavy bolster between us, but I still couldn't sleep because of his snoring.

Then he left me there, and I was suddenly sucked back in time.

The house, as I've said, was retarded, stuck back in the 1930s, but a 1930s which was defined by the Victorian and Edwardian tastes of thirty or forty years before then, being more than slightly grand and dark, its defining darkness lit up here and there with splashes of faded chintz and bits and bobs of execrable kitsch my grandmother had accumulated according to her taste.

The sense of having come unstuck in time and displaced to a period decades before I was born was everywhere. For instance, the telephone in the downstairs hall, although black like almost all phones then, apart from the occasional iconoclasm of a white or red one in trendier places much further south, was made of Bakelite rather than the later plastics I was familiar with. It seemed unbelievably archaic. It didn't have the rather cuddly curves of what were then modern phones, but sharp edges, and instead of a friendly coil of loops connecting the handset to the main bit of the phone, there was a straight cord, wrapped loosely in some fraying, wide-knit material. It seldom rang, but when it did it took trunk calls, reminding me how far away I was from anything, in space and time.

There was no TV, but instead a dark old wooden wireless, whose valves would warm up with excruciating slowness before the thing would crackle into audibility. This wasn't so bad, as I've always liked the radio, and at home we had lots of them, so you could carry one around as a constant companion, and I remember happily playing on my own or drawing or doing whatever I was doing listening to the repertory company of voices who seemed exclusively to occupy the airwaves wafted out by the BBC Home Service, people like Jack de Manio or Anona Wynn or Lady Isobel Barnett, and I can remember characters from *The Archers* no one I've ever met seems to remember any more, like Hugo Barnaby. The wireless in my grandmother's house was different. It too seemed to have been retarded in time, and defied the laws of physics because it always seemed to be tuned to a signal which took at least ten years to reach it. So I remember listening to *The Goon Show,* which I enjoyed, but which had stopped broadcasting six years previously. Even the programmes which weren't repeats seemed terrifyingly old, like *Friday Night Is Music Night* with the Northern Dance Orchestra playing tunes which you could only really dance to if you had a gas mask slung over your padded or epauletted shoulder.

The wireless was in the dining room, where most of the business of the house went on. The three old people – my grandmother, my widowed Great-Aunt Audrey and my Great-Uncle Jak – would spend several hours getting up, first appearing in their dressing gowns, great padded pink or lilac or thin plaid things, to warm up some milk to get them going for the day ahead. They'd then wash. My grandmother would spend a long time brushing her waist-length thin grey hair before pinning it up in a bun at the back of her head. Audrey would do something similar, for even longer, while Jak would get on with the housework. He'd light fires, stoke up boilers and start on breakfast.

As far as I could tell my grandmother and Audrey never did anything much while all Jak did was cook. This was because the whole day was lived round the dining table which occupied most of the room, one edge of it stuck up against another great, dark piece of furniture with a glass front, containing yet more kitschy little ornaments and trophies won for gardening by long-dead relatives in Ashton-under-Lyne. First, there'd be a cooked breakfast, after which Audrey and my grandmother would clear up, after a fashion, while Jak spent an hour or so cutting slices of white bread into tiny little cubes, which he'd then fry in the fat from that morning's bacon before feeding them to the birds in the garden.

While that was going on, Audrey would start preparing elevenses, which wasn't cooked, but usually consisted of an apple and some cheese on some buttered salty biscuits, which Jak always called T.U.C. biscuits, although I knew that they had nothing to do with trades unions. Then Jak would start preparing lunch, and if I was unlucky I'd go for a walk with my grandmother.

My grandmother was by then a shrunken seventy, although I don't believe she'd ever been much taller. When I was seven I was about as tall as she was. We'd walk down to the North Shore, slowly, and she'd often stop and chat inconsequentially with passers-by, though I'm not sure if she knew who any of them really were. We'd then walk along the seafront, and sometimes venture on to one of the piers, where my grandmother would be beguiled by some spiv who'd set up his stall hawking the latest labour-saving tat to come on to the market, like a super-sharp cheese grater or a plastic colander, while I'd sneak a look at other stalls selling merchandise more typical of Blackpool, like pairs of plastic tits or plastic dog turds.

Years and years later, I started going back to Blackpool to cover party conferences. I only went to look at my grandmother's house once, the first time I returned to Blackpool, the year of Tony Blair's first conference as leader of the Labour Party. I didn't linger. But a few years after that a journalist I know who works for the *Independent* wrote an article in the Labour conference issue of *Tribune,* describing how appalling he'd always found Blackpool to be, with its tatty shops, their cheap tatty wares, its gauche yet leeringly knowing entertainments, its damp and unfriendly hotels and its terrible climate. I remember he finished off by describing how one morning during a TUC conference he'd come out of his hotel to find, on the pavement, a pair of plastic tits floating in a pool of vomit.

It wasn't quite that bad when I stayed there, but I was probably shielded from most of that aspect of the place by my age and the indestructible aura of sweet, pink gentility emanating from my grandmother. I was safely in bed by the time the millworkers started smashing the pubs up or puking on the prom, so the only time I ever managed to punch through the cocoon of lost time and snatch a glance at the reality my grandmother constantly chose to avert her gaze from was when I saw those tits and turds. I kept the world they implied to myself, and we'd then walk back home for lunch.

I remember that I eventually persuaded my grandmother to stop holding my hand on these little excursions.

After lunch was cleared away, preparations would start for tea, then after that we'd have dinner, and then, if I managed to stay up that long, supper. This was their daily routine, and mine too, and had I been able to pick up on the references, I would have recognised that somehow or other I'd been transported to some hideous amalgam of *Great Expectations* and the Mad Hatter's Tea Party from *Alice in Wonderland*, except that we never moved round the table.

Occasionally I'd find treasures. If it was raining we'd have to stay indoors, and sometimes, if my grandmother wasn't looking, I'd be able to read. I found old books like *Redskins* by F. Antsey, a Victorian children's story published in 1898 about bored children playing cowboys and Indians in their back garden, except that the fantasy then comes alive. I also read *The Story of France* by Mary McGregor, published in 1880, where I read about Roland blowing his horn and Joan of Arc and all that stuff, along with what I later realised was a viciously reactionary and partisan account of the Paris Commune. Then there was the Lego, although that stopped being interesting quite quickly. Audrey and I spent one whole afternoon making what she called crocodiles, origami snapping heads which went from being about six inches across to be so tiny even my little fingers could hardly fold the paper, and we then fitted them all inside each other. That's the only time I can remember doing anything with Audrey, although I remember I liked her, much more than I liked my grandmother.

But I liked Jak best of all, so I'd try to spend as much time as possible with him in the kitchen, or while he clipped the hedge or fed the birds or generally kept the place afloat. My father told me that Jak, being the youngest child, never married as it was his inescapable destiny, imposed by the strictures of his class and his times, to look after his mother, and then his sisters. If it ever occurred to him to seek some kind of escape, he found it in model-making, and made the tram which sat in my parents' loft in Stanmore which I'd coveted since I was seven, and which now stands on our sitting-room mantel-piece. The tram once had rails and overhead electrical cables which powered it as it trundled around, presumably over the hall floor. My father also told me about the working gas-ometer Jak made, which went up and down telescopically, just like a real one, depending on how full it was of gas, but which also lit a little street full of tiny gas lamps running down the board it was built on. The gasometer, my father told me, would be filled with gas from the stove. I don't know what happened to it, though I can guess. But whether it was entropy or an explosion, it was no longer around by the time I was.

Now and again I'd go for a walk with Jak rather than my grandmother, and we'd go to the boating pool on the North Shore and I'd chug around the greasy water, gagging on the stench of two-stroke petrol exhaust, while he'd occasionally wave to me with his stick from the shore as he was having a fag, or we'd go down on the beach and he'd pay for a donkey ride, or demonstrate one of the truly useful skills I've learned in my life. Which is how to make a beach volcano.

(If you have a sixty-four-year-old great-uncle with you, preferably in the mid-1960s when sixty-four was still old, you take his walking stick and drive it upright into the sand, although it's possible that any stick of a suitable length might do. You then pile a cone of sand around the walking stick up to its handle, constantly patting the sand down to make sure it's very firm and compact. Then, with either your little spade or, failing that, your hands, you excavate a cave at the base of your volcano, preferably digging down into the sand so it's also partly a small pit, but making sure that you've done this on the leeward side, having already checked the wind direction by licking your finger and holding it up to the air. You then carefully withdraw the walking stick, ensuring that no sand slips into the flue and that there is a clear passage down to the pit or cave below. You now take the newspaper provided especially for the purpose by your great-uncle, and screw its pages into tightish balls, but not too tight, which you then place in the pit already dug at the base. You then get your great-uncle to use his fine old cigarette lighter to ignite the newspaper, which should commence to burn fiercely. If necessary add more newspaper as required. Soon, thick black smoke will start to issue from the top of the volcano. If you've been sensible and constructed your volcano closer to the sea than the promenade – factoring in the likelihood of there being a prevailing onshore breeze – the thick black smoke will then blow across the beach and the many other people gathered on it. If you take the precaution of doing this in 1966, when people were by and large more polite or wary of confrontation, they will then leave the beach, rather than risk tackling a chain-smoking old man and a small boy reckless enough to have precipitated such an encounter in the first place.

I've built many such beach volcanoes since, and have always silently thanked Jak for passing on the secret.)

Back in the old house, there were still some other treasures to be found. There was the tram, now kept in the lower part of another vast, dark piece of furniture, this time in the sitting room, a room otherwise filled with cut glass and china and more horrible ornaments, which no one ever went in, except when I'd sneak in when nobody was looking, open the cupboard and gaze in wonder at that beautiful, beautiful tram.

At the back of the house there was a kind of conservatory, a long room with panes of glass from floor to ceiling on two sides. It had been more or less abandoned to entropy by this stage, its cupboards, lining the third wall, now filled full of old newspapers, a large table in the middle of the room covered in discarded junk much like my father was later to cover any table he could lay claim to for more than about half an hour. Among all the stuff there was another beautiful thing, a wood-and-paper red model biplane, about two foot long, powered by an elastic band. We could never quite make it fly, but it was joy enough just to look at it.

I think Jak must have made that too, like the tram and the gasworks. He had, for a while, owned and managed a fancy-goods company, making the kind of trash the local economy demanded in Blackpool, though I think seashell ashtrays or models of the Tower would have been more in his line than plastic tits or dogshit. During the war, by which time he'd have been in his late thirties and early forties, he'd been stationed somewhere in East Anglia doing something or other, but seems to have spent all his time making an elaborate wooden carriage clock, surmounted by a white billiard ball he probably pinched from the sergeants' mess. I'm pretty certain that it must have been Jak who made another clock, which my father kept in my parents' bedroom up until he died, even though it didn't, and probably can't, work. I've got it now, and it's still at the mender's.

It's in the shape of a mock-Tudor detached house, with a dial on the front, and on top is a clock bell surrounded by various automata, including a burly-looking circus strongman with a hammer, who's meant to strike the bell to mark the hours, and a fluffy fairy-cum-ballerina, balanced on the point of one slipper, who's meant to pirouette and lasso an upright pole to operate the clock's escapement mechanism. Round these two, and the bell, a witch on a broomstick is meant to fly every hour, just missing the head of a little chimney sweep who's meant to poke his head out of a chimney, and then duck down again just before the witch collides with him. As I said, it's not working. More worryingly from a modern perspective, the little chimney sweep is actually a little woollen golliwog, although personally I think it's entirely healthy that everyone who's seen him recently recoils slightly in embarrassment.

Jak, of course, didn't have a modern perspective. I wouldn't encourage anyone to repeat them today, but the little casual racisms that peppered his conversation were typical of his time and class, and also both inventive and funny, if deplorable. He'd make references to Egyptian judo, which meant lying flat on your back doing nothing. Condensed milk, a sickly sludge I haven't seen or tasted for decades, was always called 'dago' by Jak, because it was thick and greasy. And then there was what he referred to as the nine-foot nigger that obsessed me throughout that stay in Blackpool, whom I'd seen painted on an enormous board outside a sideshow on the Golden Mile one day when out walking with my grandmother. He – it – was shown in a grass skirt standing, legs akimbo, against a vaguely tropical background, holding two white sailors in his gargantuan hands, having bitten their heads off with the mouth in each of his two heads. I wanted to see this phenomenon – who wouldn't? – which, it said on the hoarding, was on display in a glass tank beyond the glassed-in ticket booth. My grandmother wouldn't dream of taking me, so I badgered Jak for what seemed like for ever to take me instead. Just before I was due to go home he finally did, and frankly it was a disappointment. Like Jak said as we walked back to the house afterwards, it was just boot polish.

But just before I went home to my parents, we went on a last little jaunt, and again I got sucked back in time. There were still two cars in the garage leaning up against my grandmother's house, though I think only one of them was still going, although I can't now remember whether it was the bull-nosed Morris or the other one, and I never knew what model of car that was anyway. I remember it was a tall, high-sided car, probably black, with thin front seats, a wooden dashboard, an overall smell of leather, polished wood and petrol which only very few cars still have, and with a little glass-and-metal arrow that would spring out of the side and flash amber to indicate whether you intended turning left or right. Jak started it with a starting handle, and then drove us slowly and sedately to Southport, with me and Audrey sitting in the back, a blanket over our knees, and my grandmother in the front. I think I made a fuss to guarantee we ended up sitting like that. We must have looked like Norma Desmond being driven by Erich von Stroheim in *Sunset Boulevard* to any passer-by likely to pick up on the reference.

When we arrived along the seafront in Southport to go for the inevitable walk, I remember Jak put a blanket over the bonnet which was still there when we got back. I remember finding this slightly amazing, so I obviously hadn't lost all my native mid-twentieth-century cynicism during my journey into the more innocent, or arrogant, past.

I didn't go to Blackpool again until the summer after my mother's death at the end of May in 1969. My father must have needed to get us out of the way for a while, and once more I drew the short straw while my sister got to go to Bob and Beth's in Oxshott again.

I'd seen my grandmother once in the meantime. I remember my mother came to pick me up from school one day, and my grandmother was sitting in the car with her. We went to have tea in a teashop in Harrow on the Hill and, quite aware of how much my mother disliked my grandmother, I sat there in a state of astonishment, carefully watching my mother's forced politeness which hardly managed to disguise the equal measures of crossness and contempt written on her face.

Things had changed, in as much as they ever could. Audrey was dead now. Jak had had a mild stroke, and though he still did all the cooking and the housework, he seemed a lot older, and tetchier. He was now sixty-seven, and one day he and I had an argument about Judy Garland, who I insisted was dead, and he, very crossly, insisted wasn't. I remember this upset me quite a lot, not because of Judy Garland in particular, but because I knew I was right and the vehemence of his dissent from my assertion seemed so horribly unjust. I was ten.

My grandmother continued to do not much apart from flitting, smiling abstractedly, around the house. One day she asked me whether it was true that my mother hadn't liked her very much. I lied, like you do, because by and large a pretence for the sake of politeness or not upsetting someone makes for a quieter life, and I was after a quiet life at the time. But I remember, inwardly, that I was deeply affronted. My grandmother must have known what her daughter-in-law thought of her. As far as I know they can't have seen each other more than twice a decade, and even my grandmother wasn't stupid enough to think that that was just because they lived two hundred miles apart. So the question seemed to me – then and now – hideously manipulative, an attempt to make me stitch up my dead mother by squealing on her. I wasn't going to betray my mother's limitless capacity for capricious likes and dislikes and all those other irrational and rational things that had made her the woman she'd been, especially not to my grandmother, whose naive or blinkered belief that everything was always lovely and everyone was lovely too meant she was quite incapable of seeing the world in its proper three dimensions or its infinite perspectives, because she simply refused to see the shadows throwing everything into relief.

So I lied.

And I got my quiet life, a life so quiet and dull I was close to screaming by the end of the summer.

And the next time we went to Blackpool was just after Christmas in 1970, the second Christmas after my mother died. Neither my sister nor I wanted to go, but I suppose my father must have thought that it was something to do, somewhere to go. On Boxing Day my sister and I took the decorations off the Christmas tree and carried the bare little plant in its pot down to the end of the garden and chucked it on the unlit bonfire, and then we drove north. The house was freezing. Jak, now obviously iller than he'd been, would take three hours to make lunch, so we wouldn't get to eat until five o'clock. The weather was foul and trams were regularly getting blown over on the prom. At least my grandmother now had a TV set which my father had bought her, and which now sat where the terrible old wireless had once stood. I seem to remember watching Truffaut's *Les Quatre Cents Coups* on this TV in Blackpool, either on this visit or another one around the same time. Whether it was then or some other time, the film couldn't have made me more miserable than I already was, even if I'd watched it a thousand times.

Then Jak died, and my grandmother came to live with us. I can see her now as she arrived, walking into the kitchen in Stanmore with her wide-legged yet slightly mannered gait, with her great watery eyes, her hook nose and her sunny, vacuous smile, and I seem to remember my sister and me catching each other's eye with a look of resigned horror.

Memory

I can't quite decide whether memory is like a well which gets deeper because the ground level around it rises, or whether it's more like a well you keep filling up, although you never fill it up entirely, with your own bucket you've filled up elsewhere. I'm not really prepared to take the second metaphor the sufficient distance to tell you exactly what you might fill your bucket up with, or where, and it's a bit of a waste of time trying to come up with these metaphors and similes anyway. The question, of course, is how subjective or objective one's memory is, and whether what you end up getting is a synthesis of the two. This is the kind of thing which has kept the philosophers off the streets and out of trouble for millennia, and I'm inclined to leave them to get on with it. Even so, although everything I've reported so far is as I remember it, or as I remember it being told to me, there's always the possibility that I may have got things wrong in recollection, though I don't think I have.

But what do I know? And how do I explain my memory of seeing my father's corpse, about an hour and a half after his sudden death from a pulmonary embolism on 17 January 2004? The memory is clear, of him lying on his side of my parents' bed, his eyes closed, his mouth slightly open, the colour almost gone from his face to be replaced by a pale, yellowish pallor. I already knew he was dead, because my stepmother had phoned to tell me, the latest in a series of phone conversations we'd had that morning from about seven o'clock onwards, when she'd first phoned to ask me if I could come over to Stanmore and take them both to the hospital. I'd spoken to my father the night before, and he'd sounded terribly breathless, quite unlike himself. I'd said that that didn't sound too good, but he replied, in his usual way, that it was probably only a collapsed lung, and anyway the district nurse was coming round to see him the next morning, so she could check him out then. I'd phoned in the first place on the Friday night to ask about my stepmother, who had various cancers and kept getting more, and I had no reason to be particularly worried about my father's health, beyond the fact that he was, by the Saturday, three days short of his eightieth birthday. I'd asked my stepmother what she thought about my father's breathlessness, and she'd said, in a rather brusque tone, but with the tiniest squeak of anxiety behind it, 'Well, I don't know what that's all about.'

On Saturday morning I said I'd get to Stanmore as soon as I could, given the fact that we live the other side of London, and told them to ring the doctor, and thereafter ring for an ambulance and not to wait for me. If the ambulance arrived before I did, I'd catch up with them at the hospital later. At around eight o'clock I phoned my parents to make sure they were doing what I'd told them. My father answered the phone. He still sounded breathless. I asked him how he was. He gave a non-committal reply, and then I asked to speak to my stepmother, who I judged to be in charge of things. She told me she'd made the phone calls I'd suggested, so I said I'd see them later, put the phone down and went to get washed. About seventeen minutes later the phone rang again. Anna answered it. It was my step-mother, and Anna handed me the phone as I came back into the bedroom from the bathroom. I said hello to my step-mother, and she said, 'I think he's dead,' in a calm but slightly puzzled voice.

So I knew he was dead when Anna and I arrived in Stanmore. I grunted a greeting to the two police officers who'd turned up, and to whom my stepmother had been showing some cartoons of mine, but when I went into my parents' bedroom I still clasped my hands to my mouth in shock and disbelief.

The thing is, I can remember all this quite vividly, and I can scroll through the morning's events, fast-forward and rewind almost as if I was sitting in an editing suite. I remember my emotions precisely, the shock, the sorrow, the panic, the overpowering sadness as I kissed his cool forehead goodbye, my growing anxiety at my inability to get through to my sister who'd been out shopping and whom I wasn't able to contact until I got to Stanmore, found my father's address book and her mobile-phone number, or my irritation and disgust with the fat undertaker, a panting jobsworth who absolutely refused to delay my father's removal until my sister got there.

But the memory of them doesn't make me relive these emotions, just remember them. Now it's almost a pleasant memory of the last time I saw my father, as if the memory isn't a single entity with a single existence which you can choose to visit when you please, but rather it's new each time you go back there, and with each fresh visit it's received another protective coat of some kind of preservative or clear resin, transparent but, with each new layer occasioned by each latest visit, minutely thicker, until its thickness turns the reality of the initial experience, in all its different dimensions, into just a tableau of memory which you can simply look at, and then move on to another one, triggering the same process of distancing recovery.

People talk about distant memories, but I'm not sure if they mean the memory itself is distant, so it takes a lot of effort to reach it, or if they mean the memory is of a distant event. It's probably obvious that they mean the first kind of memory, but for whatever reason I don't remember things in that way, and so my memory of the last time I saw my mother is just as clear as my memory of the last time I saw my father, even though it happened thirty-five years earlier.

My father was out that night, at the kind of scientific meeting he regularly attended after work as part of his job. My mother was preparing to go out to a party with the people she knew from the children's playgroup she now worked at, now she could no longer foster babies. My sister was old enough for us not to need a babysitter, and though I don't know exactly what we were doing downstairs, we must have realised that my mother had been taking a lot longer upstairs getting ready than she should have been. I remember us finding her lying diagonally across my parents' double bed, face down over the blue, black ribbed cambric counterpane. My sister says our mother was calling out for our father but not making any sense. She remembers initially trying to call our dentist's widow but getting no reply, and then ringing for an ambulance while my mother shouted at her not to, and she remembers me tugging at her arm and screaming at her not to either, although I don't remember this part of the evening at all. At some point someone must have rung a local doctor we knew called Neville Sharples, a friend of my parents' whose children I remember I really didn't like, although that seems churlish now, considering that their mother, whom I haven't consciously met for over thirty years, sent large floral tributes to both my father and my stepmother's funerals. I remember him arguing with my mother, saying she should go into Edgware General Hospital, but I remember its reputation was so bad that my mother was forcefully, with what force she had, refusing to go. Then I remember my father arriving home, the look of shock and disbelief on his face, and then he must have taken charge, and the ambulance arrived, and I never saw my mother again.

As the ambulance men were taking her away I remember I was standing in my sister's bedroom, next to my parents' room, next to my sister in front of the large mirror my father had put up above the sink unit he'd built, and I caught a glimpse of my ten-year-old face, red and wet and pulled into a mask of grief and fear.

Perhaps a memory is clearer if you keep revisiting it, whether consciously or unconsciously, from the instant it slips from between your fingers into the past and becomes a memory in the first place, so it gets constantly refreshed in your mind. Thus recharged it retains its clarity. Then again, maybe it's just that some things stick out, like jagged spurs of rock in an otherwise flat landscape.

So I remember my father telling me my mother was dead. I was at the house of our dead dentist's widow, after school, doing my homework, when my father came into the room and told me my mother had had an operation which hadn't worked, and she'd died. We hugged each other and cried and cried. I only ever remember seeing my father cry on one other occasion. Later, when my sister, who's three and a half years older than me, got home from school to the dentist's widow's house, I'd resumed doing my homework, and I remember turning round in my chair at the small desk facing the wall in the small, knocked-through sitting room in that semi-detached house near Wealdstone as our father told my sister about our mother's death. I remember I was slightly put out because she kept asking him questions, about how, and why, and I can remember her open-mouthed expression, and the beginnings of anger in her voice and eyes and how her body was beginning to arch inwards, and I couldn't understand why she was putting things off, not realising that she wasn't crying yet because she couldn't. So, I now recognise as unhelpfully, I told her with a voice that was meant to be sympathetic but probably sounded cheery and patronising that it was all right to cry, because I had.

But there's a vast chasm of difference between being ten and a quarter and being nearly fourteen, and we all respond to all sorts of things differently.

I can't now remember what happened that night, or how I slept, or if I slept, or anything else.

Around this time, I remember standing near the bottom of the garden, by the little wall where I'd laid out my name in pebbles, next to the flower bed where the dogs were buried, and asking my sister softly whether she thought our mother had died because we'd been naughty, though I can't remember her reply. It now seems a stupid question, because I was, by and large, a good little boy.

At around the same time our dead dentist's younger daughter, aged about three, came round and asked where my mother was. I remember thinking about how her father had died the year before, so said my mother was away, lying like I would to my grandmother, to spare her feelings.

There's another clear memory from around then, which I'm sure is an accurate recollection of exactly how I felt at the time, unadulterated by later considerations or twisted by any stealthy hindsight that may have sneaked in uninvited, like a sudden draught, each time I subsequently remembered the memory. I was at school, in the corridor outside the Form 2 classroom, by the noticeboards and the little drinking fountain, when a teacher I liked called Ivan Rudkin told me he'd seen my mother's death notice in *The Times*. It was his matter-of-fact tone that immediately made me think that he was more concerned with showing off that he read *The Times* than extending any sympathy to me. I stiffly mumbled some kind of thanks, though even at the time I was conscious that the formalities surrounding the situation I found myself in, which included thanking people for their little gestures of kindness or thoughtfulness, were ludicrous and false. I also remember saying to other boys who said they were sorry to hear that my mother had died – boys I didn't like or boys I was frightened of – that they needn't worry, as they hadn't killed her. These were reactions which you can choose to read any way you like, as either understandable sensitivity, or chippiness, or gracelessness or ingratitude or maybe even rudeness, or perhaps it was just the usual kind of aggressive survival instinct which anyone would use as they grab the latest tool close at hand to hack a way through the next bit of the jungle. Whichever way, I'm certain these memories are of precisely how I felt.

Nonetheless, I was conscious for a very long time of there being a qualitative difference between my memories of life before my mother died, and afterwards. I don't mean a difference in the life, but in the memory of it: everything beforehand used to be slightly blurrier, slightly more disjointed, imbued with a thin yet slightly occluding mist, while everything afterwards was sharp and clear and coherent. For the last few years there's no longer been such a distinct division, but maybe that's just because the perspective is always getting deeper.

Although why I should clearly remember sitting in the back of the car, parked on a clifftop near Beachy Head, listening to *Mrs Dale's Diary* on a portable transistor radio sometime in 1968, at least a year before my mother died, I've no idea.

Nor, much earlier, why I remember trying to climb up Silbury Hill, the prehistoric mound in Wiltshire, or the pattern on the peeling wallpaper of the bedroom at the cheap boarding house we stayed at in Glasgow around 1964, or the bones in the bacon they served up for breakfast there, or the dowdy, dour landlady's daughter who served it up, and the way her cardigan hung from her thin shoulders, although maybe it stuck in my mind because my mother kept on berating my father (over breakfast, in earshot) for booking us into what she called a 'dosshouse'. I also remember walking down Sauchiehall Street early on a Saturday evening, and going into a cinema, although I only remember a Warner Brothers cartoon about three mice (I later found out they were voiced by Jack Benny, Mary Livingstone and Eddie Anderson as Rochester the valet) who go out for a meal at a restaurant which is, in fact, the mouth of a cat, and I remember them sitting down at little tables on the cat's tongue. We may have left then, because I don't remember any of the other films. On the same trip we hired a car and drove to Edinburgh. I remember seeing a Highland cow, and was very taken by the pets' graveyard in Edinburgh Castle.

My mother's comments about the dosshouse were typical. She was capricious in her dealings with most things, not just her friends or her family. I remember her leaving a thruppenny bit, one of those nice chunky pre-decimal brass coins with a portcullis on it, as a tip in the sugar bowl at a teashop in Esher because, she said, it was all they deserved. Earlier, on holiday in Italy in 1967, my sister and I kept getting covered in oil each time we swam in the sea, and twice we were cleaned up by fishermen who I seem to remember were either tinkering with their boats or mending their nets close at hand. I remember my mother tipping the first fisherman quite handsomely after he'd silently and doggedly scrubbed us down with bits of pumice from the beach, strewn there over the previous thousands of years from the bowels of Vesuvius, but she paid the second fisherman, performing the same service, nothing at all. I remember asking her why she hadn't paid him, as I remember thinking that this was not just inconsistent but also rather mean. And I remember her saying it was his oil anyway as she hurried us away.

Her capriciousness cut both ways. I remember we'd quite often suddenly be bundled in the car and driven miles away if a friend of hers phoned up to say they were sad or lonely or wanted a chat, and though I don't remember the conversations that then ensued, I do remember driving home one night back from Surrey and my mother getting lost round Epsom, and how we suddenly found ourselves surrounded by galloping racehorses in the middle of the countryside, presumably near stables associated with the racecourse. On another of these impulsive trips I remember we got home so late that, on another of the creamy plastic wirelesses, this one in the kitchen, I heard the recently launched Radio 1 closing down for the night. It was two in the morning. I seem to remember that my stepmother was there, so I suspect that my mother had driven us all off to pick her up from somewhere in the middle of the night, though I don't know where that place could have been, or what either of them might have been doing there.

And I remember her throwing lettuce at my father across the dining table after he'd shaken a roll of his stomach fat at her, clutched between his fists.

And I remember her running naked into my parents' bedroom in a tiny holiday chalet in Selsey after she'd come out of the bath wrapped in a towel, which my father pulled off her in order to take a photograph.

And I remember her picking up me and Richard Pitts from a Christmas bazaar in a school in Stanmore, and rather than simply driving him straight home to Harrow, she drove us to London so we could see the Christmas lights in Oxford Street.

And I remember hiding behind her in Salcombe when we bumped into Alistair Bell and his family. I didn't like Alistair Bell.

And I remember how she had a strangely personal animus towards the Queen, though I never quite worked out whether this was because she considered the Queen to be stuck-up, or remote, or in the place my mother thought that she should be.

And I remember the kind of things she used to say, like 'Hark at the wind' as it blew round our house on winter evenings, and how she used to refer to our weedier friends as 'drips of the first water', and how, when another car would overtake her, it was 'better to be a little bit later in this world than a little bit earlier in the next'. And every time we saw an ambulance or fire engine or police car speed by, its lights and sirens flashing and howling, she'd always say that they were just rushing home for their tea, although she used to carry little medals of St Christopher with her wherever she went, and give them to us and other people as presents.

And I remember her appalling habit of licking her handkerchief to clean my face just before we arrived anywhere.

And I remember her being furious when I'd embarrassed her, like when I called a friend of her friend Beryl a nosy old cow to her face, and I remember the sense of injustice I felt as I stood in a corner in the downstairs hall after we got home, because we both knew I was just quoting my mother.

And I remember her being impatient, and evasive, and funny, and difficult and, towards the end which none of us (except maybe her) saw coming, sometimes embarrassing, like when she ran down a hill on the island where the old White Russian lived off Helsinki, yelling at the departing ferry to stop, and sometimes exasperating, like when she discovered the joys of the local launderama and its advantages over the Hoover twin-tub with its vooming spin dryer, and we'd sit in that over-bright room, its exterior wall dark through the plate glass, serenaded with sploshing and whirring till midnight.

And I remember her lying in the bath for hours, with the door locked, after the Aberfan disaster in which a school full of children was buried by a slagheap in October 1966, deeply depressed and brooding on all those dead children, and she wouldn't come out. My father was travelling between scientific symposia in Japan and India at the time.

So it must have been a few weeks later that she and my stepmother tried to put on a firework display to match the usual ones my father staged (including the one when, because it had been raining heavily, he'd added petrol to the bonfire which, when he lit it, singed off his eyebrows which never really grew back again properly). And I remember standing in the back garden, next to the cardboard box full of fireworks, and either my mother or my stepmother lit one of those little aeroplane fireworks which got banned years ago, along with hand-held bangers and jumping jacks, and which whizzed round at ankle height, which is what this one did. Except that it went in a perfect circle, landing within seconds back in the cardboard box, so all the other fireworks all went off at once.

Rather crestfallen, a night or so later we went to a display at the local tennis club, a place where we'd never been before.

And I remember my mother and stepmother laughing themselves silly one Easter as my sister and I tried and tried to break the tops off our boiled eggs, until either my sister or I tried to bite the top off and found the eggs were made of sugar.

Although I also remember, one time when my stepmother was staying, my sister and I clambering into her bed and my mother bringing in some coffee, unsmiling and exuding the kind of frostiness I later saw on her face when she was sitting next to my grandmother in the car.

Of course, my stepmother wasn't my stepmother at the time.

My mother didn't go to Edgware General, but to the London Hospital in Whitechapel instead, where my father used to work in the early 1960s. My sister and I never visited her there because she didn't want us to, probably because she thought we'd be too upset by the way she looked. And then she died, following a series of aneurisms, on the morning of 29 May 1969. My father always said she died of a brain haemorrhage, which is more or less right, and was good enough for his purposes and mine.

I didn't go to the funeral either. I was asked if I wanted

to go and I said no, because I thought it would be too upsetting. I realise now – I've realised for years – that I should
never have been given the option, that I should have been
made to observe the rituals which have developed in the first
place to help us make ourselves feel better. But perhaps then
my mother wouldn't have visited my dreams so often and
admit that she'd just been hiding all along. And I can't blame
my father. He almost certainly thought he was being kind
and that he was only trying to do the right thing.

So instead I went to school that day, to my High Church
Anglican prep school in Harrow, probably pretending that
things could still carry on as usual, although I absolutely refused
to go to the bloody requiem mass they held for my mother
in the school chapel, situated above the dining hall and the
kitchens, which was why the whole place stank of incense
and boiled mince.

Stuff I've always known

I seem to have known some things all my life, or at least I don't remember ever learning or hearing about them in the first place. Some things, obviously, are instinctive, so you both can't and don't have to remember how you learned to do them, like walking, although my father must have had to learn how to walk again when he was a teenager. Nor do I remember learning how to speak, or think, or breathe, although ultimately I suppose we forget how to do all of those things.

I do remember learning to read and write, under the tutelage of Mrs Theadham, the form teacher in 1A at my prep school. We'd spend Friday afternoons copying down what she'd written on the blackboard, in our shaky infantile copperplate, which was just as purgatorial as going shopping in Watford or sitting through the masses in the school chapel, which you were more or less compelled to do unless you had the unarguable excuse of being a Jew. I remember Mrs Theadham as being a rather intimidating and frightening woman, particular in comparison to Miss Williams whom we'd had the year before.

For a start, she marked the point where I was stripped of my first name, so aged six I was summarily introduced into the world of the barracks and the prison which provided the template for how you were expected to think about yourself in English schools for generations, and also about all the children around you. I suppose this repressed surname formality was meant to discourage too much intimacy and all the beastliness, from solidarity and potential insurrection to fiddling with each other, that might subsequently arise. After all, we'd built an empire on not knowing too much about each other, and a few years ago I read about two of the first British explorers who tried to map the interior of Australia, depending more on the pluck, stoicism and taboos they'd learned from cold showers and hard dormitories than any soppy stuff about song lines. Anyway, they'd run out of food, water, energy and luck, and *in extremis* one of them asked the other what his Christian name was (it was, inevitably, a Christian name). His companion, called Carruthers, replied that he didn't think there was any call for them to abandon all standards quite yet. A century later, little boys like me were still calling each other solely by their surnames, although by now it had been hardwired into us as an enviable mode of behaviour, with the canon of schoolboy literature, from Jennings to Bunter to Molesworth, infecting and reinfecting our little minds. I suppose we should have been grateful they didn't give us numbers, and it's unimaginable that anyone, the soles of their polished shoes still damp from the ebbing tide of empire, might ever have reflected that another reason why Victorian Britain possessed the greatest empire the world had ever seen had nothing to do with hardening your spirit and your upper lip to the condition of stiff leather and everything to do with the free availability of opiates over almost every shop counter in the high street.

Mrs Theadham would certainly never have thought about it like that, although you might wonder what motivated her to tie Paul Barrow to his chair until he got his spellings right and, another time, when Mark Smith refused to eat his lunch to the point where he vomited back what little he'd eaten, make him sit at the dining table beneath that terrible painting of the leaves raked into the bonfire until he'd eaten everything on his plate, predigested and otherwise. Perhaps she'd been jaded by years in a job where almost all of the people she dealt with were unable to pronounce her surname, and being called Mrs Feddum a hundred times a day just occasionally drove her over the edge.

It must also be said in mitigation that Paul Barrow and Mark Smith may possibly have deserved everything they got. Mark Smith was one of those slightly out-of-focus, round-faced blond boys with soft deceitful eyes and a softer voice which issued gurglingly from some constricted point between his throat, his soft palate and his nose, and therefore one of those unfortunate people you just instinctively want to slap, whatever your age or theirs. Paul Barrow, on the other hand, was just a six-year-old psychopath, with a gawping mouth, yellowish skin, a lumpish yet thin posture which lent itself naturally to a loose if lithe kind of universal clumsiness, a deep, booming nasal voice, an unfocused proclivity for random violence and the kind of floppy hyperactivity which couldn't even win over the tough little five- and six-year-olds who were looking for any opportunity to make trouble. When he left the school a few years later a rumour went round that his perfidy was so great that he'd been run over, and at the time for some reason being run over was the most ignominious death imaginable, entirely brought down upon the victim through either culpable negligence or a stubborn refusal to heed the warnings of the Tufty Club. He probably wasn't run over at all, and is almost certainly now living in respectable middle age in Pinner.

I heard a few years ago that Clement Attlee, on the day he died, was able to recite the names of all the boys who'd been in the same class as him seventy years before at Haileybury. I found the idea of this utterly nauseating, evincing that rather creepy kind of *Goodbye, Mr Chips* nostalgia for your schooldays I'm inclined to guard against, in case, in constantly turning to look back you turn yourself, like Lot's wife, into a pillar of salt with your own tears of self-pity. What that kind of mawkishness neglects, or forgets, is that childhood is an age of innocence only in as much as children are usually innocent of any of the constraints we all slowly acquire and which prevent most of us from ever again hating or loving or tormenting or physically hurting each other with the cheerful and thoughtless abandon we do when we're children. But, like Attlee, I can remember the names and faces of dozens of people I haven't seen or heard of for almost forty years. I didn't much like a lot of these people in the first place, boys like Martin Lancaster, whom I was meant to be friends with because we had the same first name, but whom I actually hated, especially after he and his mother came round to our house one day and we were sent into the garden together, while our mothers drank coffee, in order to engage in a euphemism called 'play'. This mostly involved him repeatedly calling me stupid in comparison to himself and then kicking over another low wall my father had just built before running into the house to blame me. Then there were the boys I was slightly frightened of, like John Sowden, who died aged eighteen on the first day he rode his new motorbike; or Ian Harvey, who seemed big and tough until I discovered he actually made the things they showed you how to make on *Blue Peter*, which, like entering a pub full of football supporters and discovering that they're all Welsh, instantly neutralised any threatening potential he may have had; or Nicholas Snook, who at the age of seven had been kept down a year, and who every morning (being slightly bigger than me, at an age when even small proportions have a much steeper perspective) threatened to thump me unless I gave him the Milky Way my mother had given me to eat during the mid-morning break. I handed over a lot of Milky Ways until I eventually told my mother what was going on. In her typical fashion, rather than informing the school, she resorted to direct action and got my father to carve a piece of balsa wood into the rough shape of a Milky Way bar, which she then wrapped in a Milky Way wrapper. I can't remember if they painted the wood or not, but I can remember, during the lesson after break, watching Nicholas Snook unwrap his booty, and then his expression of puzzlement and dawning understanding, and then his glance of surrender to me across the classroom.

I don't remember learning to draw, but I do remember refining my technique by copying other people, and I also remember, in Mrs Theadham's class, receiving my first really useful lesson in life, when we were meant to be drawing a church tower. I'd drawn my tower, but recognised that the perpendiculars of the tower were too close together so, not having a rubber, I licked my finger and rubbed with that instead until the pencil line was sufficiently blurred for me to draw over it. Then, after we'd handed our work in, Mrs Theadham held up my drawing in front of the class as an example to the rest of them. Not only was my church beautifully proportioned, I'd even put in shading and shadows, where my damp little finger had smeared the pencil lead all over the paper. I got a star. I also got my first intimation of what you can get away with.

The next year I was in Miss Smith's class. She was a nice woman, and her class was generally seen as a year of relief between the tough regime of Mrs Theadham and the even tougher one coming up the following year under the truly terrifying Miss Treece, who'd rather brilliantly added to her already fearsome reputation by wearing a wig, an unconvincing chestnut-brown thing that bobbed above the frowning top rims of her unforgiving spectacles propped on her fat nose with its flayed nostrils, which itself sat just above her sour mouth. I remember her classroom as being permanently dark, despite having a large set of windows on one side, opening on to the school drive, while on the other side of the room were frosted windows looking on to a narrow corridor leading to the cloakrooms, where the condensation would stream down the layers and layers of green and dirty yellow gloss paint, the kind of paint that would sheer off under your thumbnail like knapped flint while you stood in line waiting to enter a classroom after break.

Miss Treece probably wasn't that bad, but she was formidable in her natural habitat of old desks and inkwells. (We still spent several lessons a week practising our handwriting with dipping pens. This was somewhere else where Time seemed to have stood still, possibly since Millais painted *The Boyhood of Raleigh*, a copy of which was hung up in the dinge.) But it was probably mostly an act. We all knew there were some teachers you could break within weeks if they even gave way an inch. Four years above Miss Treece was Mr Fraser's class. I liked Mr Fraser a great deal, but I also admired his shtick. Every boy in the school seemed to know, as an absolute fact, that in the cupboard outside his classroom Fraser kept the skull of a boy he had personally murdered. This was so well known that no one ever dared to ask him directly about it, which was presumably exactly what he intended, and he probably started the rumour himself, to balance out the fact that he taught English, loved poetry, wore soft dark flannel shirts with woollen ties and had been a conscientious objector during the war. He was one of those teachers who made a qualitative difference to my life, like my old teacher Butti. He taught me about the parts of speech, and how no one should attempt to write rhyming poetry until they could write good blank verse, and he made us learn some poems by heart so well that I can still recite Wordsworth's bloody awful poem 'The Daffodils' without a second's hesitation, though I now make it more palatable by singing it to the tune of 'For Those in Peril on the Sea'. It scans perfectly. And I remember I cried at school, though I tried my hardest not to, after he died of a heart attack a year after I left his class, three years after my mother died.

There were other things I don't remember ever having been told, so I seem always to have known. One of these was God, even though we didn't go to church, or not often enough for me to remember it. I do remember going to look at my school with my mother before I was sent there, and after I'd sat on the knee of the chain-smoking old priest who was also the headmaster, my mother and I went to look in the chapel over the kitchens. I remember us standing hand in hand just before the roped-off altar with its tabernacle containing God knows what, or possibly even God Himself, and it didn't seem that strange, though maybe I've only remembered it because it was.

Later, but while I was still at the school, I remember thinking how clever they'd been in dedicating that chapel to St Francis of Assisi, so all the little boys would be presented with a nice, easy saint who was friendly to animals, rather than trying to get us to buy into St Augustine or St Simeon Stylites or St Teresa of Ávila and all that repressed sexuality, or even St Kevin, an early Irish anchorite who earned his canonisation because one day a naked woman walked past the mouth of his cave and he displayed his resistence to the temptations of the flesh by immediately nipping out to slaughter her with an axe. Francis of Assisi was much more attractive than most of the monsters and hysterics and monomaniacs in the hagiographical pantheon, and we all remained happily ignorant of the lice in his hair shirt, the weeping pus of his miraculous stigmata and ferules and all the other impedimenta of his brand of asceticism. I suppose we were meant to think more about Bambi than all that. His statue, in a little altar to the left of the high altar, showed him looking wistfully to heaven, pulling aside a fold of his brown habit to show the wound in his side from his stigmata with one pierced hand, while the other one had a dove perched on one of its extended fingers. Candles burned in front of this, and almost everywhere else, and you were expected to dip your finger in an ornate little stoup containing holy water on the wall by the entrance as you came in, and then genuflect to the altar. The water was salty, either to deter you from drinking it or ward off the Devil, but we all used to lick our fingers after dunking them in it, as you'd expect.

The pieties extended further. The school had a chaplain, at first in addition to the chain-smoking headmaster and then, after he retired, instead of him. When I was about nine the chaplain, a nice man but with the distinctive angularity, bushy eyebrows, big nose and protruding Adam's apple of his calling, left to go to Australia. He would always wear a dog collar, but also wore trousers. His replacement didn't have the eyebrows or the Adam's apple, but wore what seemed to be a dress, twitchily pursed his lips in a kind of half-sent blown kiss every time he thought he'd made a joke, and would invite the prettier little boys to come and play with his model train set. We used to sing disgusting songs about him in the playground, knew precisely what he was up to, and had to keep a straight face as he bowed low in front of the altar during early chapel on a Thursday morning and raised the host, singing the Kyrie eleison in a monotonous baritone, while little boys in surplices swung censers and held candles and crosses, with the incense continuing to mingle with the smell of the mince. Some days, if you were lucky, mid-transubstantiation one of the younger boys near the front would wet himself and everyone around him would hastily leap out of the way of the spreading pool of piss. It would be the one note of relief in the martyrdom of Te Deums and tedium anyone knows who's sat through the Collect, Epistle and Gospel for the twenty-third Sunday in Trinity or whatever it was, and even now I can remember the effort involved, grinding my teeth and straining the muscles in my face, to stop the tears of boredom coursing down my cheeks.

And the pieties went even further than that. The school's governors were all Anglican prelates of some kind connected to Walsingham, a Marian shrine in north Norfolk near Cromer, which had been suppressed during the Dissolution of the Monasteries but rediscovered in the 1920s and rebuilt by overexcited High Churchers in the distinctive post-Arts and Crafts, Eric Gill-ish style of both the times and their predilections. Particularly pious boys – or boys who knew which side their bread was buttered – would go there on retreats prior to confirmation, but other boys occasionally got a chance to go there too, on a little holiday.

I was never confirmed, just like I never joined the 11th Harrow Scout Troop which was attached to the school. Both, like belonging to the Pioneers in the Soviet Union, were expected of everyone, except the Jews, but my father often said that you shouldn't join any paramilitary youth organisation, even one with woggles. I think this was only partly a joke, and I didn't want to join the Scouts anyway, but it seemed an odd prohibition considering that my sister had been a Brownie and joined the Girls' Brigade, pony clubs, swimming clubs and everything else going. I think that by the time it got round to me, if I expressed a shyness about joining in any extra-curricular activity, my parents sighed with relief and left it at that.

The chain-smoking priest-headmaster's replacement, whom even the teachers openly referred to as 'Hitler' within easy earshot of their pupils, took an instant dislike to me, and was always asking when I was intending to get confirmed, but by this stage I had the ultimate fallback of a dead mother to explain most of my perceived dissidence.

Still, I did go to Walsingham once. It was a sort of reward for working hard and being good, and as I've said, I was good little boy, though I'll tell you why later. We went in the minibus, the pious and the impious, and stayed in the oak-and-brick convent near the basilica. The basilica itself was centred round a chapel containing the miraculous spring where a noblewoman had seen a vision of Our Lady of Walsingham in the Middle Ages, inspiring the shrine's original foundation. In its post-Oxford Movement reincarnation, the narrow, flat red bricks of the interior chapel housed a largish doll of the Virgin Mary, black as your hat, dressed in silver and gold, just standing there and waiting to be venerated, and back at school in our prayers (no, their prayers – I mouthed the words but never really joined in) we were constantly demanding the protection and intercession and whatever else she had to offer from Our Lady of Walsingham, for what good it ever did anyone.

And I admit that I had been infected by the place – not Walsingham, but the school it oversaw and which its largish doll presumably protected – and I did pray when my mother was ill for the last time, or tried to, though I seem to remember thinking that this wasn't going to make any difference. But I also have to say, for the record, that when I was at Walsingham, two years after my mother died, I bought a little bottle of the holy water in the gift shop attached to the shrine, on sale amid the fudge and the key rings and pamphlets and pine crosses and contemplative books by or about Julian of

Norwich (a medieval anchoress who always sounded to me like a hairdresser's). I bought it for our dead dentist's elder daughter, still grieving, like me, but for her father who'd died of lung cancer a year or so before my mother. I knew she was going through a religious phase, so not completely as a teasing joke I bought her the holy water. After I gave it to her she washed her hands in it, and it cured her eczema.

I bought a bottle for myself too, and drank it when I got home, just to see what happened. But nothing did, neither my mother coming back to life, nor me growing a thick prehensile tail or being able to fly or clamber up the wall like a gecko or my grandmother dropping dead or anything. But who knows? Things might have turned out very differently if I hadn't drunk it. It's all a bit of a Mystery really.

Back at Walsingham, along the walls of the 1930s basilica surrounding the chapel containing the shrine were little side chapels, each about the size of a telephone box. One of these was the Chapel of the Ascension and in the low ceiling, in painted plaster relief, was a representation of the action itself, with two feet bearing the holes from the Crucifixion surrounded by a ring of fluffy white clouds. It always looked to me like the last course at a cannibal banquet, served up with mashed potatoes.

Not that I didn't know everything you needed to know about the Feast of the Ascension. On Ascension Day we had to go into school, sit through another interminable High Mass, and then go home again at nine o'clock in the morning, which more or less ruined rest of the day. Something similar happened on Ash Wednesday, when we'd all have some ash collected from the burning of the previous year's palm crosses daubed on our foreheads. The year after my mother died, I said something about how maybe I should leave the smuts there, probably because I thought it would ingratiate me with my teachers. My father replied that they'd just think that I never washed.

High Church Anglicanism is odd in itself, held suspended in a kind of doctrinal mid-air, the magnetic forces pulling and repelling in equal measure from both Rome and Canterbury resulting in it wobbling between being neither one thing nor the other. So on the one hand, liturgically and aesthetically, with all the usual yells, bells and smells, it was probably more Catholic than the post-Vatican II Catholics were, but at the same time it was firmly part of the British Establishment, so after the sanctus bell was jangled thrice to wake us all up, we'd swear allegiance to God and the Queen, and occasionally we sang a very strange hymn attacking the Quakers, with the rather jaunty chorus, 'You're tearing down the pillars of the Church, George Fox!', and it all reeked of 1910 and the branch of senile Pre-Raphaelitism that mutated into Anglican monasticism and thickly limbed apostles portrayed against a perspective-free background of wheatsheafs and deep blue, rather than the one that led into Guild Socialism, summer schools and, ultimately, the ubiquity of William Morris wallpaper in the country cottages of the bourgeoisie.

So it's hardly surprising that my Anglo-Catholic education didn't have quite the same effect a full-blown Catholic education has on many, including a lot of my Irish friends who suffered, literally, at the hands of Christian Brothers in almost all the ways you've got the stomach to imagine. Being a sect within a sect within a sect, the High Church Anglicans had insufficient totalitarian clout behind them to make me take any of it very seriously, a bit like my father and the Freemasons. It was too bloodless, too polite and respectable and laden with slightly distressed gentility to be really intimidating. And even though I once won a catechism prize (it wasn't that hard, and my prize, a white plaster Christ on a pale pine cross, now hangs from one of the lower canines in the jaws of the stuffed head of a one-eared jackal I was once given, a little sop to an attempted ecumenicalism between the Church of England and the gods of ancient Egypt) everything I was taught for years about the nature of miracles, red letter saints' days, the lesser and greater Forty Days, the outward-and-physical-manifestation-of-an-inner-and-spiritual-grace stuff now seems to have been as much of a waste of time as all those hours spent teaching me how to use slide rules and log tables, just months before pocket calculators became widely available.

The God stuff sank in deeper than the logarithms, but I was at an impressionable age, and all it ultimately did was give me enough information to come to the conclusion on my own that it was all bollocks, and that religion, by and large, always smells of mince.

But God runs deeper everywhere. My father told me that his grandfather used to bounce him on his knee and sing, 'Catholic, Catholic, quack, quack, quack! Go to the Devil and don't come back!', a song he'd sung as a boy, hunting down Catholics through the streets of Manchester in the 1880s.

And my mother used to call nuns 'devil-dodgers' every time she saw one, despite – or maybe because – her sister Jean had married a spoilt Catholic priest.

And when they adopted my sister, although they both agreed to her birth mother's wishes to raise her as a Roman Catholic, neither of my parents did anything of the kind.

And my stepmother, having been educated by nuns in Argentina, was full of stories about their pettiness, prudery (she said she and her sisters were never allowed to take all their clothes off, even when washing, in case it encouraged lewd thoughts) and thoughtless cruelty, although she kept the little flimsy paper portraits of saints she'd been given on religious holidays or at her friends' first communions until the day she died.

Though a month or so before that, when she was in the Royal Free Hospital in Hampstead and I went to visit her one afternoon, as I came into the geriatric oncology ward, when she saw me she rolled her eyes and, pointing behind her hand, mouthed that I should have a quick look at the bed opposite her. The old, dying Portuguese woman in it was being visited by a priest, who'd brought along a two-thirds life-size statue of the Virgin Mary, which was propped up at the old woman's bedside on one of those ubiquitous moulded plastic chairs you get in hospitals. My stepmother and I exchanged amused looks, and from the corner of my eye I later saw the priest pointing at the Virgin and saying, in that loudly half-whispered hospital voice, 'It's all up to her now, dear!'

Then again, my stepmother and her sisters finally consigned their mother to the nursing home near Letchworth which was run by nuns, though I think her daily battles with them probably kept her alive for an extra ten years.

But remember that I was born into a prelapsarian England, where Anglicanism was still the default setting for most people, even if only when they were born, got married, were admitted to hospital or died. Since then, most of us have followed the Reformation dynamic of discarding erroneous dogma to its logical conclusion and finally dumped belief in God along with transubstantiation, the intercession of saints, papal infallibility, indulgences and the power of relics, which is probably why we're now so confused and frightened by anyone who still takes their religious identity more seriously than all the other ones they could choose from.

Back in the 1960s, as I've said, the prevailing mood owed more to the previous decade; there was still a general air of church parades and harvest festivals, even if these were only the outward manifestations of something that was no longer inside. But that wasn't the point, and the powerful isotopes of conformity and suburban respectability had long half-lives. They, in their turn, owed everything to the horrors of the 1940s, and so the 1950s should perhaps be seen as a decade where a collective post-traumatic stress disorder compelled people to leapfrog back to what they might have perceived as the stability of their childhoods in the 1920s and 30s, when their parents, in their turn, and with their own post-trauma to cope with, hunkered down in their semis and tried to leapfrog back beyond the Great War to the illusion of peace, domesticity and quiet decency in the reign of Edward VII.

I was born fourteen years after it ended, but the Second World War was still everywhere, and rather than not talking about it, you never seemed to hear about anything else. Sunday-afternoon TV was dominated for years by grainy British films about it, our comics were filled with it, our playground games were defined by it, our quiet diversions – Airfix kits, toy guns and toy soldiers – were populated by it, even some of our gardens and school playgrounds still had air-raid shelters left over from it, although I remember as I grew up it was beginning to fray slightly at the edges as it came under the pressure from the only dictum of Karl Marx to be fully embraced by the English, which is the compulsion to repeat tragedy as farce. Increasingly, throughout my childhood, the War (along with the Lost Empire) was softened and made safer by whimsicality. Thus *Dad's Army* and Spike Milligan pretending to be

Hitler, or even *Monty Python*, with John Cleese, again as Hitler, shouting, 'Watch your mouth or it's lampshade time!'

Then there was Adolf Twitler in the comic *Wham!*, a character in the 'Georgie's Germs' strip who was constantly conspiring to infect the eponymous Georgie with German measles, which manifested itself in a rash of little swastikas. And then there were the little magazines I remember seeing on sale in the shop in the middle of the holiday camp filled with rows and rows of little ticky-tacky chalets, where my father took the photograph of my mother coming out of the bath. My sister and I would go to the shop to buy packets of sour cherry boiled sweets, and on a rotating wire rack were flimsy, pulpish American publications with paintings on the front covers of scantily clad women tied up in ropes, looking in horror at leering, bald SS officers with monocles and riding crops, or buck-toothed Japanese wearing thick-lensed spectacles, thus neatly reducing the whole of the Second World War merely to provide the context for some cheap and rather sordid titillation.

I remember Churchill's funeral. Somewhere or other I've still got some of the souvenir supplements the papers produced to mark the event, and I remember (though this may be in retrospect) a curious kind of intimate disjunction, as if this was something – by which I mean the entire baggage of the war which Churchill embodied then and still does – which was both remote and yet ubiquitous, and so ended up meaning not much more than the streets you walk down every day or the air you breathe, and for years my friends and I at school would try to outdo each other in making our Churchill impressions as slurry and nasal and as funny as possible. Now, sufficiently remote from the war and the postwar too, we take it all much more seriously, as we do the First World War, which when I was a child had been completely overshadowed by its bastard offspring, although my grandmother's house, caught in aspic variously in the 1930s and the 1900s, reeked of it.

In that dark, silent house I'd find old albums of jolly Bruce Bairnsfather cartoons about the comic side of life in the trenches, or little reminders of my long-dead grandfather, who'd been a second lieutenant in the South Lancashire Cycle Regiment, on active service on the Western Front until he'd been wounded in the foot. After that he was posted to a prisoner-of-war camp where one of the German inmates made him a chess set. It's in a large, wooden box with a stylised carving on the top, the letters of my grandfather's initials, 'E.R.', looping together, surmounted by what looks like a papal crown and supported by the dates '1914–1917', all this almost circled by branches of oak and olive. On the back of the chess board itself, inside an untidy red ellipse, itself inside another black one fringed with semicircles, are the words, written in green ink, 'MADE BY JACOB SENG 35 P.O.W.K.'. My father gave me the chess set years ago, as it was just another damn thing cluttering up his loft.

My mother, as we know, spent the war safe in America, apart from a brief period pulling down the blackout curtains at the beginning of it.

My father was at school went it started, and he once told me he remembered coming home from church and hearing Chamberlain on the wireless announcing the Declaration of War. The oddest thing about this is the idea of my father going to church, even though he would only have gone because that's what everyone did, for appearances' sake.

His bad leg meant that he was unfit for any of the armed forces, though I think he once said someone tried to offer him a desk job somewhere, but when he was nineteen he went to Cambridge to read medicine, so he was in a reserved occupation anyway.

As far as I can tell he did very little to further the war effort, apart from fire-watch from the college roof, for which purpose he was given an ARP warden's helmet. I remember him telling me how he and a friend used to launch each other wearing their helmets, and when I asked him to explain, he said they'd break bottles of beer over each other's heads, pretending they were battleships.

My stepmother was a nurse in London during the war and so had a much busier time of it altogether.

Indeed, her childhood in Argentina and the war seemed to provide my stepmother with her own personal, portable time capsule, and I think her experiences there and then defined both her and the way she saw the world. This wasn't a case of the past constantly dragging her back so much as providing her with the sheet anchor which gave her her safe moorings throughout her life.

This isn't such a surprise. After the brief interlude in the store in Worthing, my stepmother persuaded her father to let her train to be a nurse, like her mother. She'd started off boiling handkerchiefs in a vast cauldron in a TB isolation hospital on the South Downs, but had moved up to London by the time war broke out. I remember her stories about how she and her younger sister, by this time also working in London, would sit together on the Circle Line, going round and round and round reading books or knitting, either avoiding air-raids or just passing the time.

Another of her stories was about how she and a friend of hers, both training on the same ward in a hospital halfway down the King's Road in Chelsea, came off duty at the same time and so went to visit her friend's uncle, who owned a furrier's in Piccadilly Circus. While they were there the air-raid sirens began their familiar, slowly ululating moan (a noise everyone my age recognised, even though none of us had ever heard it when it meant anything). My step-mother, her friend and her friend's uncle went down into the basement and sat there, drinking cocoa surrounded by thousands of pounds' worth of fur coats as the bombs exploded above them. Then my mother or her friend realised that they were due back on the ward, and told the uncle that they had to go. Despite his protests that it was too dangerous for them to leave, from what my stepmother told me they obviously feared the wrath of their ward sister far more than anything the Luftwaffe could throw at them, so ran out of the shop to the comparative safety of Piccadilly Circus Underground Station and made their way by tube to Sloane Square.

The raid was still going on, and I remember my stepmother telling me how she and her friend ran out of the station and down the King's Road, ducking into doorways as they went to avoid the constant rain of broken glass showering sharply down from the windows above them. Finally, amazingly, they reached the hospital in time for their next shift.

The hospital had been built with two wings, each three storeys high, stretching out from a central building containing all the lifts and stairwells, from whence you'd gain entrance to each of the wards. The nurses' stations, along with their restrooms, the sisters' offices, the medicine cupboard and so on, were all close to the entrances to the wards, near the stair-wells. Once my stepmother got back on to the ward she checked in with the ward sister, quickly got changed into her uniform and then went to the end of the ward to check the patients, while I remember her telling me that her friend stayed by the nurses' station.

Then the central stairwell received a direct hit.

All the people at the other end to my stepmother – the nurses, the ward sister, the patients – were killed.

And I remember her telling me how it took hours to rescue the survivors, herself included, since all the stairs had been blown away in the explosion.

There were lots and lots of other stories, but I suspect that this was the defining one, and having tricked death, just by chance, aged twenty, I think it affected all her subsequent brushes with death, including the last one.

Anyway, she kept on telling stories about the war, until she could hardly speak any more, just weeks before she died.

I remember, a few weeks after my father died, and in the brief period when my stepmother tried to make a fist of living on her own in my parents' house (she lasted about a week), I phoned her to see how she was and, in passing, asked if she'd watched a recent BBC drama-documentary about the evacuation from Dunkirk. In the rather tetchy, slightly dismissive stuff-and-nonsense tone of voice she often adopted, she told me she'd seen quite enough of all that at the time, when she and her colleagues had tended to the wounded as they arrived back in London.

I'd like to have heard more of that story, but by this stage there were other stories she had to tell me, so I never got any more details.

I'd understood for a long time what very good stories my stepmother's stories were. But sometimes, when I was younger and harsher, I'd think, rather ungenerously, that I'd been told them so often that I couldn't now remember when I'd heard them in the first place. Maybe I'd always known them, like I'd always know about Churchill or Hitler or the Second World War or God, or other things I haven't mentioned here, like the Holocaust or Darwinism or the fact that I've always known that I was adopted.

When I was eighteen or nineteen or so my stepmother turned to my father over Christmas lunch and said, in a slightly conspiratorial voice, or at least in a way to suggest they knew something I didn't, 'Do you think he's old enough to be told yet?' I immediately assumed I was going to be told something really important, like I was the rightful King of Bohemia or something. Instead, they told me that I'd never been baptised. So, despite all the God stuff I'd endured between the ages of four and thirteen, at least I was saved from any possibility of salvation, even if this meant that me and God still had no idea who I really was. It was something I wasn't going to learn for years and years.

Stakhanovites

One afternoon after my mother died, maybe months afterwards or maybe only weeks, when I got home from school, I was surprised to find my father in the downstairs toilet knocking the tiles off the wall with a hammer and a coal chisel. This was the room with the toilet with the U-bend which had been stained by my mother's medication. It was also the room where I remember we used to keep the remains of the turkey, under a shroud of silver paper, after Christmas, under the handbasin, which was the same handbasin my mother used to dye her hair in, blacking out the grey hairs, just like she stopped herself getting fat by smoking cigarettes and drinking black coffee.

On the afternoon I was surprised to find my father at home, he'd already accidentally smashed this handbasin in the process of hammering the tiles off the wall.

We also used to keep mice in this toilet, pink-eyed white mice in dull, matt metal boxes, the size of two shoeboxes side by side, with the grating or bars sliding across the top, the gratings also providing small hatches or openings for the provision of water bottles and food dispensers. These boxes had come from my father's laboratory, as had the mice, whom I remember as being either permanently pregnant or effete, lying in the woodshavings with blind, spastic pink mouselings nuzzling into their pale bellies to suckle. These colonies of white mice gave off a distinct smell, a sickly sweet, slightly meaty and depraved smell which combined with the smell of their bedding and the pellets they ate and with the smells emanating from the toilet itself. I don't remember any of these mice ever having names.

I never thought much about the mice. They were just another part of the backdrop to my early childhood, like the foster-babies, but if I thought about them at all I suppose I must have assumed that they were something to do with my father's work, some more animals who'd ended up living with us, like the guinea pigs my sister and I husbanded and fed and mucked out for years, and who bred accordingly until, at one stage, we had about two dozen of the creatures, the ones we couldn't get rid of to friends or neighbours, and had to segregate them by gender into two large hutches my father built.

After my father died I mentioned the mice to my sister, and by this stage I must have rationalised their presence as some kind of freelance breeding programme by my father to augment the stocks at the hospital. My sister corrected me, and said that they were the mice she'd rescued from his laboratory.

I suppose this was the reason why, when I must have been about four, I went with my mother to my father's laboratory in the Cancer Research Department at the London Hospital in Whitechapel. I suppose I must have been told on the way there that I was going to get a pet mouse, because my mother probably thought that I shouldn't feel left out. I can't now remember that, or the journey across London, although I'm certain I'd already named my mouse 'Snowy', and I clearly remember, holding my mother's hand, both of us walking into my father's laboratory, a high-ceilinged, dark brown room with smeared and dirty windows looking out on to the brick walls of another part of the Victorian hospital. And I remember my father sitting with a white mouse pegged out on a cork board on the bench in front of him, open from throat to anus, pins through its little paws, the light glinting on the slippery coils of its exposed guts and its yellow teeth pointing up towards the grimy ceiling.

I was, not unreasonably, distraught, and it took my parents a long time to calm me down and convince me that that wasn't my mouse at all, but another mouse. The thing is, I don't remember being especially shocked by the mouse's condition, but by my absolute conviction that my father had absent-mindedly killed my mouse, perhaps because, like the Inuit tribes who believe there is only one seal – a kind of divine ur-seal they hunt over and over again – I'd got it into my head that that day there was only the possibility of there being one mouse, and that mouse was mine. After I'd finally quietened down, I was given another mouse, which I took home and called 'Snowy'.

I remember I quite liked Snowy, and was as diligent as any four-year-old can be in feeding her and mucking her out and watching her scamper squeakily round and round her red metal exercise wheel. She didn't live in one of the laboratory cages in the toilet, but in another one that had been bought in a pet shop, which was kept on the windowsill in the playroom that eventually became my father's workroom, the place where I dreamed I saw the dik-dik. Then her fur started falling out in large clumps, so my father took her back to the hospital, and I later heard, or more likely overheard, that she'd died of leukaemia.

I now realise that that probably wasn't Snowy's immediate cause of death, or that of her successor, Snowy 2, whose fur started falling out in just the same way soon after her arrival.

Whatever way they died, slowly and painfully of cancer or quickly and mercifully in a jam jar full of ether, I worked out pretty quickly that my father had, given two different circumstances, got the wrong mouse three times in a row, and I've often wondered how seriously he jeopardised whatever research programme they were all part of just to shut me up.

For years and years I also assumed that my father had killed Jock, the Scottie dog who replaced Mandy Moo-moo a couple of years after she'd been run over.

Jock was a useless dog, unfriendly, untrainable, unloving and with a hole in the heart. Once this was diagnosed, my sister and I were too sentimental to let my mother take him back to the pet shop in Harrow where she'd bought him for us for Christmas, although you couldn't take him for a walk of more than ten yards without him collapsing in a panting heap. I remember one day that he bit my sister, and that she and I went off to the local fields and when we came back Jock was dead and buried.

Although I don't remember seeing the dog that morning, I took it for granted for decades that my father had taken advantage of our absence to deploy his various scientific skills to dispose first of Jock and then of the evidence. When I was in my early forties I challenged my father directly over the dog's death, not because I'd liked Jock or remembered him with anything even approaching affection, but because this was an unresolved and enduring mystery. He just smiled and shrugged. After our father died, my sister insisted that she remembered prodding the dead dog in its basket first thing in the morning, before we went out to play.

We had lots of other pets over the years, in addition to the mice and the guinea pigs. For a long time we had a kind of double-decker fish tank, with very ancient tumorous goldfish in the bottom, wafting round and round trailing pliable pencil leads of shit behind them, while in the top tank there were tropical fish and, later, terrapins. These reptiles perked up no end the day my father thought he'd enliven what had hitherto been a dull exhibit of torpid terrapins by putting some of the guppies my stepmother had reared into the water, and I remember the terrapins swooping round like Messerschmitts as they bit big chunks out of the unfortunate little fish.

Earlier than this, my sister had some stick insects, until we finally liberated them on to our next-door neighbour's privet hedge, from whence we'd foraged for their food supply anyway.

And one winter, when I was in my mid-teens, my parents took in a young hedgehog who'd failed or forgotten to hibernate and for many months they fed him bread, milk and catfood, which he'd cough up noisily each morning while I was grabbing a sandwich for my breakfast before leaving for school. I called him Roland, because of his capacity to roll up in a ball, the better to protect himself from an unfriendly world.

As a child my stepmother had a succession of dogs and cats, as well as a pet parrot. My father once told me that, in addition to the songbirds whose birdseed grew into cannabis plants, he also had what he described as some 'very fierce lesbian rabbits'. My mother's dog remembered her and Dawne five years after last seeing them, when they returned home in 1945, and later, when their mother moved the family to run a guest house in Whitstable, they had a cat called Tim. Dawne tells me that the guest house was not a success, mostly because her mother never got up to make either breakfast or the beds. In the evenings her eldest sister Charm would serve the guests a frugal meal of tinned salmon, but first Charm would get Tim to lick the salmon on the plates of the guests she didn't like. Dawne also told me that Tim couldn't miaow. She said this was due to a wartime trauma, and he'd been found, barely alive, in the ruins of a bombed-out kennels in Carshalton.

Those animals are all dead now, probably even my stepmother's parrot. One of the reasons for having them around in the first place, but not necessarily the most important one, was to acquaint all us children early on with the idea of mortality.

I asked my father what he was doing, smashing up the downstairs toilet. I remember he said something about how there was too much to do around the house and so he'd taken the afternoon off to get on with it. After I'd helped him clear away the dust and rubble, the little room remained tileless for around seven years. It was sinkless for a shorter time, but this also stretched into years.

There was always too much to do, and there still is. The creeping entropy that had finally engulfed much of my grandmother's house, as it did my parents' house too, provides a constant background hum to all our lives. It's not so much the pram in the hall that's the enemy of promise as doing the washing or buying the groceries or paying the gas bill or getting out of bed in the morning that's the enemy of ever doing anything at all. Leaving aside for a moment the nagging question of what you're meant to be doing anyway, it's only those people with a limitless reservoir of selfishness who can afford to give it all up to pursue the creative or spiritual or ascetic life, people numb enough never to share the anger, boredom or resentment of all the other people around them who by and large are left to clear up the wreckage. So inaction, though eternally seductive, is never really a viable option.

My father, as I remember him, was never inactive. There was always too much to do, so much that a lot of it never got finished.

In the years before my mother died, what I remember of my father is his constant activity. I remember him making a huge red wooden locomotive in the spare bedroom, which at that stage was his workroom and photographic darkroom, later became my grandmother's bedroom before she was moved downstairs, and then became the spare bedroom, slowly building up coral reefs of accumulated stuff. The red train was a present for my birthday, when I was five or six, and I remember asking him what he was making as he clamped a thin sheet of wood into a cylinder to serve as the engine's boiler. He said it was a waste-paper basket, a forgivable little lie. The train was the main attraction at my birthday party, even though the roof of the footplate was likely to take your eye out if you clambered aboard without taking sufficient care.

(For years the little red engine sat in the shed in the bottom of the garden, until my father decided it would be better off cluttering up my house in Lewisham than his shed in Stanmore. It was the main attraction at one of our children's birthday parties, thirty years on, but I left it in the garden too long, and eventually the rain soaked into its chipboard wheels, expanding and warping them into a horrible, flaky kind of woody elephantiasis, so I took an axe to it.

Nothing lasts for ever.)

I also remember standing in that same room, the window blacked out with thick felt, in the orange gloom as he slopped the photographic paper from one tray of chemicals to another and the pictures slowly emerged from the pale void as the paper started to curl inexorably in on itself, with my head more or less level with the tabletop. High on the wall by the door was a clock in a wooden box, which my father may have made himself, ticking off with an excruciating slowness the seconds the paper should lie immersed in each tray.

Slowness, I remember, was part of the whole process of my father's photography: he took terrible photographs, and very, very slowly. I remember as a small child tearfully squinting forever into the sun as he fiddled with focal depths and exposures on the front of his camera as we waited for him to take the picture. Years and years later, when he'd be taking a photograph of me or our children when we visited Stanmore, even though his camera was now digitalised and incomparably whizzy compared to the ones he'd used forty years before, he'd still contrive to take an eternity to compose the shot, and I'd often observe, as I stared once more into the sun, that I could have knocked off an oil painting in half the time.

We found bags and bags of these photographs, my sister and me, photographs from the early 1960s, of us, and our mother, and dogs, and the garden, many of them rigidly curled up into greyish brandy snaps, a good number of them over- or underexposed, and many of those slightly askew, the image crooked within its white frame.

Not that that matters, or mattered, that much. The point, I suspect, was the action rather than the result. So there was the huge doll's house he started building for my sister (as opposed to the one it took him ten years to make for my daughter), and although he never finished it – never progressed much further than the shell of the building, all pale sienna hardboard – we'd happily play with it for hours, not too bothered by the lack of windows or staircases or lights or furniture or paint. And then there was the model-railway set, built, on the base that later provided him with a bench for him to fix his clocks on, with cuttings and viaducts and points, and it worked too, but he never got round to finishing the standard Lilliputian world the engines should have chugged through, never managed to construct the landscape of green grit and sphagnum moss and rows of little houses, although he made them too, from cardboard kits, and kept them in the wardrobe along with his wads of roubles. I remember he even made little tiny marrows, from green and yellow plasticine, to put in the window display of the 00-scale supermarket he built from a kit when we were on holiday one year.

When he wasn't taking photographs or developing them or making models or fixing things, he was gardening. When my parents bought the house in Stanmore in 1958, it had a standard 1930s suburban garden, divided by an enormous ancient weather-beaten oak tree about halfway down, with another equally old oak at the bottom of the garden, near the bonfire. There were crazy-paving paths, a square concrete pond, some fruit trees, clipped lawns, neat beds with roses growing in them, birdbaths and rockeries here and there, including one, in the shade of the lower oak, built over an old air-raid shelter which I never quite succeeded in digging down into. All this he slowly altered, transforming it into little forests of conifers and thick, looming banks of rhododendrons, one of which he grew from seed. Eventually he dug up most of the lawn (or, more correctly, I did), like he'd dug up the front lawn and turned it into one huge bed. The area around the middle oak, where we'd once had a climbing frame and a swing, became an impenetrable thicket of rhododendron and conifers, interspersed with dozens of compost heaps. Scattered in little clearings he'd plant fruit and vegetables, raspberry canes, blackberries, loganberries, and, at different times, maize, courgettes (he harvested 150 pounds of them in the exceptionally hot summer of 1976), some completely inedible kind of squash called a spaghetti plant, blackcurrants, mulberries, gooseberries, apples, figs, pears, bitter lilac grapes in the old greenhouse and cucumbers in the new conservatory, leaning up against the back of what became his workroom. This re-creation into planned wilderness went on for decades, and early on in the process he filled in the old square pond, while the little lawn around it was covered in the earth dug out in the early 1960s to accommodate the foundations for his eventual workroom. Most of this earth was, much later, moved by me down to the bottom of the garden, but he left a mound or bank, into the edge of which he sank the asymmetrical fibreglass pond we'd been given by our dead dentist's widow, which had once stood, surrounded by an ersatz rockery, in the hall outside his surgery to calm his patients. Into this the tumorous goldfish were exiled in the 1970s when we sold the double-decker fish tanks, and later newts would breed in it, along with frogs and toads, while foxes built earths beneath both oak trees, hedgehogs fucked gruntily in the undergrowth, robins and blue tits and yellowhammers nested in the nest boxes and pecked at the bird feeders, and squirrels constantly scampered through the interchanges and branch lines in the trees.

Later on, he managed to subvert the whole symmetry of the garden by planting a eucalyptus tree in a small triangular incursion into the main lawn, about halfway between the house and the first oak tree, and over twenty years it outgrew and then dwarfed the ancient oaks, so that its tall, straight, narrow piebald trunk somehow managed to foreshorten the focal depth, kicking the proper perspectives into total disharmony. My father didn't seem to care.

In the front garden, by the front door, he'd planted a holly tree, which also grew and grew. This didn't matter to begin with: while my mother was alive for some sociocultural reason or other we hardly ever used the front door, and everyone came in through the back door into the kitchen, down at the side of the house. At that time the garage on the front of the house, next to the front door but distant from it by the width of a window on the staircase, was only wide enough to allow room for one car (plus shelves for old squash bottles full of petrol, fertiliser, weedkiller and other deadly liquids, tools, ladders, mowing machines, foot-operated jigsaws, sledgehammers, hosepipes, buckets and hutches full of overwintering guinea pigs who in summer would graze the back lawn, reducing it to a patchwork of rectangles across the spectrum from grass green to light green to yellow to those patches where my sister and I had forgotten or hadn't bothered to move the pen, built by my father with no bottom to allow for grazing, and these would be brown, soggy and peppered with little turds).

Then, after my mother died, my father had the garage widened to fit two cars. The window on the stairs was filled in and turned into a small safe, with the new garage wall abutting the frame of the front door, so if you wanted to avoid getting scratched you had to sidle past the holly tree to get into the house now that, along with many other things, we'd stopped using the back door. My father's solution to this, with my help and approval, was to cut off all the lower branches as far up as we could reach with the long-handled clippers (about fifteen feet, I'd say), but leaving the branches at the top tapering into a cone, so that it looked like a date palm.

As I've said, all this took time, and my father was at work five days a week, usually not getting home until between six thirty and seven in the evening, either travelling home by tube to Stanmore at the end of one branch of the Bakerloo Line or, later, when he moved from the London Hospital to the Institute of Laryngology and Otology opposite the Ear, Nose and Throat Hospital in Gray's Inn Road, driving to and from work every day.

For the first ten years of my life, I have clear memories of him, which are simultaneously sketchy. It may be because I was only small, and was naturally focused on my mother, but I seem to remember that he was a bit of a blur, and I get an impression, when I dredge my memory of that time, that although he wasn't absent, he wasn't altogether there either.

Perhaps this was because he was always up to something, and perhaps, I now realise, this was because he was making up for all the time he lost in his childhood, in what he called his pram, pushed along the prom by his mother.

Of course, I spent a lot of time with him, like when he was building the little wall by the raspberry canes and upbraided me for my ignorance of Marx, or when I'd hold the other end of a piece of wood he was sawing in half or hand him some tool or other, and I remember lying with him on the dark, coarse, grass-green sitting-room carpet while he tested me on my spellings, and he kept getting simple words, like 'nine', wrong. I remember when he'd come home from work, and when I must have been very small I remember hugging him round the legs, in an infantile kind of rugby tackle, and I remember him reading to me in bed, although the only things I can ever remember him reading were the cartoons in the *Evening Standard*, 'Modesty Blaise' and the 'Bristow' and 'Billy the Bee' strips.

And I remember him on holiday with me, my mother and my sister, either with us tagging along on scientific trips or just on our own, like in Tenerife over Christmas in 1965, when there were power cuts every night and, because of my father's doubts about the cleanliness of the local water supply, we had to drink Vichy water, which I remember as being one of the nastiest things I'd ever tasted. On the same holiday one day they emptied the swimming pool over the road from our hotel, so my sister decided to take me exploring in its depths, twelve feet down at the deep end, but then they started to fill it up again, and I seem to remember we only just managed to get out in time before we drowned, though it probably wasn't as close a run thing, or as dangerous and dramatic as I remember it.

A couple of years later we went to Sorrento for another of my father's scientific meetings, and on the way we stayed in Capri and Naples, where I almost saw someone run over, or even possibly beheaded, by a tram running along the seafront, but my mother made me look away before I could really catch the full details. There were other trips, and for several years in a row we stayed in a flat in Cromer, near Walsingham, with its lifeboat at the end of the pier and the little boating pool and the lighthouse beaming its arc of light round and round, every minute or so flashing in through the kitchen window, and I have a clear memory of the innocence of the joy I felt when we topped the hill, driving between high hedgerows on narrow lanes, and saw the sea, speckling in the distance.

And although I don't know where we were going, or where we'd been, I remember we stopped one afternoon in a small village somewhere in the country, certainly a long way from London, and the kind of place most people now think they mean when they conjure up images of an idyllic English scene, with a church with a lychgate, a tea shop and a village green, bordered by dear little country cottages. I remember one of these cottages had a large and apparently vicious dog barking wildly behind its wooden gate, and I remember my father, limping across the green, his hands around the camera hanging from his neck, saying to me, 'Martin, go and get eaten by that dog so I can take a picture of it.'

A natural childish gullibility made me fall for his jokes. I remember, on top of thinking that he wanted me to get eaten by dogs, that I also believed him when he said his entire family would smear themselves in goose grease every October before sewing themselves into their underwear for the winter. He'd also told me once that every Monday the servants would boil up an enormous cauldron of porridge, and they'd then pour the leftovers into the drawer of the kitchen table so that members of the family could cut themselves a slap of congealed porridge throughout the coming week. It was only when I was eighteen or nineteen that I realised he'd been joking on both counts.

A lot of these trips involved us flying to places, long before most people travelled by plane as a matter of course, when air travel was still slightly miraculous and therefore massively glamorous and exciting, like when you'd exit a Caravel jet through a walkway which folded out from beneath its tail, as if you were climbing down from a whale's arse. Now, of course, air travel is one of the most unpleasant things most people voluntarily elect to do, but back then people could talk about the jet set and not instantly think of sitting around for hours in glass-and-metal barns before being processed through security checks like chickens in a factory, but instead be beguiled by the dolly-bird air hostesses and fondly imagine the pilot up the front, a Peter Stuyvesant cigarette in one hand and a glass of Cinzano Bianco in the other, switching to autopilot to power the flying silver eel behind him up into a heaven of the purest, clearest, cleanest, palest Technicolor blue.

And I remember how exciting it was, and playing chess with my father on a little travel set, and beating him, and the air hostesses being over-attentive to my needs while my mother looked darkly at them from the seat beside me, and even how exciting it was when they lost our luggage on our way to Tenerife, and I had to sleep in my underwear for three nights. And I remember us getting home again, although from somewhere else, and before Heathrow turned into a bench-mark for postmodern dystopias, and there'd be a man from the local taxi firm on Stanmore Hill there to meet us after we'd gone through customs, and I remember my father smiling ironically as the man from customs opened the light green plastic holdall, crammed with bottles, and saying pleadingly that all these bottles of spirits were for *my* personal consumption, and I remember the laughter just behind his voice as he said I liked my spot of vodka and that surely the customs man didn't begrudge the poor little boy a drink now and then?

Back at home, I remember when my mother and sister left me alone with my father while they went shopping, probably in Watford, on a Saturday morning when I was probably about eight, and my father decided that this was the perfect time to teach me how to drink vodka, but I knocked over my plastic beaker, the type with an integral drinking straw, spilling orange squash all over the tablecloth just as my mother arrived home.

And on my seventh birthday we all went down to the new Chinese restaurant in Stanmore, and I remember being terrified that I'd be arrested for the little glass of cherry brandy my parents had insisted I should have after the meal. Although, as the young Prince Charles had recently been caught drinking the same stuff at Gordonstoun, it's just possible they were making some satirical point or other.

And one Christmas I remember standing in the hall, by the front door, as my father stuck a cigar in my mouth and told me to suck gently as he lit it, before taking it away to smoke on his own once he was sure it was fully alight.

Then my mother died and my father came into much sharper focus, both in my memory and in my life.

I'm not aware that we ever sat down as a family – me, my father and my sister – and discussed how things were going to be run now, how we were going to cope and manage our lives or, indeed, our grief. Perhaps my father talked about these things with my sister, but then she was older than me, and I think her relationship with our father was different from mine in lots of different ways, although it's not my purpose here to speculate on any of that. That's her business, and should remain so.

We settled down with what now seems relative speed and ease. There was, of course, my inductive period into the realities of changed circumstances that I'd unwillingly undergone staying for the summer at my grandmother's house in Blackpool, a kind of airlock into the vacuum beyond. I've still got no real idea what my father did that summer, whom he visited or whom he saw or how he coped or what he changed. There was no sense of a clean break with the past, except in my perception of it in my memory, and in my memory of my memories. We seemed to just settle down into a new kind of routine.

My father would still come home from work at around the same time, and although for a while I used to go to a family friend's house after school, soon I was coming straight home and lounging around as ten- and eleven-year-olds do. A sort of demarcation of work seemed to evolve, quite naturally. My sister would do most of the cooking most evenings, although we quickly established a regime where we'd eat the same thing on the same day each week, with beefburgers one day, pork chops the next, and so on. After dinner on Thursday evenings all three of us would do the laundry, my father pulling dripping wet shirts out of the built-in replacement for the old Hoover twin-tub, and my sister or I would then put them on a hanger and rush into what had been the playroom to hang them from a length of wood straddled between two collapsible clothes dryers, where they'd drip on to folded-out newspaper for another day or two.

We'd go on shopping trips to Wealdstone to the new

Sainsbury's they'd just built, in its way a mark of the wider world changing around us, parallel to my life. I remember the old Sainsbury's in Harrow, a single room with beautiful Victorian tiles of brawny peasants harvesting and milking and being generally productively rustic, and in front of these would be burly men in white coats, standing behind marble-topped counters. The whole place smelled, I remember, of hard cheese. The new supermarket didn't smell of anything, and we'd wheel our trolley round and round it on Saturday mornings, stocking up against the disasters of the coming week. But despite its glass-and-plastic promise of the State of Things to Come, next to it there was still an old-fashioned fishmonger's, and I remember sitting in a traffic jam on top of the 114 bus one afternoon coming home from school, and seeing a live eel jump out of a bucket outside this shop and start to writhe its way down the pavement, presumably trying to return to the Sargasso Sea to spawn.

Some Saturdays my father would be on call at the Institute, and he and I would drive down to King's Cross, put the car behind the hospital in an old bomb site that now served as a car park, and he'd get on with some work while I amused myself, sometimes going to look at the laboratory animals (at the time they had a cockerel called Bobby Moore), sometimes playing with the laboratory equipment or often just reading. One day my father and I performed an experiment after he'd heard or read that the Golden Horde of Genghis Khan, as they swept across Central Asia leaving death and rapine in their wake, seldom had time to stop and cook, so as well as semi-broiling horsesteaks beneath their saddles, they'd also spin eggs round their heads in slingshots, the centrifugal action (he told me) breaking down the cell structure and therefore, to all intents and purposes, boiling the eggs. So we centrifuged an egg. It didn't work.

On those Saturday mornings, on the way to the Institute

and coming back again, we'd drive through Hendon and Golders Green, and pass lots of Orthodox Jews walking to or from synagogue, and my father would always say they were members of the Mafia, given their penchant for wearing pinstriped suits and wide-brimmed fedoras.

We even managed a holiday together once, just the three of us, to Ibiza, not then the centre for low-rent sybaritism it's become, but still being developed as a tourist destination. We arrived at our hotel, after a long coach ride, at three o'clock in the morning, and I peeked out of the window at what I thought was an enormous beach, but which proved in the morning to be a building site. The beach, what there was of it, was just a ton or so of sand dumped in a tiny inlet on the rocky coastline. I don't know how my father filled his days while my sister and I amused ourselves, playing with other children or getting drunk on Sangria or in the swimming pool or me reading Harold Robbins's *The Adventurers*, but I do remember the three of us sitting on a jetty, some distance from the hotel, our legs dangling over the side, eating a packed lunch the hotel had prepared for us of cold hard chicken, an orange and a boiled egg floating in some unspecified liquid at the bottom of each of our plastic carrier bags. Way above our heads *Apollo 13* was limping home to Earth.

Back home, the new routine carried on and on. On Friday evenings I'd slowly make my way home, often after dallying in Harrow in toyshops or record shops or Universal Stationers, a long since defunct chain whose hubristical name hinted at the lingering hope and ambition of the times. Getting off the bus a stop on from where I usually got off in Stanmore, I'd drop in at the local greengrocer's and pick up a couple of carrier bags filled with the trimmed and unwanted outer leaves of cabbages and cauliflowers, which they'd previously agreed we could have for free to feed to the guinea pigs. Thus laden, I'd walk up Green Lane and let myself into the empty and, in winter, dark house, and usually turn all the lights on, along with the TV and several radios. I'd then pull the kitchen steps over to the sink and fill it up with hot water and as much washing-up liquid as I could squeeze out of the bottle, until the suds were a foot or so high, and I'd then do the week's washing-up, kneeling on the top rung of the steps so I could reach the sink, although I was now bigger than when my mother used to wash my hair in the same sink, and rinse it by pushing my head right under the water.

And then I'd do the drying up, and put everything away, and it would slowly come out again, and get soiled and stacked up again during the week, until the following Friday I'd do the whole thing all over again.

This helped to keep an ill-fitting lid on the simmering chaos, but there were moments when things boiled over with a scummy hiss. I remember I stopped washing completely for about a month when I was eleven, and I can remember how proud I was of the embedded grime around my ankle, which I could rub off into little pliable worms with my finger. And although I now look back with both admiration and some wonder at how my father managed to cope, he sometimes got his priorities out of order.

For instance, we soon stopped eating altogether at the dining-room table, the nice ornate one, because there was a petrol mower on it, in bits, for months, so we'd eat in front of the telly, in the small, middle sitting room. The larger one, beyond it, stretching from front to back at the north end of the house, was now completely lost to us. Even when my mother was alive we'd never used it much because the room was so cold (although now and then we pretended to camp in there as my parents preferred that to the idea of us sleeping outside in tents; we always used to put the Christmas tree in there too and I remember playing in the room when I must have been very small, listening to the last ever episode of *Children's Hour* on the radio or, more likely, on a wireless). But now it was filled with junk, either on its way in or on its way out. The old wooden slide, which I'd slid down, face first with a length of dowelling in my mouth when I was five or six, pretending to be a swordfish, was in there and waiting to be sold (I still have a slight indentation in the roof of my mouth I can feel with the tip of my tongue, from the moment when I reached the bottom of my trajectory). So was our wooden see-saw and other bits of furniture. Among the stuff soon to come in were tea chests filled with the kitsch and the crap my grandmother had brought down with her from Blackpool when she came to live with us, lengths of dexion steel shelving my father and I built to accommodate their contents, as well as filing cabinets, garden tools, another mowing machine and, in the middle of it all, an old gas-and-air machine my father brought home from work one day. Its rusting trolley was still just about standing, down by the shed, on the very last day I walked round my parents' garden.

On my eleventh birthday, I remember lying in my bedroom, next to the upstairs toilet and the bathroom, and I heard my sister going into the bathroom and asking my father what he'd got me for my birthday. I remember him exclaiming with shock, and asking my sister, rather aggressively, why she hadn't reminded him, and then a minute or so later, in just his pyjama bottoms, he burst into my room with a loud shout of 'Happy Christmas!'

He bought me a present that day, and came home with it that evening, though I can't now remember what it was, and I think we probably then went down into Stanmore for a meal out at a restaurant. And I remember that I wasn't angry, or even particularly upset, or at least less for myself than I was for him, and on the whole I reckoned he'd acquitted himself pretty well with the 'Happy Christmas!' gag, defusing what I'm sure he recognised could have been my unassuageable misery with a little pantomime of studied and farcical forgetfulness, just so I'd never think there was any sense of neglectfulness mixed up in it.

Nor was there, although, as I've said, I sometimes felt he got his priorities wrong. There was so much to do, and so he concentrated on the externals, literally on the exterior, so at least the boundaries were intact, even if what they contained constantly threatened, minute by minute, to unravel completely. And I'd always help him. His practical passions, which previously he'd been at leisure to express through a magnificent kind of hobbyism, were now channelled into DIY.

His was a generation destined to fall into DIY, irrespective of class. His class, or the class his grandfather had pulled his family up into had, not long beforehand, never been occasioned to bother themselves with many of the practical facts of everyday life: they had servants and tradesmen and builders and plumbers and a whole caste of mechanicals to do that for them. Lower down the social scale, I suppose they had neither the means and nor were they encouraged to have the ambition to make much of an effort. Around the middle of the twentieth century, however, the classes – or at least all those precise strata within the middle classes – started to implode towards each other, either because reduced circumstances forced them downwards, or heightened aspirations drove them upwards, and they seem to have come together in DIY. Many boys of that generation, born between the wars, seem to have had an inclination towards practical application anyway, which may have been the last drops trickling down from the Industrial Revolution 150 years before. Anna's father, five years older than my father, was immensely practical, although professionally he'd been as louche as you could get, working in an advertising agency in Soho in the 1950s. When he was sixteen or seventeen he'd built one of Logie Baird's patented clockwork television sets, and the poet Blake Morrison's father, a GP, in retirement built his own house from scratch. My father was just another of that generation, weaned on Meccano, who ended up erecting shelves or building patios or fixing the plumbing or doing the rewiring or wallpapering the walls and painting the skirting boards (two coats, mind, and make sure the brushstrokes all go in the same direction) in their suburban homes.

I think many men of his generation were also simply awed by technology, and what the advances of their age now allowed them to do, even if it just meant they could fit dimmer switches or electrically powered curtains (my father installed both). I remember him saying, with wonder, how he'd lived through an amazing period in human history, with man's first powered flight happening just twenty-one years before he was born, and a man on the moon by the time he was forty-five, and just weeks after my mother died. He probably preferred not to dwell on the fact that the same forces had also resulted in the mechanised carnage of the Great War or the production-line genocide of the Nazis or the bombs dropped on Hiroshima and Nagasaki, when he was twenty-one. Later, by the late sixties and early seventies, at the beginning of the transition from the old Industrialism to the New Technology, from Nuffield Science Parks filled with buildings of brick and asbestos, staffed by bald men in glasses and lab coats and which leaked strange chemical smells, to business parks full of glass-and-metal barns which smelled of carpets, air conditioning, buzzed faintly with the wombnal hum of computers and were populated entirely by young men in striped shirts, the pace of change became frankly absurd. But irrespective of the aesthetics, my father went with the flow, right up to his death, and was always a fool for the latest technology, always seeming to buy the first prototype of any new machine that came on the market, despite the fact that it was invariably absurdly expensive and doomed to be obsolete within months, although having been duly gulled, he'd stick with the inkjet typewriter that could only print on special shiny paper, or the first generation of computerised chess games, or the tiny portable hand-held TV sets, until my parents' house, by the time they were all dead, was filled with stuff both more archaic, less enduring, but also more exactly and accurately indicative of its time (a week in 1977 or a month or two in 1985) than all the other, older stuff that had passed down to him from his parents or grandparents.

Then again, he was a scientist, and believed in science (though seldom in many of the people who practised it) and I remember, when he finally got round to redecorating the downstairs toilet, he and I discussed the problem of identifying where the water pipes to the replacement sink might lurk behind the tileless wall. We tried to think of various ways of locating them, just to make sure he didn't then drill through them when he put up the new heated towel rail, and for a while I remember him suggesting that we buy a Geiger counter and then put something radioactive in the water tank in the loft. I'm still not sure if this was a joke or not, although he finally compromised by buying a metal detector.

I realise now that a lot of his often almost manic activity wasn't perhaps quite as frenetic as I've always remembered it as being, but it was also clearly a classic act of displacement. We didn't sit and mope, or even just sit and grieve, because my father was either predisposed not to react like that, or because he didn't dare to, and because, for my part, I was always helping him, although I know that inside I was yearning to lock myself in my bedroom with the curtains drawn. Instead, from the age of ten onwards I'd hand him tools, hold the end of wood he was sawing through yet again, find other tools, sort screws, carry yet more tools, dig holes, hold ladders, pass him wires, put my weight behind drills, lag pipes, build shelves, lay down layers of polystyrene insulation in the loft, dig more holes, saw more wood, have bonfires, rake leaves (and each autumn I'd spend hours and hours in the dying light raking leaves into wheelbarrows through the chilling mist or thin rain, to augment yet more compost heaps), mow lawns, chop down trees, plant other trees and move those compost heaps, at least up until the day when I turned round from pitchforking another load of rotting vegetation into a wheelbarrow and saw my father sitting in a deckchair reading the newspaper. But that was when I was about seventeen.

At weekends and during the holidays I remember practically nothing except helping my father shore up against anarchy. And although I often used to hope or dream it would rain on a Sunday (though that never made much difference as far as my father was concerned), I didn't object that much. We'd talk while we worked, up in the loft, down at the end of the garden over another bonfire, measuring screws in screw gauges (and I can still tell, by sight, the difference between a three-inch No. 8 and a two-and-a-half-inch No. 6), tiling a wall, building a wardrobe or putting up yet more dexion shelving. I can't remember those conversations in detail, but snatches of them come back to me, along with their location.

We were in the bathroom, draining another heated towel rail, and I was talking about school, and I remember my father saying the chaplain who'd show the prettier little boys his model railway sounded like a quisling to him, and then we'd talk about who Quisling was. I remember talking about pollution and the environment while we lagged the pipes (all the floorboards up for days) in the sitting room, and I remember him talking about the butcher next door who showed him how to poleaxe a cow as I dug a trench in the garden between the two apple trees.

And I can remember all the little bits of wisdom he'd impart, just as a passing comment, as we toiled away, or drove off in the car to fetch more materials. How I should never obey orders, including this one (I think that was when we were pruning the raspberry canes). How I should avoid ever having to work if I could possibly avoid it (that was imparted down by the first oak tree, and I think I was cleaning the greenhouse windows, but I didn't let the apparent ironies confuse me: he was making a Ruskinian point, drawing a line between Useful Labour and Useless Toil). How you could never legislate for people's morality (that was as we were driving down beyond Belmont towards a timber yard in Harrow). How lysergic acid was actually terribly easy to synthesise, so he couldn't really see what all the fuss was about (again we were in the car, driving home past my sister's old primary school). Later, he'd say how you should always vote, as voting was a hard-won privilege, and you never knew when the buggers might take it away again; how we'd never get real, radical structural change in this country until we got rid of the monarchy, the cock (as he put it) crowing on top of the dungheap; how I was never to trust doctors, and how vast numbers of people, including entire nations, were rotten with religion; how this is the only life I'd have, so it was my sacred duty to make sure I enjoyed it.

He wasn't actively proselytising, just sharing his opinions, although I think he thought they were worth sharing. He often suggested, not entirely seriously, that he and I should start up a lengthy correspondence, along the lines of Lord Chesterfield's letters to his son, but as my father's letters were so dull it's probably just as well that we never did.

But many of our conversations, both then and for years after-wards, often had a more surreal edge to them. I remember, when I was about nineteen, after I'd left school and had a temporary clerical job at the BBC, I'd gone to see him at his laboratory in Gray's Inn Road, and we were walking down towards Mount Pleasant and the Progressive Working Class Caterers at the top of Farringdon Road, where he'd taken to having a stodgy lunch amid the postal workers from the nearby sorting office. He pointed out the trees that Camden Council had planted along the street, presumably to give this dusty and run-down area of London a slightly more Parisian ambience. They were miserable, pale, stunted things, and I remember him saying that they were ridiculous and a waste of time and money, and anyway the natives would destroy them. At first, bridling slightly, I took this to be a disparaging remark about the tenants in the Victorian council estates off the main road, but he then started describing the large, giraffe-like creatures that he imagined lived secretly round here and who wouldn't be able to help themselves, as they shyly came out on to the streets at the dead of night, from browsing the tops off the trees. I understood precisely what he meant. Down the same street was the Royal College of Dentistry, and he claimed that he kept his nails in trim by scraping them along the blocks of Portland stone along the building's grand façade.

And for years he'd create grand narratives about his colleagues, first at the London Hospital and later at the Institute of Laryngology, that were funny and weird and ironic, and best of all true. I remember him telling me about a particular professor at the Ear, Nose and Throat Hospital who was a world expert on removing cancerous growths from the nasal and oesophageal tracts – or, as my father put it, removing 'half-heads' – whom my father recreated in these narratives as a comic monster of vanity and ambition, with hundreds of diplomas and certificates on the walls of his office except, my father would observe, his birth certificate. Then there was the morris-dancing bacteriologist, who was also the World's Greatest Living Authority on the operas of Gilbert and

Sullivan and lighting in the Victorian theatre, or another colleague whom my father referred to as 'The Colonel', who was passed over for a professorship and, according to my father, spent the rest of his professional life stalking the corridors of the hospital constructing vast fantasies in his head involving his successful rival being hauled off in chains to a dungeon. To add to the layers of weirdness, the Institute where he worked had previously been the site of the *Daily Worker* printing presses, and opposite the Institute was a pub called the Pindar of Wakefield (it's now the Water Rats' Pub), where, they boasted on the beer mats, both Marx and Lenin used to drink, as Lenin lived round the corner, just up beyond the Royal Caledonian Hotel, and my father and I would create lengthy scenarios in which Lenin and Marx would argue over whose round it was, although we both knew that Lenin was about ten when Marx died.

Then there were his whimsical projects, which I don't think were ever meant to be taken seriously, although when he outlined his plans for me to dig and clay-puddle a lake in the back garden, or double-dig the entire plot, turning over the soil to the depth of two spade blades, I'd shiver with fear at the prospect of all the work he had planned for me. Other great notions were less likely to involve too much effort on my part. I remember him once saying that Mount Everest should be carved into the shape of an enormous sea lion, with a revolving spherical hotel balanced on its nose, so you could enjoy watching mountaineers clambering up its sides as you ate your lunch in warmth and luxury inside. Another time, I remember him advocating the genetic modification of human beings so they could have prehensile tails, because this would be enormously beneficial: at cocktail parties you could hold your glass, your plate of nibbles *and* your cigarette; you could have double-decker tube trains, with half the commuters hanging by their tails from the ceiling; in the same way, people could now sleep in wardrobes, hanging from the clothes rails like opossums. Maybe, deep down, he had a thing about bedrooms, because I remember, a few months before he died, him saying with apparent seriousness that despite all the scientific advances he'd witnessed throughout his life, he was surprised that no one had succeeded in eradicating human beings' need to sleep. If only they'd conquered sleep, productivity would increase and houses could be much smaller and cheaper, as they wouldn't need bedrooms.

This whimsicality often tipped into mischievousness, and he took a great deal of relish in bombarding our local Conservative MP with letters about anything that came into his head. He drove an *Encyclopaedia Britannica* salesman to distraction by repeatedly filling in a form inviting him round to make his pitch, with no intention of ever buying a thing, until the third or fourth time the poor man arrived at my parents' front door, took one look at my father and fled. He once answered the phone to a cold caller from Slumberland beds, who likewise went through his pitch, asking my father a series of simple questions leading up to a big prize, to which the answer was always 'Slumberland beds'. My father worked this out pretty quickly, and answered correctly until asked the clincher, the last question before he'd get the prize, when he said he didn't want a Slumberland bed as he always slept in a hammock. And during the 1977 Silver Jubilee, when a neighbour dropped round to ask my father if he'd like to help organise a street party to celebrate Her Majesty's Twenty-five Glorious Years, he replied that not only would he do everything in his power to prevent it from happening, but he'd also hang banners from the front of the house reading 'Death to the German Usurpress!'

These were, of course, little tiny skirmishes in the endless war of attrition we all fight, or choose not to fight, against the grosser manifestations of reality, and this aspect of his make-up wasn't really whimsicality, more a kind of quiet, rather grumpy yet always amused contempt for the idiocies around him. Nor was it ever informed by cynicism, but rather by scepticism, by a recognition of the true nature of things and the best way to cope with them to make life bearable.

It also showed itself in other, more immediately irritating ways. If you ever asked him what he'd like to eat, he'd invariably put on a pathetic, tremulous voice and say, 'Anything that's going rotten'; if you asked him what he wanted for Christmas or his birthday, he'd always answer, 'Oh, just a bag of screws and a kind word.' It was probably some comment along these lines that made my mother throw lettuce at him.

His influence was osmotic. I now find myself saying things to my children that he said to me, in the same tone of voice, so if one or other of them answers my request for assistance with whatever feeble excuse comes into their heads, I hear myself telling them to just go and lie down in a darkened room, just like my father would say, in the same circumstances, to me.

Perhaps unhealthily, perhaps disastrously, or maybe crucially, I also developed the opinion at an early age, partly thanks to his homilies, partly thanks to his sagas of life at the Institute, that I should view those people in immediate and more distant authority over me with scepticism, suspicion, amusement and, ultimately, contempt.

And as a survival tactic, his had its advantages over some of the ways that other people try to navigate their passage through life without too much damage accruing to themselves, if not necessarily to other people. And it's true that the slight air of detachment that was central to the ploy meant that, in real crises, he wasn't ultimately equipped to cope: as far as I know he did nothing to reconcile my mother and his mother, and later, more painfully for everyone, did practically nothing to reconcile my sister and my stepmother, who didn't speak for thirty years after my father remarried. But that, I realised after years of anxiety in my teens, was ultimately their business, and I suspect that my father convinced himself likewise, and if you want a quiet if interesting life, the temptation is always there to ignore loud and frightening noises nearby, and just carry on doing what you want to do as if nothing else had happened. Which, given his childhood, and then the deaths of his son and his wife, is understandable, and forgiveness isn't really an issue at this stage, and it was never an issue for me in the first place.

And for the most part, in the immediate aftermath of my mother dying, his various tactics worked. We survived, if sometimes only just. He avoided burying his grief in his work, but managed to bury it instead in Work, in Ruskin's Useful Labour, and along the way he and I forged an indestructible bond. It was built, for a short time, on a desperate kind of mutual reliance between a forty-five-year-old man and his thirteen- and ten-year-old children, but it was also built, more enduringly, on humour and irony and also on the necessity of just getting on with it.

Although of course that's not the whole of it. I don't really know what he was getting up to when I wasn't around, how he spent that summer when I was in Blackpool, how he filled his evenings when I'd gone to bed, or how he filled his thoughts day and night.

In this short interlude, when it was just the three of us against the world, he considered applying for a job in Leicester, to my horror; he often talked about moving, to Hertfordshire, to central London, to Camden, as if either he couldn't face the house in Stanmore any more, inevitably haunted by many ghosts, or he had some fleeting prescience of how the house would eventually fill up and up and up with stuff, until it came close to overwhelming him. And while he never did move, and I know that I would have found any move disastrous and possibly fatally disruptive, it suggests that he at least considered all the options, contemplating every possible chance at survival.

As things turned out, we settled into different normalities, some good, some bad, some terrible, but none of them the same as we'd had before.

This immersion into salvation through work sometimes didn't work. Or else it worked too well.

I remember, when I was eleven or twelve, feeling utterly, hopelessly miserable for weeks. This was certainly partly hormonal, as well as natural, given the events in my recent past. I remember finally telling my father, whom I hadn't told before because I recognised the unperceived but understood truth that we all still had to grit our teeth and not make too many distracting waves, for fear our little vessel would be overwhelmed. Also, the protective layers we'd built up didn't really allow for deep displays of emotion, or at least only very rarely, just to show that our emotions still worked. He was kneeling in his usual way, wielding a trowel and planting something next to our dead dentist's pond, and I remember, rather nervously, telling him how I felt, probably hoping that he'd be able to do something about it. And I remember him saying, rather jauntily and without looking up from his digging, 'Ah, you must be a manic depressive! That's interesting!' In a way his response did the trick; at any rate, after toiling at his side for the next three hours, I felt slightly happier.

Worse than that, though, was the weekend when the DIY took over completely. He was painting all the windows on the ground floor of the house, and had been, I seem to remember, since Friday evening. I'd helped a bit, but I also had homework and other things to do, and I remember, still with a shudder, the Sunday night, and coming downstairs after I'd had a bath, at around seven o'clock, and it was November, and dark and cold because all the windows were open because the paint wasn't yet dry, and there was no food, and the rooms were all too bright because he'd taken down all the curtains and the viscous wet white paint glinted back the lights with a hideous harshness, and the place was filled with the choking stench of gloss paint. Whenever I smell that slightly yeasty petroleum smell, I'm instantly transposed back to that dismal evening, when I really thought that chaos had finally triumphed, and everything really was going to fall to pieces.

And that's the reason why I was such a good, compliant, helpful little boy, almost from the start. It was fear, a terror that if I didn't cooperate everything would crack and crumble, be it into a harsh word, or a stern disapproval, or into total and utter disintegration. So I worked hard, was always polite to adults, spoke nicely, for the most part did as I was told, and it took a long time for me to wise up and work out the wisdom of my father's words: never obey orders, including this one, and make sure that I enjoyed life.

But naturally it was also about infinitely more than just fear. And I remember, a few months after my mother died there was a thunderstorm in the middle of the night. I was ten, and I was frightened, and eventually, rather nervously, I went into my father's bedroom, although I knew he'd dismiss my fear as nonsense, but even so I asked if I could get into bed with him. He let me in and went back to sleep again almost straight away, while I lay there, kept awake by the thunder and my father's snores, but also feeling perfectly, sublimely safe.

The Nomenklatura

Look, I need to get something straight before we go any further. I've left some important things out.

My name's Martin. You'll have worked that out from the cover, and I've used it several times already. But it isn't, or at least wasn't, Martin Rowson. There was, for a brief moment, a possibility that I might have had the same surname, but a different first name or, if my parents had had me baptised, Christian name. But my mother wouldn't let my father call me Humphrey, which he wanted to in honour of Humphrey Bogart. Anyway, I arrived with the name I've still got, which had been given to me by my mother, but by a different mother to the one we've already met.

My mother and father did give me my second and third names, George and Edmund, in honour of one estranged grandfather I only ever met once and the other dead one who'd died eight years before I was born. Both these names were hand-me-downs from my dead brother Christopher.

My parents also gave me my surname, or at least my father did.

The name Rowson has been a burden to me for most of my life. It's not that I resent it, or don't like it, or am embarrassed by it, like it was Hitler or Twatbottom or something like that. In fact, I think it's rather a good name, slightly out of the ordinary. The problem is entirely practical.

It's one of those strange English words that always seem to fall into the slim gap between written and spoken language, a common enough phenomenon that any child would recognise, with a stinging sense of the injustice of it all when someone older, apparently wiser or just more at ease with the illogicalities involved, corrects their pronunciation of Geoff or gaol or the way they've spelled yacht. The name isn't exactly like that, but there always seems to be disjunction between its existence on paper and when it's said, before it eddies away into the air.

To put the record straight, the first syllable rhymes with crow, not with cow. It might seem to you to be no big thing and that I'm making too much of a fuss about this, but for nearly five decades I've winced inside whenever people get that the wrong way round, and I have to make an instant judgement call on whether I politely correct them or let it go and prepare myself for the next time, the error now compounded and beyond reach. Even at my father's funeral the humanist minister got it wrong, and although it didn't seem appropriate to correct him, my stepmother, my sister, my children and I were all secretly grinding our teeth with growing rage and frustration each time he said our name wrong. Even Dawne, who's been familiar with the name for over fifty years, gets it wrong as often as she gets it right. And even people whom I've repeatedly corrected keep getting it wrong, like the senior journalist on the *Guardian*, who at least admits that it's his problem, not mine, the result of a tiny and specific dysphasia he can't control, or the former Tory Cabinet minister whom I like a lot but who always says my name wrong while more or less implying that I'm the one who's in error.

It's even worse, or at least leads to even greater confusion, if heard but not seen. Then the name Rowson is almost invariably transcribed as Rosen, and the assumption is immediately made that I'm Jewish. I've got no problem with being a Jew, except that I'm not, although over the years hundreds of people have concluded, having not wasted too much time thinking about it, that because the name is Jewish, I therefore look Jewish, and so therefore I am, even though I'm not. My friend Charlie, who is, says I'm obviously not, and that all these people's Jewdar is hopelessly out of kilter. Even so, I was once pursued round a party by the writer Howard Jacobson who accused me of being a self-denying Jew, and each time I gainsaid him he said I was just making matters worse: when I spelt out the name, he said my forebears had obviously Anglicised it because they were self-hating Jews too, and when I finally said I was adopted, and it wasn't my fucking name anyway, and told him my real, or at least original, name he just smiled, rolled his eyes and clicked his tongue, having proved his point conclusively, to himself at least.

Not that I'd mind being Jewish, and for a long time I rather hoped that I was. There's a certain quality of cool about being a Jew which the goyim just don't have, but I've now got it in black and white, on my adoption papers: 'No Jewish, Negro or Irish blood.' I was rather disappointed when I read that for the first time.

The name was never Rosen, and I remember my father telling me that his grandfather, being a prosperous, self-made man at the turn of the nineteenth and twentieth centuries, naturally hired a hack genealogist to draw up his family tree. Although it's now been lost for years, my father told me that this was a long and beautiful document, which traced the Lytham plumber's ancestors all the way back to Row, a Norman knight who came over with William the Conqueror in 1066 and whose descendants, being the sons of Row, were rather unimaginatively called Rowson.

All of this was entirely untrue, as you'd expect, and my father told me that the genealogist had only been able to go back through four generations of legitimacy to a farm worker in Lincolnshire.

These days genealogy is more thorough, and has developed into a kind of popular movement or folk art as people spend hours and hours on the Internet filling in the gaps in their backgrounds like stamp collectors or trainspotters, as if this might finally help them to work out who on earth they are. I'm inclined to think that this is what many people now have instead of Christianity, allowing you to connect to an older, purer religion with no arcane rules, rituals or devotions to a grumpy, speculative and largely unresponsive Higher Authority, just the mild veneration of, or simply a vague interest in, the generations and generations of people who ultimately led up to you. This used to be called ancestor worship, though my father always used to describe my grandmother as an ancestor worshipper, because she claimed to be a Spiritualist. Thousands and thousands of people now worship at this wafer-thin, self-generating Church, and every few months I get a phone call asking if I'm related to some Rowson or other. Invariably I'm not, or not enough to really count. About a month and a half after my father died, I got an email from a man in New Zealand called Don Rowson, who was closer in than most, and after a brief email exchange he told me that somewhere down the line a member of his branch of the Rowson family had met my father when he was a small boy in his invalid carriage. This is quite interesting, but it was too late to afford my father any fleeting moments of diversion or reflection, and Don Rowson's too far away, and all of it too long ago, to detain me for too long, even if I count as a Rowson in the first place.

I've no idea how Don pronounces his surname.

And after all, what's in a name? Neither my father, nor my mother, nor my stepmother used the names they'd been given by their parents for large parts of their lives.

My mother was christened Angela Eve Bovill, but she hated both her first names, and Dawne says that when they arrived in America my mother turned to her and said, 'My name's Ann now.' In the address book she started filling up when she was in Ohio, which I found in my father's desk, there's a photograph cut out from a magazine and stuck down inside the back cover. Above it, in green ink, and along the side of it, in pencil, is written the date, 'May 29th 1945', and it's a picture of Dawne and my mother standing on either side of a third girl, all of them wearing rather stylish twinsets of the cut of the times, and printed underneath is the caption 'These Three Misses, from Left to Right are Dawne Bovill, Audrey Hamilton and Angela Bovill'. My mother had crossed out the word Angela – completely obliterated it, in fact – and written Ann above it.

The photograph was taken exactly twenty-four years to the day before she died.

I always called her Annie, as did my sister and father, and Annie was what she called herself. I still always think of her as Annie, but she was never Mum or Mummy, and I remember my father and stepmother telling me independently of each other that if I called her either of those names when I was very small, she'd say that she wasn't my mummy, though I don't remember this ever happening. When we were children we'd sometimes call her Angela Eve to tease her, and it always worked.

She was – and is – Ann or Annie to Dawne as well, and although I don't know what her mother or father called her before she renamed herself, the renaming seems to have stuck.

Her mother's name was Eva Jessie, but she was always called Bunty or Bunt.

My other grandmother's name was Gwendoline May, but she was always known as Gwennie, sometimes shortened to Gwen by her brother and sister. My father always called her Gwennie, as did my sister and I. I don't remember ever hearing him address her as Mother, Mummy or Mum.

My stepmother's mother's name was Edith, and my stepmother called her Mother, although I recently found a letter from her to my stepmother, written when my stepmother was in her early thirties, signed 'Mummie'. I don't remember that I ever called her anything when I spoke to her, because I wasn't sure how she'd like to be addressed, even though I liked her and got on with her pretty well. I've no idea how my father addressed her, although Gwennie, who was living with us when my father and my stepmother got married and was getting steadily madder by the day, quite often addressed her opposite number as Mother too.

My father was christened Kenneth Edmund Knight Rowson. I found his christening mug up in the loft after he died, though he ended up as godless as me. He was Edmund after his father, who gave me and Christopher our third names, and I gave the same name to Fred. Knight was Gwennie's maiden name. I don't know where Kenneth came from.

I always knew him as Ossie, and I always think of him as Ossie, though I don't know where this name came from either, except that I know that Annie gave it to him. Apart from the fact that, in my subjective judgement at least, he looked like an Ossie, slightly owlish and amused, the name remains something of a mystery. By the time I was old enough to start wondering about things like this, Annie was dead, and all Ossie would say, when I asked him why he was called Ossie, was that Annie always renamed her pets, often adding that she had a compulsion for looking after sick animals, implying that that included him. I don't even know when she started calling him Ossie, although I found a letter she wrote to him a day or so before they got married that started out 'Dearie'.

I never called him Dad or Daddy, although for the last twenty years or so of his life I usually called him 'governor' or 'squire' or 'chief' or 'the old man'.

Gwennie called him Kenny, as did Jak, and I remember him wincing slightly at this. His oldest friends, and some of his colleagues, called him Ken, though most of the later ones, once he got married, called him Ossie. I remember him signing off the letters he'd write to Gwennie after Sunday lunch with Ken. Dawne oscillates between Ken and Ossie. Some people called him Oz.

My stepmother didn't know his name wasn't Ossie – a diminution, she must have thought, of Oswald – until the day they got married on 1 March 1973 and they were saying their vows. For the last twenty years of their lives, she called him Kenneth.

When I was in nice Miss Smith's class, one day she asked everyone what they called their parents. It seems now to have been an odd thing to do, and I can't imagine how it would serve any curriculum you could ever think of. There were a few titters from the tougher boys when someone said they called their parents Mummy and Daddy rather than Mum and Dad, but the whole class collapsed in hysterics when I said I called my parents Ossie and Annie. Miss Smith treated them all very sternly on my behalf, but I don't remember feeling embarrassed, just rather contemptuous of how childish they all were.

My stepmother was christened Eva Jocelyn Smith, in Buenos Aires, in the Anglican Church in Belgrano. The christening was merely a ceremony, however, as prior to this her father had had to register her with the Argentine authorities, who refused to let him call her Jocelyn because it wasn't on their list of officially approved names. From what she told me, he told them to call her whatever the hell they wanted, so they chose Eva, with Jocelyn as her second name.

She never used her first name, however, and the only people who ever did were the doctors and nurses and social workers who beset her in the last months of her life, despite the fact that she and I both told them repeatedly that this was a name she never used and wouldn't answer to, simply because neither she nor anyone else had ever used it. Presumably it never occurred to any of them that Mrs Rowson might have done just as well, though inevitably they would have got that wrong too.

She was always known to everyone as Jos, which some of her oldest friends spelt Joc. Sometimes, for jovial or ironic effect, they'd call her Jocelyn. Her mother and sisters alternated between the two.

I always called her Jos, from before I can remember.

She was four days short of her fifty-second birthday when she swapped the name Smith, which is impossible to mispronounce unless your class or age compels you to replace the last two letters with a double f, for the perennial pratfalls of the name Rowson.

The business of names is an odd one, and I'm not quite sure why I get so annoyed by my son calling me Martin. I suppose, like most things involving the way human beings deal or cope with each other, it's because it's ultimately about power and control. People have a tendency to thrash endlessly about trying to find anything that might mark them apart from being at heart little more than a mutated marmoset, and one of the things that always used to be cited in evidence was our capacity for naming things, for nomenclature. It's in the Bible, it's in Linnaeus, although I think it might just be evidence of another of our many shortcomings as a species, as we've evolved in such a way as to deny ourselves the rich variety of senses by which other animals have no difficulty recognising each other, and how do we know they don't have a swirling vocabulary of smells and tastes and sounds and sights by which they name each other, which we're too stupid even to guess at? Anyway, as a species we name everything in sight in order to control it all, and as individuals we rename things and people for the same reasons. My sister, when she was very small, had a little private language of her own: she called lights 'lugs' and aeroplanes 'airybuzzers' and, most inventively of all, renamed tube trains as 'gubgoes', which I've always thought was onomatopoeically perfect, and that's what we used to call these things for decades. It made them private, as if they belonged solely to us. Likewise, it's pretty obvious that's why my mother renamed my father, so she could wrest control of him from his mother, and it's just as clear why my stepmother renamed him again.

Oddly, after my mother died, my father started calling me 'Fred' or, more often, 'boy', but I suppose the change in circumstances demanded a few name changes too.

We all call each other all sorts of things, to denote degrees of intimacy or distance, and although unstructured, it's as tightly governed as the difference between how you should address a duke or a marchioness, which is probably why I don't like Fred calling me Martin, because he should be sufficiently intimate with me to call me Mr Bunnykins or something. That he prefers not to only means that I'm not quite up to speed on the rules he's revised, for his own reasons, which is more or less as it should be between parents and their children.

But I also really don't like the name at all, and I never have.

Not that it's one of those names one can't help associating with factors far beyond, and far beyond the control, of the people who bear them. For some reason or other, I've always associated the names Simon and Jason with babies, and so it's obvious that only babies should have these names, and it's just my bad luck that two of my brothers-in-law are called Simon and Jason. Similarly, I always associate Nigel with a very slobbery and grubby boy at school who had appalling table manners and a tongue too big for his mouth, so I can't help assuming that all Nigels have the same repellent misfortunes. Only recently have I been able to convince myself that everyone called Dave or Steve isn't a smooth lout in a trench coat, hanging out in Northwood looking mean and menacing in 1975, because all of that lot seemed to be called Steve or Dave, although two particularly violent and frightening boys at school never quite managed to be ultimately terrifying, because they were called Julian and Tim, and as I remember it the former wasn't quite bright enough to reinforce his potential by renaming himself Jools.

But as far as my name goes, by this stage I just have to lump it, and equally, at this juncture, I can't foresee any circumstances where I'd have the opportunity to rebrand myself, either using the Atlantic as a huge, fresh baptismal pond like my mother did, or joining Equity, or assuming an alias to pursue a life of crime. I'm simply not cut out for that kind of thing. Had I thought about it at the time, I could have chosen a nom de plume when I started out in my career as a cartoonist, but back then the kind of cartoonist I wanted to be had abjured the Spog or Pronk or Splut monickers, and I very consciously wanted to identify myself with the fully disclosed bylines of artists like Ralph Steadman, Gerald Scarfe and Steve Bell. But I should also say that in the early 1980s, although I knew I must have had an alternative name, I didn't know then what it was.

As I've said, I've always known that I was adopted. There was no secret about it at all, and I was even told stuff about my birth mother and my real father, again from before I can remember, though it never ever occurred to me to wonder how these things could be known. More than simply knowing about it, I was made to feel rather pleased about it too. We had a nice picture book, illustrated in a style that I'd later recognise as similar to Shirley Hughes's, published by the Adoption Society and called *Mr Pennyweather Gets a Family*, all about a thin bespectacled man who chooses first a daughter and then a son for her to play with. Later, when I got older, I started to work out some of the implications of being adopted, the first one being that I must have been illegitimate, but that was fine too, and made me feel rather special, definingly different from the crowd, all those sporty little prep-school boys I got on with well enough but viewed with a certain level of disdain. I didn't even mind much when I told Ian Harvey as we walked home from Stanmore Station one day when I was about twelve, and he crossed the road and started chanting 'Bastard!' at me: we've established that he actually made the stuff they showed you how to make on *Blue Peter*, so I'd got his number already.

And I never did much about it, although whenever I told anyone that I'd been adopted, they'd always, always ask if I'd tried to trace my birth family. I'd usually tell people if it came up in conversation, or they asked me something that implied a genetic link with my father or sister, or because I thought it was just quite interesting, or because, on the whole, it was also quite funny. I'd always been told that my birth mother had been an electrical engineer with the Post Office, and that my father had been a Canadian architect, so I wove a complex narrative that culminated in a night of passion up a pylon sometime in the late spring of 1958. (I was later to find out that my wife Anna was born exactly nine months before me, which added to the fun with the possibility that I'd been conceived the day she was born. Also, for the record, although this is entirely irrelevant to anything, the Soviet Army began its withdrawal from Afghanistan on her thirtieth birthday, and concluded it on mine.) Other times, I'd tell people that I'd been reared by wolves in the woods, while playing a nice, private game inside my head imagining who I might really be. Like people who claim to have lived previous lives, I always imagined myself to be the child of someone of significance, like Peter Cook or the Pope or Prince Philip or someone, although I also knew that this was just a game, a little secret to fill the minutes as I waited for a bus or needed to occupy my mind as I scribbled away at my drawing board. And after all, a void can be filled with anything you care to imagine, which was another good reason to let things remain a bit of a mystery.

But more importantly than that, and uppermost in my mind, was the fact that I thought any attempt on my part to dig into the truth would upset my father, and that there was the terrible danger that he might interpret anything I did as a rejection of him and how he'd brought me up, a kind of ultimate, and possibly unforgivable, rebuke. And I had nothing – and have nothing – to rebuke him for.

Still, when our children were born I'd hold them and look at them and occasionally feel a terrible inner sadness for my unknown mother, who'd given up a baby like this – a baby, moreover, genetically with more in common to me and her than anyone else I'd ever met. With Fred, our first child, the compulsion to find out more about his grandmother was strong, but mitigated slightly by the fact that he took, in looks, after Anna's side of the family, and at five months old, when you looked at him next to Anna's father, who was then sixty-nine, they looked like Before and After pictures warning of the terrible consequences of good living. Then, when Anna was pregnant with our second child, we'd occasionally talk about what the genetic tombola might throw up this time, and I remember there was a running joke about the unknown and unknowable possibility of a dominant gene sneaking through from the mysterious Granny No-Nose, an outcome we didn't relish at all as we rather like big noses in our family. Rose now has a beautiful nose and looks a lot like me, only considerably better, although she thinks like Anna, just as Fred looks like Anna but thinks like me.

The obvious physical similarities between me and Rose made me think once more about that unknown gene pool, but it didn't really detain me, and worries about possibly upsetting my father still prevented me from doing anything to find out.

Then, for no particular reason, but aware that time was passing, in 1998 I applied to see my original birth certificate.

I remember it was a Friday morning in October, a grey, dull, warm autumn day, when I drove to the social services offices just beyond Catford. They're in a row of rather grand, late-Victorian houses edging along the main road to Bromley, although inside the house had been decorated in a flat, neutral, 1970s kind of bureaucratic blandness that a committee once must have decided had the virtues of being both cheap and inoffensive. They were wrong on the second count, but this didn't bother me too much. I remember that I felt vaguely ill at ease, which was probably just nerves, but when I was finally seen by the social worker who'd been handed my case, she seemed, after a few questions, to be satisfied that I was sufficiently stable, middle-class and middle-aged not to give her too much cause for concern. And so she gave me my birth certificate, and that was that. It was all she had to give me, and it stated some things I knew, like that I'd been born on 15 February 1959 in Queen Charlotte's Hospital in Hammersmith, and that my name was Martin. What I hadn't previously known was that my mother's name was Kathleen Ann Gould, and that her surname had originally been mine too. I also discovered that I'd been adopted through the Church of England Adoption Society, but there was no more information to be had. I filled in a form saying that I was content to have forwarded to me any letters Kathleen Ann Gould may have left on my file, but I had to get any further information I might want or require from the Church of England Adoption Society. I thanked the social worker and left.

And all the way home I was growingly conscious that sitting next to me, in the passenger seat, there was a barely formed yet vividly palpable spectre called Martin Gould, the ghost of who I might have been, an alternative thirty-nine-year-old me, and he dogged me for the rest of the weekend until, by the Sunday night, he started to fade away.

At this stage I told neither my father, nor my stepmother, nor my sister, what I'd done.

A few weeks later my friend and old schoolteacher Butti died. His name was really Dr Robert Arthur Buttimore, but I'd long since called him Butti, like his wife and children did. Other people, depending on the depth or shallowness of their earnestness, would call him Bob or Robert. Like my father, he didn't seem to care what he was called, and in a way he filled that hole, which is hardly a void but more like a painless if gaping wound, which many people find in themselves in their late childhood, when with the callousness and ingratitude which naturally blossom at that age they seek out an alternative to make up for the shortcomings of their own fathers. The people you find to fill that role probably don't, or wouldn't want to, even acknowledge that they fulfil that need, and I never stated it, either to Butti or, indeed, to myself, until I told his sons at his wake that he's been like a second father to me. But it was, of course, an almost entirely different kind of relationship: it was intellectual rather than emotional, based on friendship rather than the bonds that tie, or sometimes shackle, families together. Nonetheless, after my father, Butti was the man who had the greatest influence on my life.

It was influence through example, but also through instruction as he was, after all, a teacher, although he never actually taught me in a classroom, but I'm inclined to think that those are the best kind of teachers there are. Among the things he taught me were the subversive powers of slight scruffiness, that the plural of miasma is miasmata (and also why it's so strangely wonderful to know that); he taught me the qualitative difference between a Catholic and a Protestant atheist, that you should never say 'hopefully' when you mean 'it is to be hoped'; that Carl Jung was set on the path of his life's work in psychoanalysis aged ten when he had a dream about God shitting an immense turd on Cologne Cathedral, but also why Jungian philosophy is such obvious crap. He also taught me the value of books at all times, why it's cool to be clever, that everything is serious, but that almost everything shouldn't be taken too seriously, that the very highest attainment of human civilisation and culture is the ability and capacity to enjoy sitting and eating and drinking (nothing but bad red wine) and talking intelligent bollocks until late, late into the night; that the poetry of A.E. Housman and all that misty-eyed English rural lyricism is, in his words, just so much etiolated bourgeois faggotry, and that the proper name for a specifically heterosexual paedophile is an 'omphacerast', from the Greek for an unripe grape, a word he'd invented but – as he was a classicist – with perfect semantic credentials about a minute before I heard it.

He also said one of the wisest things I've ever heard, as wise as anything my father told me. They say that you should stick to your principles, but who is better, the SS officer who sticks to his principles and continues murdering Jews, or the SS officer who abandons his principles and stops?

He also said some of the silliest things I've ever heard, and when I was in my late teens and early twenties, I hung out a lot at the Buttis', at Butti and his wife Ann's, over long and wonderful and crowded lunches, drinking and talking too much, and we'd try to outdo each other in excruciating puns or immensely contrived jokes. I went to many of these lunches while I was still at school, and they allowed me into a world I yearned to join, a world of other opportunities, different and wider vistas, a chance to stroll along a path that would lead me to the me I wanted to be.

For years Butti's wife Ann and I had had a running joke that she was really my mum (which she was, in a small way), even though I now knew different.

A week or so after Butti's death I went to a cartoon festival in Skibbereen in West Cork, in Ireland. I was then still working for the Dublin paper where I'd drawn 'Fuck the Pope' in Cyrillic script at the back of a cartoon, so I more or less counted as an Irish cartoonist. There were a lot of other cartoonists there, most of them Irish, whom I'd met before and liked a very great deal, and at around one o'clock in the morning we were sitting around drinking in the hotel where we were all staying when a young woman, probably in her mid-twenties, came up and joined us. Almost immediately she started berating me, as an Englishman, for working for an Irish paper, for being an Englishman telling the Irish what to think, and how I was thus perpetuating eight hundred years of English oppression and the Saxon yoke. At first I tried to engage her in some kind of conversation, but it soon became clear that she expected me to do nothing more than flinch beneath her diatribe. She was incredibly cross, and not, or so it seemed, that drunk, and while my Irish friends by and large told her to fuck off, I tried to be more emollient, and when that didn't work I tried to ask her what her real problem was, and when I got nowhere doing that I began to get rather annoyed, and told her that she was demanding a kind of ethnic purity that would shame even Slobodan Milosevic. Even that cut no ice with her, and by now my friends were beginning to wander off. So I said that she accused me of being English even though she had no way of knowing whether I was English or not, and for that matter neither did I. And I told her that I was adopted, and a few weeks previously I'd got hold of my birth certificate, and that my mother's name was Kathleen Ann Gould.

The young woman suddenly beamed at me, gave me a friendly rub on the shoulder and said, 'Oh, you're Irish! Well, that's all right then!'

Except that I'm not. I'm no more Irish than I am Jewish. It says so on the official documents, even though for a while I hoped and wished that I was both, as that would be doubly cool. In fact, my mother came from Portland Bill.

I didn't find that out for another two years. After I shook off the ethereal Martin Gould, I tried to look up the Church of England Adoption Society in the phone book, and subsequently on the Internet, but it wasn't there. Then, a year or so later, my friend Blake Morrison wrote something for the

Independent on Sunday about adoption and adopted children's reunions with their birth families. He phoned me while he was writing the article, to pick my brains and to ask if he could mention my experiences of finding out about my origins as far as I'd got. This was fine with me; I've always been a firm believer in full disclosure, probably more than I should be, more than is entirely wise or prudent, but I also tend to think, what the hell? So Blake started his article writing about me, and about how I'd found out about my mother's name (which he gave, with my agreement) and the name of the agency through which I'd been adopted, but how I'd thereafter drawn a blank. The article was duly published, and a woman from the Adoption Society then phoned me to tell me that the Church of England Adoption Society had changed its name too. She gave me its contact details, and I got in touch with them, but they said they couldn't access any of their files right then, because they were undergoing major refurbishment, and would I mind waiting about six months? It didn't really matter whether I minded or not, and for the time being I left it at that.

Meanwhile Anna's father died. Then my friend Jon died, and I went slightly mad for a bit. There was a quite genuine grief in there, but I now recognise that my compulsion, that May and June, to sit out in the garden until the early hours of the morning, drinking and talking to myself, was because Jon's death, and the uncomfortable coincidences in the cause of it in the cancerous catastrophe in his brain, and how his son Joshua was just the same age as I'd been when my mother died, meant I was also dealing with a lot of stuff I'd deferred for far too long, and at the same time how I was just doing the standard, boring, modern middle-aged mawkish thing of grieving for my extended youth. Jon deserved his due, which is about half of what I invested from my emotions after he died, because the other half was all about me. I call it a kind of madness because it was an aberrance of self-indulgence in some things which were well overdue, while others were just plain wrong.

I said earlier that I deluded myself into thinking that Jon's death marked the end of my childhood. It was a delusion, even though our relationship, when we were little more than children, had been of an intensity you get when you're sixteen or seventeen, and was as intense, although obviously in different ways, as the intensity of my relationship with my father between Annie's death and when he married Jos. But it was a delusion because I now, with hindsight, don't buy all this stuff about divisions between childhood and adulthood, about maturing and growth and all the other stuff we kid ourselves runs in judgemental parallel to the irreversible onward trajectory of our lives. And while I've also never bought into any of that other sub-Cartesian dualist nonsense, about a division between our physical and spiritual beings, it's clear to me that, while the body grows and then starts to decay, the mind – the physical mind, that porridge of electrical discharges and connecting and disconnecting synapses – is harnessed to something else. It's not God, or alternative universes, or anything metaphysical, but it doesn't track, yard by yard and year by year, the depredations of the rest of our bodies.

On his seventy-eighth birthday, I asked my father how he felt to be seventy-eight. He replied that he didn't feel any different from when he'd been eighteen, except that his body didn't do what it used to be able to do.

When I was approaching my thirtieth birthday, I went into a terrible kind of panic. This was because I'd been told, when I was a student, that if I didn't stop drinking and smoking so much I'd never make it to thirty. But I was fine, and by then I'd remembered that the person who'd told me that, my own personal Cassandra, was smacked out of his head at the time, and gobbling acid like it was lemon drops.

For the record, I've never wittingly taken LSD, although many people seem to think that I must have done.

But forty was fine. I remember it was half-term, and so I indulged myself by having a long, long bath as I didn't have to take the children to school, and lay there in the nice hot water, realising that I didn't have to pretend to be grown up any more, and I could now simply enjoy the rest of the toboggan ride towards death.

You may think that this is just more self-indulgent nonsense, and you may well be right, but things are never as simple as you think, and it's far healthier to work on the basis that they never should be. The geometry between mind and body isn't a parallelogram, but a jagged and infinitely irregular tangential polyhedron, and I'm inclined to the conclusion that a personal notion of maturity is just a confused by-product of adolescent insecurity, and that almost all of us are better off sticking where we started, in an endless childhood, albeit qualified by experience into reasonably good behaviour, but still with all that capacity for wonder, laughter, larks, caprice, forgiveness, love and malice.

Then again, what do I know?

The renamed Church of England Adoption Society got back in touch with me about seven weeks after Jon died. They seemed to be very anxious that I get in touch with them as soon as I possibly could, which seemed to me to be a bit rich after I'd been left on hold for so many months. Even so, I made the appointment. It was a very hot July day, and I drove over to their offices in Clapham feeling just as nervous, or trepidatious, as I'd felt two years earlier when I'd gone to Catford. I remember that I'd joked to the children, as I'd walked them to school that morning, that this was the day

I'd discover about the previously unknown werewolf gene that kicks in when you're forty-one, but it was a joke which was just an attempt to muffle a deeper uncertainty and anxiety.

Their refurbished offices looked very nice, in a late-nineties, postmoderny plush sort of way, and I was directed up some nice new pine stairs to a room where I met the social worker who was on my case. She seemed to be very excited, almost overexcited, and started off by telling me that my birth mother, Kathleen Gould, was dead. I remember my lower lip trembled a bit when I heard that, but she then said that I had two older siblings, a brother and a sister.

This was something else I'd known for a long time, another bit of that information that somehow or other had trickled down as a part of family lore. I think it was Dawne who first told me that she'd heard that the reason I was put up for adoption was that my birth mother's parents, my grandparents, hadn't been prepared to 'rear a third bastard', although again I'd never really wondered how she could have known this.

The social worker asked me how I felt about all this, so I told her. I said that mostly I felt rather sad, for my unknown and unknowable mother, but beyond that I didn't feel all that much, and I said that on the whole I doubted that I'd get in contact with my older brother and sister, and I thought that that was that. But then the social worker, who was still very excited, said there was more, a whole lot more. She said that my younger sister had left a letter on my file, but there was still more to it than that. She, too, had been adopted, and this was the first case the social worker had ever come across of two children, adopted by separate adoptive parents, being reunited. My sister's name was Jan, short for Janette, although our mother had originally called her Madeleine, but this had been changed by her adoptive parents. Jan had started the search process years before I had, and she'd therefore done all the work. She'd discovered me, and she'd also discovered that, after she'd been adopted, our mother had finally moved to America, where she'd had seven more children, all sons.

The social worker asked me how I felt now, and the oddest thing was that I now felt wonderful.

That was partly down to the kind of bipolarism you often get after a series of shocks. But there was something else to it, something which is a cliché but is nonetheless valid for all that. After all, clichés are only clichés because, by and large, they tend to be true. This particular cliché is that adopted people never feel quite complete, but I did now, and it was almost a physical sensation, that I could feel a small but important piece of the jigsaw puzzle finally being put in its proper place. The place I felt it going into was on my right side, just at the bottom of my ribcage.

I'm not entirely happy with the idea of being classified as an 'adoptee' or 'adopted person', not because the condition itself bothered me, but because I don't like labels. They're another aspect of that lazy human trait of classifying everything, and then pigeonholing it all in a further largely futile effort to take and keep control. It's entirely understandable why we do this, but it makes things appear much simpler and more straightforward than they truly are. Knowing what I've just told you, it would be forgivable for you hereafter to earmark me as 'adopted' as if that explained everything, and that that is really all this book is about, whereas I've meant it to be about much, much more than that, and about infinitely more than just me.

That was another reason why I was so tardy in getting round to finding anything out about my origins. It was too much all about me, and any journey I chose to embark on to 'find my family' would inevitably exclude the family I'd found already.

The literature of adoption stories is growing exponentially all the time (and forgive me for adding to the pile), but although I know there's an almost prurient fascination among the majority of the unadopted, it's a genre that's inherently solipsistic, and in order to avoid slipping into being unreadably and exclusively personal, there's a temptation to talk up adoption as if it's something more than it really is, almost as if it's a bid to recruit the adopted to the legions of other victims who trumpet their victimhood as another way of making everyone else shut up in embarrassed awe while the victims make a quick getaway to be the first ones down the fire escape.

During my own process of discovery, I was tempted to think the same way myself. I spoke and wrote a lot about the history of adoption in Britain throughout the first two-thirds of the twentieth century; about what, in one article, I described as a mini-holocaust of child abduction by well-intentioned but fundamentally misguided philanthropists who failed to recognise that they were managing a programme that was pure eugenics, seeking to purge the Original Sin of illegitimacy through the redemptive sacrament of stealing the babies of powerless women and imposing some kind of 'respectability' on them. I still think that that's a largely accurate analysis, but I was over-egging the pudding, adding to the growing feeling that adoption was in some way a kind of crime, with its victims scattered everywhere in its wake. Worse still, I think this attitude makes a glib assumption that the experience of adoption should always thereafter be assumed to have wrought a defining trauma on all those people – mothers and babies

– who went through it. And while it's certainly true that I suddenly felt more complete that July lunchtime than I had previously, my former state of incompletion was never a real problem, was never even remotely traumatic enough to prevent me from functioning on a daily basis, or from being both successful and usually happy. My status hadn't haunted my childhood, and if I was ever haunted by the idea of a missing mother, you already know the source of that. My sudden sense of wholeness was, I think, down entirely to the information. The one thing I wasn't after was an instant new happy family, as I already had one of those.

Of course, some people's experience of adoption has been truly terrible and horrible, but that's not true for all of us, just as it's not true that only adopted people uniquely suffer the exquisiteness of loss, betrayal, abandonment, uncertainty, ignorance or any of the other routine emotions concomitant with being both human and alive.

Still, it's objectively interesting by anyone's standards suddenly to find out that you're one of eleven children, at least four of whom were born illegitimately back in the days when that was still a major taboo.

I got overexcited, even more so than the social worker. I was put in contact with Jan, who's married to an officer in the RAF, and because they were then stationed in Cyprus there was an agonising wait of two weeks before she learned that I'd surfaced. The renamed Church of England Adoption Society rang me and gave me her address and phone number, but counselled caution, suggesting that I write to her first, and that I take it slowly. After I finished talking to them, I remember staring at her phone number while I was drawing a cartoon for the *Racing Post*, with a deadline looming, but even though I hadn't finished it, I thought fuck it and phoned her. We spoke for about three hours, while I held the phone in my left hand and carried on cross-hatching with my right.

I found out contradictory things, from Jan, from my adoption papers and also from subsequent conversations I had with three of our brothers. Our mother, Kathleen Ann Gould, was the daughter and only child of an unskilled labourer in the naval dockyards in Portland, that strange spit of land that sticks, like a mosquito's proboscis, into the English Channel from the south coast way beyond the Isle of Wight. She was born in 1934, and in 1954 she had her first child, my brother Andrew, and then, a couple of years later, she gave birth to Alison. On my adoption papers it said that she told the lady almoner at the Church of England Adoption Society that the father of these children was a sea captain who was estranged from his wife and who kept promising to marry Kathleen, but he eventually returned to his family, leaving my mother in the lurch. Andrew later told me that in 1994 he asked his mother on her deathbed to tell him who his father was, but she refused. She then went to London, having been educated at grammar school and thereafter trained as a technical assistant. According to my adoption papers, she was a technical assistant to the Central Electricity Generating Board. According to my family gossip, she'd worked for the Post Office. According to another of her sons, she came to London to work at the Admiralty, and Jan told me that several of the brothers told her, during her earlier research, that she sought work in London to pay for medical treatment for Andrew, who'd been born with webbing between his fingers and toes. Her move to London happened around ten years after the foundation of the National Health Service. Once in London, according to her testimony on my adoption papers, she met a young Canadian architecture student from Vancouver University (which doesn't exist) who was called Edward

Burden. She gave his date of birth, and said that she had had a long and steady relationship with him, but he had always maintained that he was sterile, due to an accident while he'd been in the army. When this proved not to be the case, at first he didn't believe that she could have become pregnant by him, and then told her (she said) that he wasn't yet ready for the commitment of marriage and, I presume, fatherhood. When I was born, when she was twenty-five, she therefore reluctantly agreed to put me up for adoption, although she told her interrogator that she was very sad to have to give me up and loved me very much. She also swore that this would never happen again, although she admitted that she found it difficult to remain celibate.

Less than two years later she gave birth to Jan, or Madeleine as she called her. We've already established that Kathleen called me Martin, which you need to keep in mind as we get deeper into the story. Jan was adopted privately, and the way she told me her side of the story, or how she understood it, she seems in some way or other to have been sold by our mother to her new parents. Because of the private nature of the arrangement she has no legal basis for finding out anything more about the circumstances of her birth, and no possibility of discovering who her father might be.

Then, less than a year later, Kathleen had her fifth illegitimate child, another boy, whom she called Martin.

On his birth certificate his name is Martin Gould, but he's not the Martin Gould who rode ghostily home with me from Catford in 1998. This time, she married the father, who was an American serviceman stationed at the American Embassy in Grosvenor Square in London. Martin was therefore retrospectively legitimised, and soon thereafter they moved to California, to the Bay area around San Francisco, although she left her two eldest children with their – my, our – grandparents in Portland. Then, when her mother – my grandmother

206

– died, her father – my grandfather, whose name was George but whom Kathleen apparently called Kingdom – wrote to her to say that he couldn't or wouldn't cope, so the three of them went over to California too, reuniting Kathleen with her first two children. Kingdom then remarried several times and lived into his nineties. Kathleen died of cancer when she was sixty, her husband having predeceased her. Before then, however, she had six more children, three of whom, like me, Madeleine/Jan and Martin, also had names beginning with the letter M.

When Jan made herself known to the rest of the family, a lot of the younger brothers simply refused to believe her story because, she said, they saw their mother as a saintly figure, and no doubt she was. I'm told she was widely loved, especially by their friends, and her funeral thronged with young people. It's clear, however, that she never told any of them about the two missing youngsters. But though there's no way of knowing now if she told her husband about me and Jan, he clearly knew about the first two, and to his credit ended up raising them as his own. But I'm also told by one of the brothers that for as long as he could remember there was a little photograph of an anonymous baby on the mantelpiece in their small, crowded house in California, and one day when the boys were having a scrap the frame and the glass got broken, and he said he'd never seen his mother angrier.

That may have been Jan, or maybe it was me. With my adoption papers were some letters from Kathleen to the Church of England Adoption Society, one of which thanked them for the photos of me which my parents (though I imagine it was just my mother) had passed on to her via the Adoption Society. Though it's possible, as I've since discovered, that if

207

that was my photograph, Kathleen might have got it another way.

Then again, it could have been anyone. I once read that the writer Jan Morris's mother used to carry a photograph of a baby around with her in her handbag, and show it to strangers on buses. They'd ooh and aah for a while, but when they asked her if it was her grandchild, she'd reply that it was a photo of Hitler as a baby, and then relish the reaction as her new friends recoiled in disgust. Jan Morris changed her name from James in the early 1970s, although when I was a student I once persuaded a friend of mine that before his/her sex change Jan Morris had been Johnny Morris, the comedy zookeeper from *Animal Magic*.

I met my sister Jan. She looks a lot like my daughter, and we noticed, as we sat over lunch, how we had the same little mannerisms, although in many other ways she's a lot different from me. She's a Christian and a Tory for a start, and she subsequently told some of the other brothers that I was 'very posh', even though both she and I are, on our mother's side at least, of Dorset peasant stock. We had a nice time and I liked her, even if I didn't share her feelings of resentment against Kathleen. We haven't met since, though we exchange Christmas cards.

I met Martin, too, about a year after I first found out about him and the rest of them. He was then serving as a chief petty officer aboard the USS *Enterprise*, an enormous American aircraft carrier which was then, in July 2001, moored off Southampton, and he came up to London especially to see me. We met in a pub on Millbank, near to Tate Britain, where I'd been on a panel discussing the satirical art of James Gillray. Halfway through the talk the fire alarms all went off, and the panellists and the audience all had to leave the building and stand outside until someone worked out what was going on. As we were standing in the sunshine, I said to one of my fellow panellists that I hoped that this didn't go on too long, as I was due to meet my brother, and the thing was we'd never met before. My fellow panellist, an art critic, expressed the usual quiet amazement at my story, and then told me his, which wasn't about adoption, but about secret families, unknown cousins, lies and late discoveries, which confirmed my growing feeling that the adoption experience is just a formalised version of most people's family lives, where you can hardly hear yourself think for the noise of skeletons rattling in cupboards all around you.

By the time I got to the pub, Martin was drunk. In fact, he was very drunk. I generously put this down to nerves or apprehension, but an American friend of mine later pointed out to me that he would have been used to American beer on an American aircraft carrier, which would have had a minimal alcohol content, unlike the export-strength lager he'd been drinking while he waited for me. I showed him my birth certificate to prove my credentials, and then tried to catch up with him. We got on reasonably well, although getting him into a restaurant later on that evening wasn't at all easy, and he finally came home with me and passed out on the sofa. I didn't like him that much, and I suspect he wasn't that taken with me. At one point in the evening, as we walked up Whitehall (I was more or less carrying him by now, which wasn't easy as he's about five inches taller than me), he said that if I hadn't been his brother, I'd just have been another 'drawin' faggot', which is probably true. When I saw him off at the station as he caught the train back into London the next morning, we hugged each other, but I've hardly heard a word from him since.

I liked John, one of the younger brothers, and the last of

my long-lost siblings I met. He was stationed in Iceland with the US Air Force, and caught a plane down to an airbase in East Anglia and then came down to London to see me. He came back to Lewisham for dinner with us, although when we said goodbye to each other at the station later that evening, we shook hands rather than hugging. Again I haven't really heard anything from him since.

I speak, about twice a year, to Andrew in California, when we can work out the time difference. After the first, three-hour-long conversation, we haven't really had that much to say to each other, although I like him too. He was in the US armed forces as well, although he told me that he's still a British subject and is forbidden from becoming an American citizen because he was dishonourably discharged from the army for possession of cannabis.

Neither John nor Andrew seemed to have much time for Martin.

After I met Martin, but before I met John, I wrote an article for the *Guardian* about the whole business, and I finished it off with a gag about whether or not irony was a shared gene by saying that I hadn't shared with Martin my thought that I could think of no other circumstances in which an American serviceman would get drunk with a left-wing member of the London media chatterati, except possibly for sex. I sent him a copy of the article, and he sent further copies on to his brothers, but although he told me via email that it had made him laugh, he made no comment on the sex joke. In the same article I digressed a bit about families, asking why we think they mean so much anyway, particularly as most people who are murdered or physically or sexually abused get murdered or physically or sexually abused by members of their own families. I think I then repeated the old line about how your friends are God's apology for your family. When I met John, he brought up that section over lunch, and asked me why I'd written it. I remember that he looked genuinely puzzled and upset.

He probably thought I was being unnecessarily cynical.

I think I'm just being realistic.

You, for your part, may think that various experiences in my life have warped, or at least coloured, my view of things. I think that that's too glib an analysis, and I think the apotheosis of the family into a paradigm of perfection by politicians, both profane and religious, is too glib too, as well as often being truly cynical and frequently sinister. Every year or so another bloodless and highly regarded moralist will deplore the condition of society, and call for returns to family values coupled with the rigorous application of an older, tighter morality. Twice in recent years I've heard apparently serious and thoughtful people say that this necessarily involves the forcible discouragement of single parenthood through the confiscation of lone parents' children, in order to improve the moral health of society at large. One of these moralists, an American sociological Dr Strangelove called James Q. Wilson, was given breakfast by the then childless Chancellor of the Exchequer Gordon Brown in early 2001, who praised Wilson as a 'towering authority', whose books he had read with profit. The next day the *Guardian* summarised Wilson's comments to Brown and the other breakfasters as follows: 'Moral revival may involve locking up single mothers in institutions to ensure their offspring are taught virtue, and [he made] repeated references to the way moral decline is related to the growth of single parenthood.' During my father's four years of single parenthood, which wasn't the result of any moral laxity on his part, would this wholesale abduction or internment have included my sister and me? And, bearing in mind my father's homily about how you can't legislate for other people's morality, what fucking business is it of anyone else's anyway?

The earthly accoutrements of respectability, scholarship, office, position and intellectual contortionism have a tendency to make people nod politely or keep quiet out of embarrassment that gainsaying this garbage will expose them to a response that will make them look either rude or stupid. But don't be either gulled or badgered by the smart boys: the agenda is always too transparent, and the snarling of the dogs rounding up the scapegoats is always too loud, however loudly the rest of us keep whistling, pretending that this kind of cruel nonsense about respectability comes even close to being intellectually respectable itself.

Families, like everything else humans touch or which touches humans, are too complicated to regulate except when you're firefighting. Kathleen, in happier circumstances, probably gave John and the rest of them a happy and stable family life; in unhappier times, she didn't or couldn't or wouldn't give me a family life at all, for all sorts of different reasons I can guess at but choose not to judge. Others, at the time, probably refused to allow themselves the luxury of not judging, although of course I have absolutely no way at all of knowing to what extent she was pressurised into giving me up for adoption, and if that pressure was personal or was sloshed out by the societal and cultural forces of the times. Given the fact that she'd already had two illegitimate children, maybe the pressure to conform to the standards of respectable society weren't that great; maybe, given what she'd already done, they were greater; maybe her parents really weren't prepared to bring up a third bastard; maybe they never knew she got pregnant a third and fourth time. And maybe she should have had the opportunity to keep Jan and me along with Andrew and Alison, in a happy family in Portland, and maybe, just maybe, it was a huge relief all round, for everyone concerned, that there was also the opportunity available, and a system in place, that meant that she didn't have to.

I'm not sure what I now think or feel about my birth mother, six years after finding out all I'll probably ever be able to about her, at least in relation to me. Nor am I entirely sure what I ever thought or felt about her. For a long time I turned her and the fact of my adoption into a bit of a joke, another plate in the armour. But I also, before I knew anything about her, sometimes felt sad for her and about her, and a little bit sad and sorry for myself. But it was in an oddly abstract way. I was also curious about her, but again in the abstract sense that it would just be interesting to know who she was and what she was like, to see if the little fantasies I indulged in inside my head matched up to the reality. And in a way, finding out has robbed me of the pleasures of mystery, deprived me of that favourite fallback of huge numbers of children, in moments when they hate their genetic and still present parents more than anything else in the world, that they might, please God, have been adopted themselves.

Mystery still surrounds my birth father, however. A few months after I found out all about Kathleen and my ten siblings, I hired the services of a private detective who specialises in adoption cases and in reuniting children with their long-lost parents.

Having got my mother, I was now more interested in my father, in the way you get when you're sated but you still want more. The reality of Kathleen failed to explain various things about me, and the reality of her other children failed even more. Where, for instance, did I get my skill in drawing, which I know is innate, if subsequently honed? Where did I get my brains, my imagination, my memory, the interior things which I assumed were as genetic as my stubby Dorset peasant fingers and toes, or my nose and jawline which I

213

could clearly see in the one photograph of Kathleen which Jan sent me?

When I found out about Kathleen and the brothers and sisters I was, as I've said, overexcited. Too many people I'd known and loved had recently died that I felt energised by the new vista of fresh hellos opening up in front of me. So I told everyone, and probably talked about it too much. Among other people, I told Jon's widow, although she must have had other things weighing on her mind at the time. I probably convinced myself that this was a life-enhancing story, and as such needed to be told to everyone. I told her what Jan had told me about our younger brothers, how many of them served in the American armed forces, and how others worked on production lines and drank beer all weekend, and as usual she cut straight to the business in hand and said that I had to find out about my father, as so far it all sounded 'a bit knuckle-scraping'. I didn't mind the comment, because it was true.

So a few months later I hired the services of the private detective. I went to her flat off the Gray's Inn Road, close by the College of Dentistry where my father claimed to file his nails on the Portland stone. As she looked at my adoption papers she winced slightly and told me that there was too much information. This wasn't one of those little social tics people fall into instinctively when we're embarrassed by being invited too deeply into the life and secrets of another person, but an observation, born no doubt of long experience, that women didn't usually volunteer that much about the absent father. In other words, Kathleen's testimony about my birth father was too good, or at least too complete, to be true.

The private eye spent several months searching for Edward Burden, but drew a complete blank. As far as she could ascertain, the Edward Burden my mother had said was my father simply didn't exist, or had left no discernible trail of existence. He'd sunk into the earth, or gone back to the mothership, or she'd just made him up the first place. If so, maybe the name holds the clue, and suggests a capacity for mischievous inventiveness I'd rather like to ascribe to my mother, even if she didn't have one. But nonetheless it's a good, clever name, with the father being a Burden, just like his son.

Anna thought the private detective hadn't tried hard enough and was insufficiently thorough in rendering me an audit of what she'd done, where and how, to justify the sizeable amount of money I'd given her, but by that stage I wasn't so bothered.

In a way I relish the remaining air of mystery, the infinite scope for possibility, and we all secretly love mysteries. It used to be the unfathomable and sublime mysteries of religion; now it's crime shows on the TV, and you never really want to find everything out too soon in case you ruin the ending, even if there's no ending in sight.

Of course, within that infinity of possibility, there are some probabilities you can guess at, from the sordidness of a one-night stand to the sadness and cruelty of abandonment. And there are others – like rape or incest – which you hardly dare to think about at all.

I remember going to Portland Bill on our last family holiday before my adoptive mother died, at Easter in 1969. We were staying in Eype, a little village a mile or so inland from the concave arc of the Dorset coast, and one day we drove to Portland, through Weymouth, parallel to the thin, sharp needle of the Chesil Beach sticking like a hypodermic from Portland Bill into the belly of the mainland. I remember it was a sunny day, and as Portland then still had a naval dockyard – the one where my grandfather had once worked – we got stopped by a military policeman at a checkpoint, asking our business. My father, in the same slightly apologetic tone he'd used when he tried to blag the bag of booze past the customs officer, said that we only wanted to look at the military cemetery. I remember the spring sunshine on yew trees and conifers, and how I thought it wasn't quite proper that the tombstones of named and anonymous German Luftwaffe pilots, shot down trying to pulverise Portsmouth nearly thirty years previously, should have swastikas carved on them. It seemed like a dishonourable, and probably undeserved, symbol to bear into eternity. What I don't remember was any sudden atavistic awareness that this was the land of my forebears. There were no bat squeaks from any song lines stretching from Southwell through Fortuneswell and Castletown up the A354 over the Ferry Bridge. And there's no reason why I should imagine there might have been.

The bedrock of the whole process of adoption back then was that there should be a clean break. The first step on the path to salvation from illegitimacy, or abandonment, or the chance of the unsustainability of any hope of that elusive happy family life, was that you were, in a way, born again, and I suppose that it wasn't unreasonable to compel you to forget about your first birth if the second one was going to be viable.

And yet, as I've said, there were those family stories, about my birth mother and her job and the attitudes of her parents. I just took these for granted, without ever thinking much about their provenance, although when I started going out with Anna and started telling her all this stuff about myself and where I'd come from, she asked the obvious question, which was how anyone could possibly *know*.

When I first found my adoptive mother's old address book in my adoptive father's desk after he'd died, I didn't read it all the way through. I saw the photo of her and Dawne in the back, and flicked through it, noticing the names of all those friends in Ohio. I lent the book to Dawne for a while, as I thought she'd be interested and those names would bring back happy memories.

I visited Dawne again in doing the research for this book, and went to see her down in Kent on a damp and miserable Monday in January 2006. I took a few of the things I'd found and kept, as I wanted to talk to her about my adoptive mother, filling in the gaps where I couldn't depend on my memory. There was a nice photograph of Annie kneeling between two enormous poodles, one black and one white, and there was also the address book, which might provide some aides-mémoires about Annie and Dawne's time in America during the war. But there were other names and addresses, from later on. One of these, Mrs Sarah Knight in Ashton-under-Lyne, is my adoptive father's grandmother, though I may be wrong, and there are other names, with addresses in nurses' homes from when she was training to be a nurse. But my father isn't in this book, or any other members of his family, or any of her friends like Bob and Beth or Beryl or my stepmother, so she must have had another, later book for everyday use, although I didn't find that one.

The night before I went to see Dawne I was standing in our kitchen boiling the kettle and I absent-mindedly started looking through the address book, conscious that I hadn't previously read through it properly, although I didn't really expect to gain any great revelations from it, but I suppose I thought I might see a name from America that might mean something to Dawne.

Then I got to the names and addresses listed under the letter G, and on the second page I found written, but not in my adoptive mother's handwriting, the words 'Kathleen

Gould', and on the next line the single word 'Friend', written in block capitals, but with a dot over the 'I'.

I went into psychic shock, and was shaking when I went into the sitting room to tell Anna.

But it made sense of a few things, like where that stuff about my mother came from, and it made more general sense too. It's exactly the kind of thing Annie would have done, despite or maybe even because there were strict rules to prevent even the possibility of my two mothers meeting.

Some of the information may have got scrambled in the retelling, like what Kathleen's job was. Some of it may just have been wrong, as she covered her trail. I can only speculate, just like I can only speculate and just brush the fingertips of my imagination over where they met and for how long; when it was they met, and whether Kathleen was then yet pregnant with Madeleine/Jan, and what they made of each other. I'm certain that it was Kathleen who wrote her name and that word 'friend', and Dawne said it was definitely not Annie's handwriting.

But what are the wider implications of that meeting? Did they ever make contact with each other again? Did Annie tell my adoptive father? Did he find out? Did Kathleen continue to keep tabs on me, until the last, thin ties that connected us withered away when she moved to America? Did one of my mothers tell the other one about her childhood in America, and paint a tantalising picture of a land of reinvention? Why did my father keep this address book and not any other ones? Did either of them know more than they ever told me? And if so, why didn't they tell me? Or was it just that Annie knew, before everyone else wised up, that the gnawing itch inside each adoptee is the ignorance, that the sense of incompleteness is almost purely to do with information, and so she was simply finding out as much as she could, entirely on my behalf?

There's other, deeper stuff caught up in all this. For years and years I was told, first by my adoptive mother and then by my stepmother, that the reason for Annie's final break with her parents, ten years before she died, was that she'd taken me to see them, just after I'd arrived, and her father had said to her, 'I don't like the look of that one much; I'd send it back if I were you.' I never questioned this: given what had happened to Annie, with Christopher's death and then Naomi's, it was an unforgivable thing to say, and I suppose I was always rather pleased by the other implication, that she'd sided with me against her parents. But Dawne tells me that all this is quite untrue, and that her parents were delighted with me.

That's not the only lie I grew up believing to be true. I'd always been led to believe, possibly by Annie, but it was often repeated by my stepmother who must have heard it from her, that at the end of the war Annie's mother had written to her and Dawne's American foster-parents saying that she'd be obliged if they could send Dawne back, but they could keep Ann. Dawne tells me this is untrue as well, because her mother never wrote a single word to anyone in America throughout the war.

We all build up our own mythologies to justify our lives and smooth the path, and anyway, full disclosure isn't necessarily in everyone's best interests.

It was a few months after I received my adoption papers that I told my father and stepmother. I was nervous about it, and slightly embarrassed, but over lunch one day at the Royal Society of Medicine, of which my father was a member, I said there was something I had to tell them, and then prefaced what I had to say by saying how much I loved them both and how grateful I was, almost beyond words, for how they'd raised me and all the support they'd shown me ever since. After I'd told them everything I knew, and emphasised that all I'd been after was just information, my stepmother showed an almost excessive curiosity about it all, while all my father did was half raise his thin eyebrows and say, 'I'm surprised it took you so long to do anything about it.'

But later, after I'd told my sister, she was having lunch with our father and started talking about the whole business, including the circumstances of her own adoption, and she told me afterwards that our father seemed to get genuinely upset, and made it clear that he didn't want to talk about it.

But I don't think that was about me. My sister has told me that she's quite aware that her private adoption happened suspiciously soon after Christopher's death, that she knows that she was what our parents got to assuage their grief, or even what they got instead of grieving. I think that's what upset my father so much. And there was also, as I've said, a qualitative difference between my sister's relationship with our father and mine. But that's her business, not mine. She decided not to make any further enquiries about her own origins.

One last thing. After my stepmother's funeral, as her cousin Gwyneth was leaving our house, she said that, although I didn't know it, we'd met before. I was about to say that I remembered meeting her several times after my stepmother married my father, when she interrupted and said that it was a lot earlier than that. She'd been with my stepmother when she'd gone to pick me up from the Mother and Baby Home to take me to my new parents, and had held me in the taxi as all three of us were driven from Chiswick to Stanmore.

So, let's just run through all that again.

I was born, illegitimately, on 15 February 1959, in Queen Charlotte's Hospital in Hammersmith, which has now been knocked down, its place taken by blocks of luxury apartments. I was the third child of Kathleen Ann Gould, who died in California in 1994, after having given birth to a further eight children. My father was possibly called Edward Burden, although he doesn't seem to exist. Kathleen Gould gave me up for adoption to a Dr and Mrs Rowson, being their third child, although their first and only natural child had died in 1955. Dr Rowson died in 2004. Mrs Rowson died in 1969. I was delivered from one mother to another by Sister Jocelyn Smith, a midwife, who subsequently became the second Mrs Rowson, and also died in 2004. Prior to her marriage to Dr Rowson, she'd always been known to me as my godmother. I was never baptised, and so officially I never had any god-parents.

All clear now?

Which leaves a lot of stuff unexplained, and probably inexplicable, and in the end, so what? I think we put too much store in the power of genetics, just like we used to invest too much trust in God. There are other ties, just as strong as the ties of blood, and this emphasis on the journey of discovery undertaken by the adopted inevitably sidelines the third party to the contract, the adopters. I know that some adoptees have had appalling experiences with their adoptive families, but then again many, many people have had appalling experiences with their own flesh and blood, and part of me thinks there's too much else to be getting on with to allow us the luxury of constantly seeking to reduce our lives to an I Spy book of personal trauma. Nor should we overlook the altruism and magnanimity of most adopters, albeit based in an initiating self-interest. It's not always easy or perfect for them either, and that shouldn't be forgotten.

For instance, my adoptive father told me when I was about thirteen or fourteen that he'd felt very uneasy about adopting me, because I was a boy. Whether that was because of Christopher or was more generally Oedipal I can't now say, but after he died, my stepmother repeated the story, and said that at the time he'd said that no one should have to rear another man's son. Yet he did, even if I suspect that he just went along with what my adoptive mother wanted. But after she died, had he been a different man who knows what might have happened? I could have been sent away to boarding schools, or far worse than that. But that didn't happen.

Throughout all of our lives we're constantly hemmed in by countless ribbons of alternative lives running in parallel to our real ones, the hints of what might have been. It's a largely pointless game wondering how things would have turned out if this had happened, or that hadn't, but you can get a life-time of largely harmless fun out of playing it.

I have wider scope than many when I play the game, and a higher probability, or greater risk, that the phantom alternatives could easily have ended up as the reality. To start the game rolling, there's the throw of the dice that governs us all, and what we'd have been like if a different sperm had fertilised a different one of our mother's eggs, so one set of genes would become more dominant, another lot would have been more recessive, and somewhere someone's nose would be slightly longer, and somewhere else someone spawns a psychopath. If you go back *ab ovo*, and start trying to calculate the probabilities, quite quickly you start going mad, so let's move forward a few months, and make this more about me.

There's a good chance, if my mother had been more ruthless or desperate, then that would have been it for me. I could easily have been aborted, in some backstreet in the late fifties by a wise old woman or an unscrupulous or disgraced doctor, and knitting needles or gin and a hot bath would have meant my little tiny bones would have ended up flushed down the drain.

Or failing that, Kathleen might have decided to keep me, and I'd have grown up in Portland, and she might have called it a day, and that's where I'd have stayed. Or she may have strayed up to London again, had Jan, kept her, and we'd have carried on, or she may have met her American, gone to America and left us behind, or taken us with her, and then may or may not have had my seven other brothers.

Each twist and turn would have changed my life utterly, made me another infinite series of possible Martins, each one of them further and further away from the me I am the further back you go. And who knows if that would have been better or worse, or happier or unhappier? And Christopher may not have died, so my sister and I may have been adopted by completely different people. And my adoptive mother may not have died, and my father may not have remarried, or married someone else, and I may have moved to Leicester, which means I'd have gone to a different school, had different friends, gone to a different university or not gone to one at all, married someone different, had different children, had a different job and lived a different life.

Or maybe, when I went down the slide with that bit of dowelling in my mouth, it might have hit the ground harder and sheered straight through my careless four-year-old brain, just like the handle of a trombone should do, and that would have been that. Or go-karting down our road aged seven, maybe the car that was backing out of a drive halfway down would have been going a fraction faster, or would have gone a foot or so further, and I wouldn't have whizzed past, just inches away from its approaching back wheels. That would have been it for me too, just as it would have been if the swimming pool in Tenerife had filled up quicker, or I hadn't braked in time speeding out of a lay-by in Scotland when I was nineteen, or I'd crashed the car, up to my eyeballs on speed, driving home at seven in the morning when I was twenty-two, or when I drove home stoned from Cambridge one afternoon when I was twenty, unable to remember a single thing between Grantchester and the end of the A1. And on and on it goes.

As I said, there's little point in entertaining any of this what-might-have-been, so let's stick with what we've got. And part of what I got was a thoroughgoing endorsement of the prime purpose of the whole apparatus of adoption as it was practised for most of the twentieth century. It was, quite simply, social engineering, and on a grand scale, the point of which was to redeem thousands of innocent babies who were nonetheless congenitally if circumstantially guilty of the besetting sin of illegitimacy. Twenty years before I was born, unmarried pregnant women were still being put in mental hospitals, mostly to get them out of the way, but probably also because their dissidence from the moral ortho-doxies of the time defined them, like political dissidents in the Soviet Union, as quite simply mad. Adoption provided a way of avoiding that at least, and also, given all the rules about clean breaks, the option for the mother to move on and reinvent herself, and the child to become a blank slate, and you can hardly blame the well-intentioned people who managed the system for the fact that this left out the writhing tangle of other factors that subsequently make the process of adoption such an issue for the people who under-went it.

Still, as far as instant respectability is concerned, in my case the system worked perfectly.

Recently the English have started to pretend that class no longer matters, although we all know that it does, from whichever position you approach it. It's true that in my lifetime the rigidity of the class system has broken down a great deal, but just because it's looser doesn't mean that it no longer exists, or that class no longer defines almost all our dealings with everyone else around us in tiny, possibly subconscious yet incremental ways. Indeed, the loosening of the shackles has served to make everything far more complicated. We're told that we're all middle class now (those that aren't are generally portrayed as either almost feral members of the underclass, beyond hope, or archaic and vaguely funny relics of feudalism), yet within the middle class the defining strata are almost infinite, and within them different perceptions and preconceptions about our own position and how it's perceived by other people on either side make us twist ourselves into a bone-cracking yoga of embarrassment or resentment.

Here's a story where you'll run out of fingers counting off all the inherent class signifiers.

When I was at Cambridge I went to meet a friend of mine in a pub beyond the medieval centre of town, dominated by the colleges, beyond the bus garage, in an area known as the Kite, filled with rows of artisans' terraced cottages, many of which were now occupied either by academics or by the elderly or students living on the cheap. The pub was very crowded, and the person I was meeting hadn't yet arrived, so I started elbowing my way to the bar to buy a drink, although the last few feet of my quest were blocked by two young men standing at the bar with their backs to me. They had shaven heads, were wearing donkey jackets and were drinking lager. As a middle-class student (albeit unshaven and dressed, shabbily, by charity shops) I felt that instinctive apprehension I'd grown up with of people who might potentially do me violence because of the way my class had determined that I look and speak, but then, standing behind them, I overheard snatches of their conversation. One was asking the other which house at Marlborough he'd been in.

It cuts all ways. There were other people at Cambridge who didn't don disguises, but who haw-hawed and ran with the beagles and had the kind of haircuts dictated by genera-tions of differing factors in the Home Counties and whose vowels could crack the chapel windows at Winchester. I liked some of these people individually, but as a whole I despised them, for their money, the way they looked, their attitudes and, most of all, for their easy complacency. Part of what defined my politics, which were pretty firmly entrenched by that point anyway, was a desire to have this whole class of people swept away by history. Even now, several counter-revolutions later, I'm still always slightly amazed when I meet some young man called Rupert, working as a barrister or in PR, with a voice that's loose and nasally and open-mouthed as the 'yaaaars' and 'gneeurghs' fall effortlessly out, because I assumed everyone like that had slunk away in shame when the Sex Pistols' first single came out. But who am I to speak?

My sister Jan described me as posh. Many of my contem-poraries at both my private schools, having cultivated their glottal stops to avoid being beaten up at bus stops, mocked the way I speak. At another cartoon festival in Ireland, my Irish colleagues called me Lord Snooty, just for a laugh. But where did my 'posh' accent come from?

Genetically, I'm Dorset peasant stock. From what I've learned, it seems that my biological grandfather was more or less a member of the lumpenproletariat. By adoption, I'm middle class, but I've already said there is an infinity of middle classes in England. My adoptive father was second-generation professional middle class, but his father's family's acquired respectability didn't manifest itself in the way he spoke, which was accentless, with a slight Lancashire intonation here and there. My adoptive mother was lower middle class, and even then quite lowly, and although her mother's pretensions made her insist they change her husband's job on my mother's re-issued birth certificate, that didn't alter her social standing. When she married my father, because he was a doctor she immediately shot up a ladder on the board of social snakes and ladders to join the professional middle class, and Dawne tells me that their mother bragged about her daughter's good fortune. But although I remember her sometimes putting on a slightly posher voice in certain company, none of this really changed the way she spoke or thought or behaved. My step-mother's case was different, if only because her semi-colonial upbringing skewed everything, but on returning to England she settled quickly into a kind of provincial lower middle class, and that's essentially where she remained.

My education marks me down as solidly middle class too. I suspect I was sent to my High Church Anglican prep school because of my mother's aspirations, and before she died she'd also put my name down for the public school I eventually went to. This was just as well, because after she died, my father spent a long time coaching me for the eleven-plus, although with no encouragement from my school, which I always assumed didn't want to miss out on another two years' worth of fees. He coached me from old papers, so it was unfortunate that hours and hours spent working out how many buckets you need to fill up a swimming pool while Janet eats all of John's apples proved to have been in vain when I actually sat the exam and was faced with pages and pages of new-maths numbers. I was also quite hopeless at weird things that were meant to test your intelligence or aptitude, like turning the word LIGHTHOUSE into HEDGEHOG in five moves, and so, like John Prescott and Martin McGuinness, I failed. Had I passed, I would have gone to the same school, at the same time, as Michael Portillo, Clive Anderson and Diane Abbott, and there would have been yet another possible, alternative me, and then another one if I'd accepted a place at the secondary modern school which would have been my destiny had my mother not planned ahead.

None of which really helps explain how I speak, or how I think, or draw, or where my political outlook comes from, even if we factor in all that stuff I might have had bequeathed to me by my unknown biological father. And even if we added him to the stew, that wouldn't explain it all either, because it can't and shouldn't. We're no more determined exclusively by our genes than we are by Jean Calvin's God or the God of the Koran. As to the way I speak, that's probably how you end up sounding if you listen too often to the BBC Home Service at an impressionable age.

When I was still overexcited about finding out about Kathleen, I was about to start telling the whole story yet again to some more people over lunch, when my then twelve-year-old son Fred rolled his eyes and said, 'Oh God! Not this again! How many more times do I have to listen to this?' It hadn't even occurred to me that I was getting boring, but that's probably what defines a bore in the first place.

On the whole, I think Fred was probably right. By the way, my father was rather pleased that we'd named Fred after his grandfather, Frederick Gittings Rowson, happy that the name had been revived in the family, even though I told my father many times that we'd named the baby boy after Fred Astaire.

The Doctors Plot

By the time he died most of my father's books were about clocks or gardening or travel. I'd long since requisitioned all the other ones, including the books published by J.M. Dent in their Everyman Library series, with beautifully ornate frontispieces after the style of William Morris, in which my grandfather had written his name, sometimes prefacing it with his rank at the time, either Lieutenant or Captain, sometimes adding the name of his regiment in case he lost his copy of Marcus Aurelius or Lamb's *Tales from Shakespeare* in the trenches.

But my father had kept his red Penguin copy of George Bernard Shaw's *The Doctor's Dilemma,* one book in an edition of the complete plays published to mark Shaw's ninetieth birthday in 1946. The paper's now browning slightly, and was always thin and quite coarse, as you'd expect in any book from those austere, utilitarian times. Inside the front cover he'd written his name, in his sloping but legible signature, 'K.E.K. Rowson'. He was a medical student when he bought it, and though I vaguely remember him telling me that one of his lecturers recommended the play, I think he probably only read the preface, which is a sustained and vitriolic attack on doctors, written in 1907. It contains the famous line about all professions being a conspiracy against the laity.

My father's tastes were far more catholic than you might have guessed if you judged him by the interests of his old age. I remember when I was about twelve and we were on holiday that I offered him Mario Puzo's *The Godfather* to read, but he gave up after a few pages, saying he couldn't make head or tail of it, and he much preferred something far more straightforward, like Henry Miller. During the four years he was solely responsible for me, he and I would often go to the theatre together in the West End. I remember we went to an Alan Bennett first night, and we also went as a family to see *Hair* and sat in a box at the side of the theatre, and I remember a clearly drunk, red-faced man in a pinstriped suit getting up from his seat to dance with one of the Afro-haired hippie actors.

As he got older, his cultural interests seemed to narrow, shouldered aside by his other pursuits, and I don't remember him reading a novel in the last thirty years of his life, but he had a wide frame of reference, and I remember him often saying that the best thing about Shaw's plays were his prefaces, although he may only have ever read the preface to *The Doctor's Dilemma*.

I read the preface shortly after my father died, as a little act of homage. It confirmed all the suspicions I'd felt about the medical profession for as long as I could remember, and all of which I'd first received from my father.

His father wanted him to be a lawyer, which is why he was a member of Gray's Inn and ate his three dinners in hall there. He told me that he'd wanted to be a chemist, but that his father had told him that he had to belong to one of the professions (which then meant being a doctor, a lawyer or, possibly, a clergyman), so he studied medicine. After graduating from Cambridge, he went to Bart's Hospital in London where he was on the team of Sir Geoffrey Keynes, brother of the economist Maynard Keynes. As a junior houseman at Bart's he was interviewed on BBC Radio on the day the National Health Service started. From Bart's he went to be a house physician at Epsom District Hospital and Kent and Canterbury Hospital, where he met my mother, and then he was resident pathologist at the Royal Berkshire and North Middlesex hospitals. In 1953 he joined the Public Health Laboratory Service, from which he resigned in 1959, and when they refused to let him withdraw his resignation, he moved on to the Cancer Research Department at the London Hospital, where he worked as a virologist, and where he killed a succession of my mice. In 1968 he moved on again, and became Senior Lecturer in Clinical Pathology at the Institute of Laryngology and Otology at the University of London, where he had the title Reader in Virology conferred on him in 1977, and where he stayed until forced into early retirement in 1981, aged fifty-seven, but then spent several years working three days a week as the locum director of the Public Health Laboratory in Chelmsford, until finally retiring for good in 1985, aged sixty-one.

Along the way he became an MD and was later awarded a PhD by Cambridge University, based on his published works. He was also an MRCS, LRCP, MB, B.Chir., Dip.Bact. and MRCPath, qualifications whose letters outnumbered the number of letters in his own, long full name. He was also a member of various prestigious scientific societies including, as I discovered after his death, the Antibody Club, which sounds like something that drifted from P.G. Wodehouse into a Sherlock Holmes adventure. He published nearly fifty scientific papers, many of them on lactate-dehydrogenase virus and Riley virus, and in 1970, assisted by his colleague Iris Parr, isolated a new strain of mouse leukaemia virus which was called Rowson–Parr virus. In 1981 he published his *Dictionary of Virology*, which he'd compiled with Terence Rees, who ran the bacteriology department at the Institute, and Brian Mahy, a friend and former colleague from the London Hospital.

Considering that he didn't learn to read until he was ten, this is an impressive summary of a long and distinguished career, but it's the stories between the facts that flesh my father out.

For instance, I remember him telling me that when he was at Bart's the junior doctors had a strange kind of challenge or initiation rite, which entailed the inductees buying a drink over the bar of a different licensed premises for every hour of the twenty-four hours in a single day. He said this was relatively easy for most of the period of the challenge: you'd start at Smithfield at six in the morning, where the pubs were open to victual the porters at the meat market, and then you'd move on to Billingsgate and Covent Garden until the pubs opened at ten thirty. When they closed at three o'clock in the afternoon, it was easy enough to talk your way into one of the drinking clubs in Soho until five, and then it was a different pub for each succeeding hour until chucking-out time at ten thirty. After that, it was more dingy drinking dens, all brindled brown and black with Naples yellow bulbs feebly filtering thin light over the drunks, then maybe blagging your way into a hotel bar, and so it went on until around two or three in the morning. This was the tricky part, their dark night of the arseholed, but he told me one of their number knew about a hotel in Maidstone, or it may have been Maidenhead, so they drove off into the countryside, bought the obligatory drink, and made it back to the London markets as the pubs there opened at four, providing a safe haven until six.

I presume they all then went back on the wards later that morning.

I remember him telling me that later, when he was at the Royal Berkshire, he was doing his rounds in one of the wards and happened across an old man in one of the beds, wheezing and gasping away and obviously about to breathe his last. My father prescribed him some penicillin, still not widely available at the time, and a few days later the old man was sitting up in bed and reading a newspaper, almost fully recovered, as the consultant did his rounds. I remember that my father told me that the old man's continued survival drove the consultant into a fury, as the bed was meant to have been 'cleared' by this stage, although, from what my father told me, I don't think the consultant had considered that it could be cleared just as effectively by sending the old man home, alive, to his family.

I remember him telling me how when he was at Canterbury he'd run a paediatric clinic which was the envy of his colleagues. They couldn't understand how he managed things in such a way that his patients not only never had to wait beyond the time of their appointments, but also that he and the other doctor in the clinic would often have time for a cup of coffee and a cigarette between patients. I remember him telling me that it was quite simple really, and all he'd done was ignore standard procedure and just staggered the appointments, so each patient was allotted ten minutes to be seen for each consultation. His colleagues, meanwhile, told everyone to turn up at ten in the morning, and allowed five minutes per consultation, so everyone waited around for hours and hours.

And I remember him telling me several times about a typist who'd worked at the Public Health Laboratory in Colindale when my father was there, who was a very good typist but a deeply depressed woman, and who cried all day long, smudging the carbon copies of the letters she was typing. According to my father, one day one of the doctors this typist worked for told her that he could cure her problems with a simple operation, so they gave her lobotomy. After that she laughed and smiled all the time, but could no longer type to save her life.

Later, when he was at the London Hospital, he worked for a group led by Myer Salaman. I remember, as a small child, hearing things about Salaman that led me to build up a portrait of him in my mind as a monster of vanity and incompetence, although I remember trying to forget all that when I met him at the opening reception of another international scientific junket we'd all gone to. I think it was in Helsinki, and I remember sitting on a sofa, surrounded by scrubbed pine, talking to Salaman for ages, and I think we were talking about Anglo-Saxon longhouses, and how I didn't believe one of my teachers who said he'd visited one of these, when I knew, empirically, that its wooden structure must have rotted away centuries ago. Because Salaman had been happy enough to talk rubbish with a nine-year-old, I liked him, although I also remember, a few years previously when we were on holiday in Norfolk, we went to have lunch with Salaman in his country cottage, a converted windmill. All I remember about the lunch was a certain indefinable yet palpable frostiness between my father and his boss.

Years and years later, shortly before he died, I remember my father telling me about how he discovered his virus when he was working for Salaman at the London Hospital, and he said he'd brought in his friend Iris Parr to help with the research so they could call the bug Rowson–Parr virus, so it would sound like Epstein-Barr virus, the viral cause of herpes in human beings. Perhaps he'd hoped that this might lead, subsequently, to a degree of diagnostic confusion.

And when he was at the Institute of Laryngology, I remember him laughing at the statue of St Blaise they erected in a little niche in the entrance to the Ear, Nose and Throat

Hospital the other side of the Gray's Inn Road. St Blaise was a fourth-century Armenian bishop who lived in a cave and healed sick animals who came to him of their own volition, but were careful never to disturb him when he was at prayer. When Agricola, the governor of Cappadocia noted for his assiduous persecution of Christians, sent his huntsmen into the forests of Argeus to collect animals for the games in the arena, they found dozens of sickly beasts patiently queuing up outside Blaise's cave, and the saint was apprehended at prayer inside. When he refused to recant his Christian faith, Agricola had him thrown into prison, where he healed many of his fellow prisoners, including saving a child who was choking on a fish bone; Agricola then had him thrown into a lake, but Blaise just stood on the surface of the water, inviting his persecutors to walk out to him and prove the efficacy of their pagan gods. Obviously, they all drowned. But when Blaise walked back to the shore, Agricola's men set upon him, beat him, tore his flesh with wool combs and then beheaded him.

Thanks to the fish-bone incident, St Blaise is the patron saint of throat diseases, coughs, goitres and whooping cough. Because of the nature of his martyrdom, he's also the patron saint of wool-combers and weavers, in the same way that St Elmo became the patron saint of sailors because his tormentors martyred him by winding his guts out on a windlass, and one of the St Lucys is the patron saint of opticians because she had her eyes torn from her head before she was stabbed to death with a dagger.

My father clearly thought this invocation of the miraculous potential of St Blaise was clinically questionable, which was why he laughed. Years later, when I was covering the 1992 Irish general election in Dublin, I was following Albert Reynolds, then the Irish taoiseach, as he glad-handed his way round the Crumlin Children's Hospital, and noted with the same, slightly detached amusement that the hospital's patron was the Blessed Virgin Mary who, despite her interesting obstetric history, probably couldn't cut the mustard as far as modern paediatric best practice is concerned.

Later, when my father was at Chelmsford, one weekend Britain's second victim of Aids, the chaplain at a borstal in Essex, died. I was living in Stanmore at the time, mostly because my stepmother didn't like to be in the house on her own during the two nights of the week my father was away, and I remember that weekend the phone ringing more or less constantly, as the pathologists and morbid anatomists doing the autopsy on the unfortunate chaplain rang my father over and over again, asking how many pairs of surgical gloves they should wear, how to dispose of their instruments afterwards, how they should sterilise the air-conditioning system and so on. Aids was then a new, unknown and, because of that, terrifying disease. Their caution, care and fastidiousness was therefore understandable in the circumstances. But I remember having dinner with my father in one of the restaurants in Stanmore a few weeks later, and I remember he said that in epidemiological terms Aids was an uninteresting disease, and the current panic − gravestones thonking down on government adverts on telly, growing talk about corralling whole sections of the population into things like concentration camps − was mostly down to the complacency of the medical profession, who'd imagined that infectious diseases had been wiped out by stuff like penicillin, the stuff my father had used to save the old man's life in Reading thirty years previously, and so all those isolation hospitals that used to lurk on the outskirts of most largish towns, the kind of place where my stepmother had started her nursing career boiling the blood and sputum out of the handkerchiefs of consumptives, had long since been pulled down. The sites were now occupied by ticky-tacky Barratt Homes and Wimpey Estates, the double glazing repelling any possible pathogens. So a new infectious disease had caught them on the hop, even though Aids could only be transmitted in specific circumstances, and my father told me that, with only a minimum of care, you needn't worry much about any infectious disease you couldn't catch either drinking a glass of water or standing at a bus stop in daylight.

The real problem, he went on, was a cultural one. The medical establishment had seduced itself so successfully with its belief in its own abilities, it simply couldn't react calmly when it got caught out. And then its panic infected all other parts of society, from the media to politicians to the general public, all of them as compromised as the doctors had been when they realised they simply didn't know what to do.

I may be overstating my father's case here, but not by much. We had this conversation twenty-two years ago, but it segues seamlessly with Shaw's line of argument in his preface to *The Doctor's Dilemma*. At his funeral, my father's old university friend said that I'd caught my father's spirit perfectly in my address, because I'd caught his scepticism, because his friend remembered that my father had always been sceptical about authority including, he added, the biggest one. He then pointed to heaven, a bit like John the Baptist.

A few months after the autopsy weekend my father told me that he went to a scientific symposium on Aids, where the main business was a discussion of how the virus had crossed the species barrier from other primates into humans, and I remember my father saying that several of the scientists there expressed shock and outrage at someone's suggestion that you could probably trace the point of crossover to missionary nuns in the Congolese jungle who'd had sex with monkeys. I think my father rather liked that idea, less because he thought it was actually true than because their reaction to it showed the narrow-mindedness of his scientific colleagues. I don't know what my father would have made of one recent theory about how Aids was first transmitted to humans as an unforeseen result of researching the polio vaccine using apes and monkeys in the African jungle in the 1960s, though I can guess.

At some point in our lives, most of us make some kind of bid for emancipation, from our parents, our childhood, or from the way we've lived previously, when we're constantly constrained by the wishes of others, so that we can live the way we want to. Sometimes this process is so quiet and subtle you don't even notice it, although the nexus of power and control shifts nonetheless. Other times, the bid for emancipation can be ruinously destructive. Often, the opportunity is missed altogether, and people carry on much as before, building up their stores of resentment and bitterness.

I think my father spent his whole life in a series of little emancipations as soon as he was able to. I don't know whether his scepticism was innate, or whether he'd learned it through experience, or if those experiences included him quietly watching the doctors swathe him once again in gallons of plaster of Paris, from his knees to his chest, or if the scepticism was just a mechanism, a catalyst to allow him to unshackle himself from whichever yoke he found himself under at the time. Maybe that explains why he defied consultants and despised his bosses and resigned from jobs and viewed his whole profession with an amused detachment which, despite the smiles, often slipped into contempt. Or maybe, being a good scientist, he was also simply a good empiricist, and recognised that you can't explain the world unless you see it clearly in the first place.

Though, again, that detachment which came from the clinical side of his character sometimes worked too well, and I always felt uncomfortable when he described my mother, after she was dead, as mad, or my stepmother, when she was alive, as being good concentration camp commandant material, because she was good at obeying orders.

But they, too, had had their emancipations. Unable to escape back to Ohio or Argentina, my mother finally succeeded in escaping from her mother and the perfume factory by training to be a nurse, while my stepmother escaped from the job in the department store her father had made her take by becoming a nurse too, although both of them, because of their educations in different parts of the Americas, could have blown it all early on. Neither of them had good written English, but luckily both of them were given dispensations, and when my mother sat her written nursing exams, one of her supervisors wrote, at the top of the paper, 'This nurse was educated in America and spells phonetically.' They both qualified. Both of them then trained to be midwives.

My mother ended up working as a district midwife on the south coast, near where my stepmother's parents lived in their bungalow, although this was before my stepmother and my mother met. I'm told that one day one of the babies she'd delivered died shortly after birth. Dawne tells me that my mother was riven with guilt, quite convinced that the baby's death was her fault, although I don't think that anyone ever thought that that was the case. Dawne says my mother had a kind of breakdown; that she didn't or couldn't speak for months; that she tried, unsuccessfully, to commit suicide, though I don't know any of the details about that. I was told by Dawne that my mother thought that Christopher's death was a kind of judgement on her for the death of the baby in Hove, a sort of balancing up of dead babies. All of which would, in part, explain the foster-babies, and how she brooded in the bath behind a locked door about all those dead children in Aberfan. And then she moved to Canterbury, met my father and they married, and she stopped being a nurse.

My stepmother almost certainly delivered babies who died, but she didn't repine. She often said to me, after telling a particularly gruesome story about a neo- or post-natal catastrophe, that you couldn't let it get to you and that you had to move on. To an extent my father was right. She was good at obeying orders, although I'd prefer to see it as her doing her job and her duty. But she, too, developed tactics for making things bearable. One of the ways she did it was by wrapping herself in an archaic kind of slang, a joviality that allowed her to distance herself both personally and generally from all the specifics of each individual tragedy. So when she talked about a baby that had died, it would have 'grown wings and gone to heaven'; premature babies, many of whom probably also died, were all nicknamed 'Horace' by my stepmother and her colleagues, though I don't know why. Some people were 'funniosities', psychiatrists were always 'trick cyclists', and men with beards (probably the same group) had their 'face in a frame'. She didn't have much of an original sense of humour, unlike my father, but knew the importance of humour and, like many people of her and all previous and subsequent generations, traded catchphrases to put herself and other people at their ease. As she got older, hearing her say 'TTFN', an abbreviation of 'Ta-ta for now' from the wartime radio show *ITMA*, sounded increasingly odd. Then it started to become endearing.

As I've told you, she'd already seen some terrible things, and she coped with each successive if smaller terrible thing she witnessed by telling stories, reciting second-hand humour and getting on with the job without pausing to think too much about what had just happened. It worked, I suppose, but it also came at a cost.

That said, she worked her way up her profession, from

nurse to district midwife to ward sister to assistant matron. Along the way she worked in the Elizabeth Garrett Anderson Hospital, King's College Hospital, at Hampstead, Dulwich, Leeds, Burnley and, at the end of her career, just before she married my father, at Lewisham Hospital, where she was the matron in charge of midwifery. After she got married she started again at the bottom, aged fifty-three, as an assistant at the antenatal clinic at Edgware General, the hospital my mother had refused to go to on the last night I saw her. It was said that her years of experience meant that, when no one else could, she'd be able to extract blood from the most shrivelled, collapsed veins of the most raddled, if pregnant, junkies, like getting blood out of a stone.

My mother and my stepmother met in 1955, when my mother was pregnant with Christopher and suffering from high blood pressure. My stepmother was the ward sister, and the fact that they were both midwives, even though my mother was retired, must have attracted them to each other in the first place, and ease the way to them becoming friends. And it was my stepmother who took Christopher to have the operation on his blocked oesophagus, and she also took him, after the operation had failed, to the hospital morgue. But I think it's just coincidence that my father subsequently worked attached to an ENT hospital, specialising in, among other things, conditions of the oesophagus.

And it's probably just coincidence that both my father's wives were midwives, and that both were childless, one through bereavement and the other through accident or oversight, although they both loved children, worked with them and, through different mechanisms, acquired them. Just like it's a coincidence that they both spent crucial, defining parts of their childhoods in the Americas, and both bore the name Eve, or a variant on it, names which they hated and never used, and it's also just a coincidence that they both died in the month of May, albeit thirty-five years apart, and it's pure coincidence that May was the middle name of their mutual mother-in-law, whom neither of them could stand.

But that probably wasn't a coincidence.

Had my mother still been alive I don't think there's any question that my father would have brought his mother to come and live with us. But in that precarious period when he was solely in charge, I suppose he thought he had no alternative, and that she might even help. I remember that she now used to do the washing-up, although often I'd have to wash up again after she'd done it, and I don't remember her being any more real help around our house than she'd been around her own. Then again, she was seventy-five when she moved in, and her behaviour was increasingly erratic. Soon after she arrived I remember coming home from school one day and discovering that she wasn't in. This didn't surprise me that much, as she'd go on at considerable length about what a great walker she'd always been, and would often prove the point by walking into Stanmore or often much further. This time she'd left through the back door and taken the key with her. She still wasn't back by the time my father got home from work, and was eventually brought home in a police car, having been found, still going strong, somewhere near Ruislip.

Despite this, I remember she went through an extraordinary rejuvenation after she first came down from Blackpool. When she arrived she still had the long, long grey hair women of her age had always been tying up in buns, and a wardrobe just as archaic, but then my father, or possibly my not-yet-stepmother, who'd come and visit us most weekends, took her to a hairdresser's and to buy some clothes. As she was still, at this stage, apparently as sane as ever, they consulted her about her makeover, so she ended up with bright pale, yellow-blonde hair in a Marlene Dietrich cut, and a wardrobe of ladies' suits, all subtly different but all equally garishly pink. That was what she looked like when she said that Georgi Dimitrov winked at her, so in the circumstances maybe he did. What was going on underneath the pink I didn't like to imagine, but I remember my mother telling me years before that a mark of her mother-in-law's awfulness was that she didn't wear a bra. It was later that I learned, through unsought but frequent observation, that instead of seeking uplift she tucked her drooping breasts under the high waistband of her enormous knickers. The rejuvenation didn't, however, halt the speed of her decline.

The year my father married my stepmother we went on a tour, by car, round the country, mostly as an opportunity for my stepmother to introduce her new family to her old friends or colleagues, and en route we took in south and mid-Wales and Yorkshire, as well as the Lake District. We stayed a couple of nights at a hotel in Ambleside, a large Victorian pile with a granite exterior, doubly grey in the unrelenting down-pour, while inside it was all gloomy, dark brown, echoingly silent as only an old but slightly out of sorts English hotel could be, and damp. I remember small young women, little more than girls, in black dresses, white aprons and stupid little curly white hats, probably embarrassed to the point of implo-sion, who had to summon us to meals of uniform grey by beating an enormous gong. It was my grandmother's natural habitat, which is just as well as she was the only reason we were there. For months she'd sighed, with a contrived and manipulative wistfulness, about what she always called 'Lakeland', and how she yearned to be there once more. I think this arch gaucherie was how she'd always behaved, but on the way to Ambleside we'd stopped in Blackpool and I remember my grandmother showing us the state of things to come.

Softening us up to take her to the Lake District, my

grandmother had also gone on and on and on about how much she also wanted to visit her very best friend in Blackpool, a woman called Mrs Tapley. I remember us driving to Mrs Tapley's house, and going past my grandmother's old house, and her leaning across me in the back of the car and looking at the place with her great watery blue eyes and a bleary, mindless smile on her face. And I remember sitting in Mrs Tapley's front room or sitting room or parlour (at the time my social antennae weren't sufficiently well developed to tell which one of these it might be). I remember it was another of those awful social occasions I'd got used to. I'd known variations on them all my life, though when I was younger and more innocent I'd occasionally liven things up by calling someone a silly old cow to jolly things along. Since my father had married my stepmother I'd now, in adolescence, sit silently in a corner and notice how my father was sitting, slumped because of his leg, usually chewing a corner of his lip and, like me, not saying much either. These occasions usually involved meeting another family friend or relative of my stepmother's, old women with names like Mrs Streetly or Great-Aunt LittleGlad, and although most of the old women were perfectly nice and kind, the event would always mean there'd be another of those excruciating little petit bourgeois pantomimes, where the old woman would offer me another gypsy cream, and I, being polite and well brought up, would decline, and then there'd be a little dialectical struggle, well mannered but just as intense as those that led to the collapse of empires, as the old lady sought to break my will until I'd finally accept, even though I knew that in so doing I was bringing disgrace upon my family. Why this might be I didn't know: all I knew was that you always politely declined the offer of more food, perhaps in case my hostess imagined that I was literally starving and we were just a step away from the workhouse.

Tea at Mrs Tapley's was just like that, except that the

conversation wasn't propelled by my stepmother as it usually was (and it was usually funny and almost uproarious: the point was that it had nothing to do with me). My grandmother just sat there and quite literally stuffed her face with cakes, hardly saying a word to her very best friend in all the world, and Mrs Tapley would now and again look up to one or other of us with that bright-eyed smiling expression which needs no words. The words, needless to say, were 'You poor luvs! You've got a right one 'ere!'

And we had.

It was a peculiarity of my grandmother's condition that she began to display two completely different characters day by day. It was actually rather spooky. One day she'd be hyperactive, opinionated, interfering, infuriating and would never stop talking, most of it being blithe gibberish of the kind I'd first encountered when I was seven, but occasionally she'd become quite malicious. Then, the next day, as regular as clockwork, she'd seem to be a completely different woman: timid as a mouse, obliging, very quiet and apparently completely lost at sea. You'd be able to plan for months ahead on how she'd be on any particular day, and I remember standing next to my father as he consulted the wall calendar in the kitchen to choose a date for a forthcoming outing, several months in the future. Each day on the calendar had a Q or a B written in its little square, to mark down what my grandmother's mood would be that day, and I remember my father picking a day with a B for Busy in it, and I remember my dismay at the prospect of the inevitability of the day of disorder and embarrassment he was letting us in for as we tried to keep my grandmother under control. I protested, but he said that she'd enjoy it much more if she knew what on earth was going on.

The point is, we'd taken my grandmother to see her best friend on the wrong day.

245

I think my grandmother's personality had somehow or other split in two, and one of the two halves would take over from the other once she fell asleep, a bit like in *Invasion of the Body Snatchers*. The mind, like everything else, is far too complicated to come up with a neat explanation, and anyway her Jekyll and Hyde condition soon became the least of our worries.

She'd stuffed her face at Mrs Tapley's like a hamster. On her quiet days she'd eat and eat, although on her busy ones she was too busy talking or fiddling or interfering to have time for food. However, over dinner she'd quite often find that the mass of food in her mouth was proving a bit of a problem, so she'd remove her dental plate, untangle the half-chewed bolus from it, replace her teeth and then start again. I used to sit opposite her at mealtimes and try not to notice, and certainly not to comment.

The thing was that while she was infuriating, deeply annoying, often disgusting, she was also ill, although that's not the reason why I kept quiet. It was, I now realise, a horrible kind of illness, and while I doubt she suffered much, in a way that just made it much worse for the rest of us. My father would occasionally talk, with his usual clinical detachment, about hardening of the arteries, arteriosclerosis, senile dementia (although not, in those days, about Alzheimer's disease), but I didn't talk to him about it that much. I remember my sister telling me that he'd told her that his mother was no longer recognisable as the woman he'd previously known all his life, although I couldn't see much disjunction in the slow declining trajectory from the smiling airhead in Blackpool, via the miniature Barbara Cartland in Bulgaria to the much reduced old woman whose dinner I'd later bring on a tray most nights, in the room she now occupied on the ground floor.

She'd started off sleeping in my father's old darkroom, but soon she was in constant danger of falling down stairs, so she was moved to the room which had once been the front part of the cold sitting room, the one that had become piled high with junk until my father rearranged the rooms on the ground floor, had a wall knocked down and a long, large new sitting room created at the back of the house. She was now in the little room left over from the rebuilding, and she ate there too, given her increasing frailty, confusion and the business with her dentures. I'd often take her her food, and ask how she was and change the TV channel if she wanted me to. The room contained her bed, an armchair (which doubled as a commode), a wardrobe and various ledges for knick-knacks and this and that. She'd taken to wrapping many things in tissue paper, and squirrelling these and other stuff away in different crevices around the room (this was how my father and stepmother had found her gold watch, which she'd sighed and sighed about losing; they gave it back to her for Christmas and she was delighted that they'd found another watch exactly like her old one). One day I came into the room with a bowl of ice cream for her pudding, but couldn't find the plate from her first course. As I was used to her propensity for hiding things, I started looking round the room, until I opened the door to the cupboard. There, on a shelf level with my eyes, I saw a large, dried human turd sitting on a black-and-white postcard from the Isle of Man. I think I screamed. I then asked her what it was doing there, and she replied with a smile that the Germans had put it there.

Then she became doubly incontinent. Most mornings I'd take her her breakfast and then mop up the pool of piss by the front door, something I'd also often find myself doing just at the moment when friends of mine would turn up and ring the doorbell. Soon thereafter my father got her a place, on weekday mornings, at a day centre for the elderly in Harrow. I don't know what they did there, but it was probably the usual combination of singing 'Roll Out the Barrel' and sitting in a plastic upholstered chair staring at the cream paint on the walls, but it meant that she wouldn't be alone in the house when I was at school and my stepmother and father were at work (my sister had long since left home by this stage).

My father was trying to teach me to drive at this time. He'd never taken a driving test himself as he'd learned to drive during the war and there'd been a general amnesty afterwards, but he always said he'd successfully taught my mother to drive, and she'd passed her test first time. Then again, she'd taken it in her nurse's uniform, an option I didn't have, and although I learned how to drive, I learned how to drive like him: I rode the clutch, and tended to whack the car out of gear at every opportunity and then coast, in order to save petrol, and the first time I took the test I failed on almost every count (though it wasn't my father's fault that, turning right at a T-junction, in the process of changing down from third to second gear, I got the car into reverse). Early on in the learning process, I'd drive to school each morning, with my father, denied the technology of dual control, frequently jerking up the handbrake each time we diced with death. My grandmother would be in the back of the car, as once we'd got to school my father would drive her to the day centre, drop her off and then drive on to work. Quite often we'd also give a lift to my friend Charlie, who lived not far away.

Charlie remembers these journeys with a combination of fear and horror: fear of my driving and horror at my grandmother, sitting next to him on the back seat. One day, as he pressed himself as close up against his side of the car as he could, my grandmother hoisted up her skirt, pulled down the top of her tights, pulled out a half-eaten lemon-curd sandwich and offered it to him with an inviting if blank smile.

Earlier, in the Easter holidays before my O levels, we went on a barge holiday on the River Wey. I remember that I had to sleep in the top bunk, above my grandmother, so one morning, moored somewhere near Godalming, I woke up to see her standing next to her bed pissing into a teacup. I think I just shuddered and turned my face to the wall of the cabin.

Perhaps you think I'm being unnecessarily harsh or callous about my grandmother. Maybe I am. I remember, as she was getting worse and worse, lying awake in bed one night when I was about fourteen or fifteen, weighing up in my mind the pros and cons of pushing her downstairs. Adolescents tend to be prone to deranged ideas, and I was no different. I remember thinking that I should try to make it look like an accident, but even if I was found out, years and years in prison might be worthwhile, because it would take the strain off my stepmother, newly married but now an almost full-time geriatric nurse, and how all in all taking my grandmother out of the equation would be good for my father and stepmother's marriage. I think I was just beginning to realise that I might get indefinitely sectioned under the Mental Health Act when I fell asleep.

It never occurred to me for a single second that my father might object to me murdering his mother even though, as I was ever the pubescent Hamlet, it would obviously never, ever happen.

Eventually my father agreed to have his mother placed in a nursing home in St Albans. He'd go and visit her each Saturday morning with my stepmother, and they'd take her out for a little drive around the ring roads and bypasses beyond the Green Belt, before stopping in a layby for a cupcake, a sandwich and a mug of scaldingly hot coffee from a Thermos. I went on a few of these expeditions, and I remember the car shaking and rocking from side to side in the wake of the enormous juggernauts thundering past on their way to the A1 or the M1. Once or twice I'd help my father plant a bush or shrub by the side of the lay-by, as he'd decided to take advantage of these little outings with his mother to do a bit of guerrilla gardening. It's possible that the rhododendrons and azaleas quickly choked to death in the grey scree of dust, mud, plastic, rubber and general trash that's swept to the fissuring tarmac at the sides of our great arterial roads, but then again, maybe a forest of exotic flora now encroaches on those same roads, and one day will cover them entirely, long after the last of the oil has gone and the last Espace has long since whizzed past, its dreary Doppler effect marking its passage to another ballet lesson in Elstree.

I didn't see my grandmother much in her final years, and I doubt if she'd have known who I was if I had. She lost her false teeth soon after she arrived in the nursing home, and her beard grew longer and longer. I remember, when I was seven and she was seventy, she'd keep it in check by ripping the hair off her chin with strips of Sellotape, thus pre-empting later cosmetic treatments by decades, although at the time I thought it was just another of her disgusting habits to hold against her. From what I'm told they looked after her properly, and on the few occasions I saw her she was well presented and clearly well cared for.

She died in 1981, aged eighty-five. She was cremated in St Albans, in a crematorium near another thundering road, and I didn't feel a thing, except possibly mild relief.

I don't know what my father thought or felt. He and I were going through the only period of any strain or difficulty in our relationship, although all of it was my fault. In 1978 I'd gone to Cambridge, to his old college, to read English. He'd said that if I went to any other university, I'd have to read Law, which was an incentive for me to work hard to get a place, because I knew that I'd make a very, very bad lawyer. As things turned out I also made a very bad English student, and after a year and a half I'd had enough. Precisely what I'd had enough of is a moot point. At the time I thought it was the course, my supervisors, my director of studies, the whole heady miasma that Cambridge gave off, of self-satisfaction, corruption, condescension, complacency, callousness and that deadly medieval prettiness, the façade of charm behind which the students got bored, took drugs, went mad and killed themselves. In my first week a maths student, described in the student newspaper as the most brilliant mathematician to have matriculated at the university since Newton, killed himself by drinking Paraquat. No one could understand why someone would have chosen to cut short a life so full of promise, and in such an horrific way, though it seemed pretty obvious to me. At the end of my first year, during finals, something like twenty-eight students killed themselves, a record beaten only by the University of East Anglia, which at least had the excuse of having a campus built in the New Brutalist style where some of the rooms in the halls of residence had no windows because, the architect had argued in a lengthy written justification of his vision, the students shouldn't be distracted from their studies. In Cambridge, I suspect, the light dappling on the Cam and the sun-kissed ancient stone and the clipped lawns and the general beauty just made it all worse.

I never got remotely close to feeling suicidal, but I was miserable and, I now recognise, bored. Halfway through my second year I decided that I wanted to jack it all in, get out and move on. Despite the way I justified it to myself and other people at the time, I now know that my main motivations were boredom, arrogance and sloth, meshed in with a realisation that I'd obeyed orders and done what other people expected of me for too long, so it was high time to cock things up and blow myself out of the water probably just in order to see what happened next. It was, in short, my emancipation, and after that everything would be entirely, and rather wonderfully, my own fault.

I wanted to go straight away, and I wrote a long, self-justificatory letter to my father. The next day, the day he received the letter, he immediately drove up to Cambridge to see me, and I remember him sitting in my room as we tried to understand each other's point of view. That was the second and last time I ever saw my father cry, and I'm more ashamed that I was responsible for that than for any of the many other shameful things I've ever done. I know now that he was trying to do what he thought was right for me; he was being kind, and thoughtful, and doing his best. I also now appreciate that I was thoughtlessly adding to the encircling chaos.

We eventually got over it, but I gave him a hard time for too long, although none of it was directly his fault: he just happened to be in the way.

I was persuaded to sit my Part I exams, but got bored after the first one so I wrote deliberately nonsensical answers to all the other papers, just to mess things up once and for all. Even then, the college let me back to finish the tripos after I spent a year living in a slum out in the town, beyond Parker's Piece, and I was halfway through my final year when I went to my grandmother's funeral. I'd borrowed my father's car, and got there late, just in time to see her coffin carried into the chapel. I remember jokingly apologising for being late, but adding that at least I wasn't as late as my grandmother. I remember my sister laughed when I said that, and she laughed again when

I pointed out, rather cheaply, the irony of the No Smoking sign above the door into the chapel. I didn't bother to think what my father might have thought of my behaviour.

I doubt he'd have told me about how he felt or what he thought about his mother's death even if it had occurred to me to ask him, and not just because I was being such an oaf at the time. It was a quality neither of his generation, nor of his personality, nor of our relationship. And maybe he was simply as relieved as the rest of us. Or maybe he'd stiffened himself, during her long living death, against the final day of reckoning, and so had long since grieved in his own way. Or maybe he just shrugged, marked it down as another catastrophe and pulled the coat closer round his throat in preparation for the next one. At his funeral my father's old university friend told me that they'd met at a reunion dinner around this time, and had gone for a sentimental walk in Grantchester Meadows, and my father had said, with a quiet ironic smile, that I was having some arguments with the English faculty, though I don't think he mentioned his mother, whether she was still alive or yet dead. So he probably just got on with things. As I say, I don't know.

I do know that before she died he started taking precautions against going the same way, changing his diet as a prophylactic against his arteries hardening till the supply of blood to his brain and mind slowed down to a useless trickle. He avoided cholesterol like a vampire shunning garlic; he ate bran with everything; only drank skimmed and then dried milk; upped his roughage; cut out eggs and butter. And it worked for nearly another twenty-five years, although it was a blood clot that killed him, five years younger than his mother had been when she'd died, but nineteen years older than the age at which his father had died.

I doubt whether anyone intervened too aggressively to ameliorate my grandmother's condition in her last years, mostly because it was chronic, untreatable and, at the end of the day, terminal. After my father died my stepmother told me that as far as she knew my grandmother had died of a heart attack, which makes sense, and I imagine no one did much to either prevent it or to help her survive it. But I'd been brought up to have low expectations of the medical profession anyway, so I didn't really expect them to be able to do much in the first place.

In retrospect it seems rather strange that my father should have been so insistent in impressing on me his profession's many shortcomings, because in other respects my upbringing was largely informed by medicine, as it was a family of medical practitioners, and even long after they'd retired or gone into research or retired again you couldn't stop them putting their training into practice at the slightest excuse, whether that meant overdosing me with cholera vaccine or, when Fred was about eighteen months old and coughed during lunch in Stanmore, compelling my stepmother to shove her fingers down his throat before marching back into the kitchen announcing, just audible over Fred's unassuageable screams, that 'the airways are clear'.

I remember that my father, my mother and then my stepmother would talk shop over dinner, and I remember one evening when I was around sixteen and we were eating spaghetti bolognese as my stepmother was describing a particularly gruesome parturition involving the birth of twins at Edgware General, where one of the babies had been crushed to death in the birth canal by the other, a monstrous foetus who was dead already or, as my stepmother described it, 'just a lump of meat'. I just carried on twirling the spaghetti round my fork, and absorbed the information in the same way I absorbed the vocabulary and the attitude. And I always thought it was quite funny when my father used medical terminology to describe passers-by, like a man with a heavy footfall who was clearly suffering from general paralysis of the insane, or someone with a big head was either hydrocephalic or an over-large achondroplasiac dwarf, or like the nice mixed-race children we made friends with on holiday in Selsey, whom my father described as rhesus hybrids. The vocabulary bobbed and weaved. For my father and stepmother, if a woman had a termination or abortion she'd have been 'scraped out', but a gippy tummy would be 'D & V' (for diarrhoea and vomiting), bruises were contusions, and swellings were always oedematous.

This stuck with me, and I learned early on that you can always get further if you know the secret language, and a little learning is a useful thing. So I can talk to printers and win their trust because I know a very small amount about fonts and layout, and I once instantaneously got some zookeepers on my side by referring to their sea-lion pool as a pinniped facility, and on several occasions, when I've taken one of the children to the doctor and mentioned their oedematous ankle or something, I've been asked where my medical practice is.

Maybe my father didn't like the Freemasonry of it all, the secret and exclusive language, and most of all the assumption of both rectitude and infallibility. A phrase he'd often use when talking about politicians was that their real problem was that they'd started to believe their own propaganda. I suspect that he thought the same thing about the medical profession, who've been ill-served by their public image.

For centuries doctors were seen as the epitome of venality and incompetence, but slowly, thanks to mass entertainment and in spite of Shaw, our perception of them has changed, as has theirs of themselves. Perhaps it's all caught up in the decline of Christianity, and we just need new priest magicians who, instead of offering us the prospect of eternal life after we're dead, promise to make us all live for as long as scientifically possible. Consumerism's mixed up in there as well, the idea that you can have whatever you want – health, potency, a baby, a different gender on top of a patio heater and a car the size of a bus – whenever you want it. And of course power and hegemony and control further pollute the brew, and so we all prefer to forget that doctors, by and large, are often just as stupid, lazy, greedy and incompetent as the rest of us, and alongside every Dr Kildare or lurking somewhere on the set of *ER* or *Casualty* there's also a murderous nurse with Munchausen's syndrome by proxy or another Harold Shipman playing God. At least Dr Shipman made house calls.

Anna's now a barrister, although when we started going out she was a station manager and I was signing on and had just been summonsed by the bank for an outstanding overdraft of a couple of hundred quid. These days, every summer she invites some of her colleagues from her chambers round for dinner. I like these people, and I also rather like teasing them now and again, when they start getting too lawyerly or talk too much shop.

The year my parents died, when we were all quite drunk, I suggested to them that, all in all, lawyers had done more good for society in general than doctors had ever done. They looked at me in some astonishment as I warmed to my theme, pointing out that lawyers provide a public service for people either too ignorant, powerless or obstinate to sort out their problems for themselves, be it divorcing couples, murderers, shoplifters, squabbling parents or neighbours who've fallen out over a hedge. In this regard, I went on, lawyers are essentially rather grand plumbers, although unlike plumbers they almost always turn up when they say they will and, by and large, charge less per hour. By now my audience was staring at me in disbelief, so I turned to doctors.

Although, like lawyers, they are an elite, jealous of their standing and privileges, who conduct their business in a secret and arcane language, doctors are pretty much useless, and if they achieve short-term successes, ultimately they have a 100 per cent failure rate, whereas lawyers do far more for their clients, are more caring, efficacious, considerate and generally useful, with on average a fifty-fifty chance of success. Now my guests started complaining loudly. How could I say such things? Everyone knows that lawyers are just a bunch of money-grubbing leeches, exploiting the public left, right and centre. I raised a hand for silence, and pointed out that they had proved my case. Lawyers know that they're the scum of the earth, whereas doctors think that they're God.

So that's probably why my father impressed on me from an early age that every time I went to the dentist I should never allow him to give me any injections, or any gas, because, he explained, a general anaesthetic was likely to be far more dangerous than anything I had wrong with my teeth.

That was also why I never had my tonsils or my appendix taken out, despite there being a fashion in the 1960s for surgeons to whip out vestigial organs that didn't appear to have any function any more, without really thinking about it too hard or for too long.

And I remember him telling me about how they used to administer general anaesthetics by dosing the patient with up to fifty aspirin, which knocked them out all right, but also often resulted in massive stomach haemorrhages, after which the patient usually died.

And I remember him saying how you should go to almost any lengths to avoid going into hospital, because more people died in hospital than anywhere else. Statistically, of course, he was quite right, but that wasn't quite what he meant.

I remember my father showing me an article in either the *Lancet* or the *British Medical Journal,* sometime in the early 1980s. It was a decade since most of the profession had, under pressure from each other, given up smoking. I remember, aged eleven or twelve, hiding my father's cigarettes, under his instruction, and I'd pretend to be asleep as he sneaked into my bedroom to rummage through my drawers seeking out a fag, though he finally quit by having the effort of will to stop buying the things, so that eventually his friends got sick to death of him bumming off them. Anyway, by now they'd had time to do the research and draw up the statistics, and these showed that the incidence of alcoholism, drug abuse and suicide among doctors had risen exponentially.

He showed me another article, around the same time, by a thoughtful doctor decrying the fact that advances in antibiotics meant that very few people now remained ill for long enough to manifest one of the main symptoms of tertiary syphilis. In the past, General Paralysis of the Insane had been the catalyst that had sparked the latent genius of Van Gogh, Schubert and Nietzsche, among many others, but these days the unquestioning belief in treatment in all circumstances was depriving the world of the arts of an unquantifiable number of possible geniuses, whose potential output could only serve to enhance the human condition, even though there would inevitably be a sizeable proportion of untreated sufferers who were just dullards, whose bones and noses would rot away without a hope of a cantata or a beautiful sunset.

And I remember that when the government made the wearing of crash helmets compulsory, there were some muted protests from transplant surgeons because they would now be denied a steady supply of healthy organs from young men who'd died of massive head injuries but were otherwise more or less intact.

And I remember my stepmother telling me about an old midwife she'd met when she was a trainee nurse, who'd prowl the delivery rooms at night checking all the recently delivered babies, and she'd gently ease on their way any of them that she'd didn't think were quite right.

As a child I suffered a series of accidents, to the point where my parents would refer to me as accident-prone, as if this was a chronic medical condition. Maybe it was, and maybe I wasn't quite right either. There was the swordfish down the slide incident, and when I was about five I took the stabilising wheels off my bike, hurtled down the garden path, fell off and landed in the undergrowth where a piece of flint, the shape and size of an orange segment, nearly sliced off my left kneecap. As I had blood pouring down my leg I didn't immediately get back on, as they say you should do, and that's why I still can't ride a bicycle. I still have the scar on my knee, and for years as a child I kept the piece of flint too.

Later, when I was around seven or eight, I'd got out of our car which my mother had just parked by the new shopping parade in Stanmore, and slammed the car door on my thumb. I remember asking her if she could open the door, as it was now stuck around my bent and mangled thumb. In order to effect some first aid, my mother took me to the chemist next to where she'd parked, where they looked at my injury and suggested my mother wrap it in cotton wool and give me some milk of magnesia. Instead, she took me to hospital, cursing the chemist all the way there. My thumb was broken. It was my writing thumb, now my drawing thumb. I can still remember the deep dent in it, and now it's about a centimetre shorter than the other one, even more stunted than the rest of my stubby little Dorset peasant's fingers.

Shortly after that I was running along another of my father's little walls at the bottom of the garden when I stumbled, put my hand out to balance myself and fell through the shed window. I went to hospital then too, and I still have a V-shaped scar on my left middle finger, and on cold days I can make out the little pinprick scars left by the stitches.

I remember my various trips to hospital, and what the hospitals were like. The corridors were still lined with shining tiles, the Victorian brick buildings still buttressed by iron fire escapes, the nurses were still decked in starched linen, the doctors wore ties and had stethoscopes hanging like chains of office round their necks, and always seemed to have their hairy hands in the pockets of their white coats. There was cream paint and parquet floors and chipped enamel kidney bowls and low-watt bulbs, and what kit there was, like X-ray machines, were massive bits of industrial plant, like something cannibalised from a traction engine. And everything smelled of surgical spirit, down to the sad bunches of flowers on the reception desk and the torn comics in the waiting rooms with their hard wooden chairs.

After that, apart from visiting my father or stepmother at work, I didn't go near a hospital for about ten years. In my late teens and early twenties I visited my father in Northwick Park after his hip replacement and visited my friend Charlie in Stoke Mandeville after he'd smashed his femur to pieces coming off his motorbike, although because he'd been wearing a crash helmet others, perhaps ultimately more deserving than him, were deprived of many of his essential organs. I spent a couple of nights in Mount Vernon Hospital in Northwood after I dislocated my left elbow clambering out of a field after getting drunk at a beer festival, although I then discharged myself, against medical advice, because I was being driven mad by the patient in the next bed who wouldn't stop talking and talking. I'd had enough when he started to tell me how he'd put a Triumph Spitfire engine into a Reliant Robin, and how the thing now went at 250 miles an hour.

Then there was another gap of about ten years, and now I was visiting Anna in Guy's after the children were born, and when she had a uterine haemorrhage after Rose was born, and when Rose had some mysterious ailment when she was about three months old, which we thought was meningitis, but which the doctors were unable to diagnose. Anna was still breastfeeding, so she had to stay with Rose in Lewisham Hospital children's ward, where a cockroach lay dead in the toilet for a week and the hierarchies were so blatant they were almost unbelievable. The nurses were black, the sisters were white and working class, and the doctors were so young and middle class they wouldn't have looked out of place scarecrowed on a length of barbed wire on the Western Front, a slim volume of their own poignant poetry stuffed in their knapsack. None of the doctors ever spoke to or even made eye contact with Anna.

And a few months earlier I'd spent a couple of nights back in Guy's, so they could extract some wisdom teeth which were curling round like tusks in the back of my mouth.

Each time I went, I noticed how things were changing. Northwick Park, Stoke Mandeville and Guy's were all new buildings, rather than the Victorian workhouses I'd gone to as a child (although Lewisham was still like that, with a few feeble essays in Formica facias in the corridors). There were no more bricks, or tiles, or parquet floors; the equipment was far more up to date and space age, the wards were smaller and more intimate; the nurses were no longer stiffly outfitted in white starched linen, like off-duty nuns, and almost everything else was now plastic, from the panels on the walls and the surface on the trolleys you ate your dinner off to the specimen tubes and the wires coming out of your own personal radio. The smell was different too. The overpowering stench of surgical spirit had gone, and because these were new hospitals it had been replaced with vaguer, gentler smells of flooring and flowers and a distant canteen. But also, barely discernable but getting stronger all the time, until it would become the defining odour of the modern hospital, was the smell of dilute shit.

Ten years further on, I became horribly overfamiliar with hospitals, and by now they all smelled of shit. I visited Anna's father in the Charing Cross Hospital, after he had elective keyhole surgery to correct an injury when he'd fallen over on holiday in Madeira. He then got MRSA, and then got transferred to a geriatric rehabilitation unit in Acton. That was an old cottage hospital, a kind of missing link between the old, tiled and parqueted workhouses and the new gleaming plastic-and-shit hospitals, and Russell got worse and worse. One day when I visited him I thought that that would be the last time I saw him. He sat slumped in a wheelchair, his eyes screwed shut, hardly able to speak. Then, one Sunday night, he had a stroke, which perked him up no end, and soon, albeit with a Zimmer frame, he was going down the pub again, and Anna and her sister set him up in sheltered accommodation in Fulham. Then, a year or so later, he had further elective surgery in Charing Cross, started haemorrhaging internally after the operation, got pneumonia and then died of sepsis on Christmas morning 1999. Had that winter's 'flu' epidemic broken out a week or so earlier, in order to free up a bed they would have cancelled his operation. You never know. He might still be alive today.

Around the same time I visited Jon in the same hospital, as he went in and out for treatment for his brain tumour. I remember I was there the day the consultant came to examine him, to see if he was a suitable subject for a new and radical treatment. It turned out that he was, and he probably lived another six months as a consequence, although what I remember was the consultant, and the awed deference of the doctors and nurses as he came into Jon's room, and how he didn't acknowledge or make eye contact with either me or Jon's wife, but just silently examined Jon and then left, his staff nervously scurrying after him in his wake.

As they got older, my parents went in and out of hospital too. Often, I'd only find out about these visits later, and I'm still not sure whether they didn't tell me because they didn't want me to worry, or because my father didn't, for whatever reason, want to surrender any of his area of expertise to me. So when he fell head first and backwards down the stairs on a bus going to Watford, as he lay on the floor, bleeding from his head, he told my stepmother not to tell me, and I only found out by accident six months later.

Earlier, in 1990 and just after our daughter Rose was born, I phoned Stanmore one day and, after talking to my father, I asked if I could speak to my stepmother. At the other end of the line my father hesitated for a moment before saying that she was in the Royal Brompton Hospital, having just been operated on for a carcinoma in her left breast. An hour or so later, sitting at her bedside, I asked my stepmother why they hadn't told me, and she said that we had enough on our hands with the new baby, although I think I replied that I'd have had more on my hands if she'd died during the operation.

Then, a month before my father died, my stepmother phoned me early on a Tuesday morning, asking if I could come over to Stanmore. I was meant to be going to a meeting at London Zoo that day, but she explained that he'd collapsed in the upstairs toilet during the night after bleeding profusely from his rectum. Apparently this wasn't the first time he'd had this anomalous bleeding, but now he was insisting that it was nothing, although she thought he should at least see a doctor, and better still go into hospital. To complicate matters further, she had an appointment that morning at the Royal Marsden, to check up on the various cancers that were now growing inside her. I said I'd be over in an hour or so.

When I arrived my father was lying in bed, and my step-mother's sister was coming up from Hove to go with my stepmother to the Marsden. As I walked into his bedroom he turned over, peered at me over the edge of the duvet and said I'd had a wasted journey, that I had better things to do, that there was nothing really wrong with him and that I might as well go to the zoo. I smiled and replied, with heavy irony, that if there was nothing wrong we'd have a nice cup of coffee and a chat, and maybe we'd call the doctor as well, just for a laugh and to pass the time. He grumpily agreed to that, as I tried not to look too often at the red-brown stain on the carpet, or notice the cloying, sweet smell filling the room.

We had quite a nice day, all in all. After my stepmother left, he gave me various things he'd found while tidying his desk which he thought might interest me, like a journal he said his father had kept in France during his demobilisation after the First World War. I got some clocks out of a chest in the bedroom, and we talked again about how after he died my sister and I should sell off his clock collection, a few pieces at a time, so other collectors could have as much fun as he'd had in acquiring them. We'd talked about this before, so it didn't strike me as being particularly morbid. Nor was the conversation we had about where his will was, as he reminded me where he'd placed it in the loft, and where the keys were, although immediately after he died this was the one detail of

264

our conversation that day I couldn't remember, and it was months and months before my sister finally found the will.

Then the doctor arrived, assumed that I was the Dr Rowson she'd been referred to and asked me where I practised. I told her I was a cartoonist and that I practised at home. Then she examined my father and told him he should be admitted to hospital, so I packed an overnight bag for him and we waited for the ambulance to arrive, by which time my father was dressed, wearing his short, pale raincoat and the fingerless mittens my stepmother had knitted for him, and holding his walking stick. Then the ambulance workers arrived, dressed in dark green nylon safari suits, and asked if the patient needed to be stretchered downstairs. I stood back from the door and indicated my father, standing behind me.

The chief ambulance man leaned forward and smiled, and said slowly and too loudly, 'Hel-lo, Ken-neth! All right are we then? Can you make it to the ambulance on your own?' My father smiled back at them and walked down the drive, and we got into the ambulance, where they strapped him into a chair and wired him up to various machines to take his temperature and blood pressure. The chief ambulance man leaned forward towards me and asked, in a hushed tone, if I could tell him my father's medical history. I shrugged, said he was a retired senior lecturer in virology and that he was therefore far better qualified to tell them than I was.

They didn't quite click their heels, but their entire attitude changed. At first they stiffened, and I think I remember one of them actually grimacing as they realised they'd made a wrong call, and potentially a big mistake. This was one of their own, and a senior one at that; a made-man; a hierophant in the Freemasonry; what they used to call in the old Soviet Union one of the '*nomenklatura*', one of the untouchables in the Party. They stopped being patronising, stopped talking to my father as if illness or accident had sucked his brain down into his spinal column; stopped calling him Kenneth. Instead, they started being *deferential*.

It was the same when we got to Northwick Park Hospital, where they'd recently introduced a revolutionary new system for speeding up admissions. A doctor came to see him very quickly to assess him, and said she'd read his *Dictionary of Virology* when she'd been a student. They gossiped for a while about people they both knew, and he ran through his medical history. He told her about his Perthes' disease (and I realised for the first time in forty-four years that he hadn't, as I'd always thought, had polio), and then he said he was taking aspirin for his arrhythmia, his uneven heartbeat, and I didn't know about that either, and he told her some other stuff, including why he'd recruited Iris Parr in the naming of his virus, so it would sound like Epstein–Barr. He was on good form and in good spirits, and while we waited for the next couple of hours for them to find him a bed, we talked about all sorts of things. I remember there was a patch of something brown and gooey on the sidebar to his gurney, and he pointed at it, pulling a nasty face. I went off to find some antiseptic wipes and mopped it up, so we pondered for a while if anyone there had ever heard of Semmelweiss, the father of antiseptic, who'd drastically cut the number of women dying of childbed fever in his Viennese hospital by suggesting that the doctors wash their hands between each examination. I then said how all hospitals had smelled of methyl alcohol when I was little, and my father said that when he was a junior doctor everything – the floors, the walls, the bedframes, the tables and chairs – was continuously slooshed down with alcohol. He said that alcohol was excellent and versatile stuff, and almost certainly good for you, and the only reason why they said it was bad for you was because they didn't want people to have a good time.

Semmelweiss's story would have appealed to my father: it was about common sense, science, scepticism and the stupidity of the prevailing medical establishment.

Then we talked about other things, and Semmelweiss had led on to childbirth, and that made me say, for no particular reason, how pleased I was that life's twists and turns had resulted in me ending up with him, rather than stopping with my birth mother and then slugging it out with all my brothers and sisters in that possible and alternative reality in California. He smiled and grunted non-committally, but he wasn't the kind of man to say any more than that.

When they finally found him a bed I went with him to the ward, patted his shoulder and said goodbye, pausing on my way out of the hospital to phone my stepmother and my sister to tell them what was going on, and how everything seemed more or less under control.

They thought he had diverticulitis, and gave him an endoscopy to find out. When I went to see him a few days later he was lying on top of his bed, reading a book on clock escapements, his lips moving as usual. I asked him how he was, and he told me how interesting it had been watching the TV pictures of his lower bowel as the little camera passed up inside him, and then he said they didn't seem to have much of a clue what was wrong with him or what had caused the bleeding. We then talked for an hour or so, again about all sorts of things, and I remember I told him about someone we both knew whose major problem, as she grew older, was how she was getting more and more self-satisfied. 'Oh no,' I remember him saying, 'you must never get self-satisfied.'

It was coming up to Christmas, and I was rather anxious about the lack of a diagnosis. I'd come across cases before where people got stuck in hospital for weeks, with nothing apparently wrong with them, but the doctors wouldn't discharge them until they'd worked out what had been the matter. My parents always came over to us on Christmas Day, and I was conscious that this might easily be my stepmother's last Christmas before she was overtaken by all those cancers. I didn't want my father still to be stuck in hospital, but I needn't have worried. The day after I visited him, as a nurse was going round the ward taking orders for dinner, she passed by my father, who called out to her asking why she hadn't asked him what he'd wanted off the menu. She told him that he wasn't allowed any food as they were operating on him the next day, which was the first he knew about it, so he kicked up a fuss until a doctor finally came to see him to explain what was going on.

As they hadn't been able to locate the precise cause of the problem, and although there'd been no recurrence of the bleeding, the consultant had thought it wisest to remove my father's bowel – to perform a colostomy on him – and send his guts to the path lab to see if they could find out what was up. My father discharged himself on the spot.

But he followed the doctors' advice and stopped taking the aspirin for his arrhythmia, in case the pills had been causing the bleeding, and doing that probably caused the blood clot which killed him a month later. As he was getting dressed to go into hospital the morning he died, my stepmother asked him what he thought was wrong. Almost the last thing he said to her was: 'I don't know, but I think it's terminal.'

I wasn't expecting my father to die before my stepmother and neither, I suspect, was she. I know that they were both deeply anxious about the prospect of him being widowed a second time, though they kept it between themselves and I only heard about it from her sister after my stepmother had died.

When we eventually got to Stanmore on that Saturday morning, I remember my stepmother saying, 'What a terrible thing,' and then, later, more to herself than to anyone else, 'What will become of me?'

We were all in a state of shock, but I did my best to try to make her feel as good as she could in the circumstances. He'd collapsed while shaving and fell dead on top of her and she'd dragged him to the bed and laid his corpse out on her own, but continued to be exercised by the fact that she'd failed to close his mouth, as she'd been trained to do sixty years previously when laying out the dead. And of course she was also continuing to think that there was something she could have done to have prevented him dying. When the autopsy showed that he'd died of a pulmonary embolism, I told her that there was nothing she could have done, and when we talked about how he'd been the night before, I told her that even if they'd admitted him to hospital then, there was every possibility that the imminence of his death would have gone undetected, and he would have died anyway, alone and in a hospital ward. This way, at least, he'd died at home, in her arms, and had bucked the statistic he'd been so fond of citing.

Later, but not that much later, a lot of people said that it seemed to them that it was the perfect way to go, quick and painless. They may well be right, except that he probably didn't want to go in the first place, and none of the rest of us wanted him to go either.

Earlier on that Saturday morning, while I was getting washed and after I'd first spoken to my stepmother and told her to phone for an ambulance, my stepmother tried to phone their GP. He'd been their GP for decades, and had been mine too when I'd lived in Stanmore. I'd last seen him when I had chickenpox in 1982, when he'd come round and told my parents that sweating the disease out of me was a rather old-fashioned approach as far as patient comfort was concerned. That Saturday morning my stepmother kept getting the outgoing message from his surgery's automated switchboard, which failed to give any contact details about locums or emergency doctors, and merely enjoined his practice's patients to ring NHS Direct. My stepmother did that, but also phoned the district nurse, who'd been due to visit anyway, and she told her, like I had, to call for an ambulance.

Nearly a year before, walking down into Stanmore, my stepmother had been struck in the side by a motorcyclist who'd shot the lights as they were crossing the road down by the bank. My parents didn't tell me about this at the time, although they did eventually tell me when my stepmother complained of increasing pain on her right side. She went to see the GP, who misdiagnosed the problem as post-traumatic bruising, and thus failed to refer her for X-ray for nine weeks, by which time the tumour in her kidney was firmly established. She'd had a nephrectomy – removing the cancerous kidney – the summer before my father died.

That Saturday, my sister turned up, and then my stepmother's sister, who again came up from Hove. My sister and Anna and I stayed until about six, occupying ourselves with the things you have to do after someone dies, although because it was a Saturday there wasn't much we could do except just sit around. My step-aunt stayed with my stepmother, so I felt that I could stay at home on Sunday, although I can't now remember what I did, apart from feeling numb. On Monday my sister and I went back to Stanmore, and started sorting things out in earnest. We needed a lawyer, we needed an undertaker and a death certificate and to stop his bank account and his pension and his direct debits and his membership of the Antibody Club and CND and all the rest of it, and I remember that I was, once more, on the phone, on hold, when my step-aunt answered the front door to my parents' GP.

He had less hair than the last time I'd seen him, twenty-two years previously, but he was still tall and lean and rather lank, and his smile and the way he said 'Well, none of us saw that coming, did we?' made me want to murder him on the spot. But I just grunted a greeting and kept on holding.

Between my father's death and his funeral, my sister and I went over to Stanmore most days. My step-aunt was still there with my stepmother, and they were sharing what had been my parents' bed. When I found time to think about it, I found the idea of these two old ladies in their eighties, both widowed, both with cancer, but both tucked up together, almost unbearably moving. But most of the time my sister and I were too busy, visiting undertakers, calling banks, arranging to see lawyers and still looking for the will.

We took a day off on the Tuesday after he'd died, as we'd decided to keep the booking for lunch at the Gay Hussar in Greek Street, a booking I'd made a couple of weeks earlier when my father, my sister and I were going to celebrate our father's eightieth birthday. When I'd made the booking my sister and stepmother still weren't speaking, although things had changed now.

We had a nice lunch, and my father had been quite insistent that he wanted to have lunch at the Gay Hussar. This was partly because I'd then almost finished a four-year-long project to draw sixty of its celebrity patrons, whose caricatures now cover a whole wall of the downstairs part of the restaurant. The previous autumn, the fifty drawings I'd done thus far had been unveiled in a little ceremony by Michael

Foot, and it transpired that both he and my father had eaten there regularly, if separately, in the 1940s in its previous incarnation as a Serbian restaurant called Johnny's. I've still got a nice photograph, taken that evening, of my father and Michael Foot deep in conversation on one of the plush banquets, Foot in his customary state of careful dishevelment while my father's looking both sophisticated and neat in his suit and bow tie, an item he often wore because he said he thought it made him look like A.J.P. Taylor.

Over lunch my sister and I talked and talked about our father, and we often laughed out loud as we remembered things about him, and I'd like to think that that's what he would have wanted. At around four thirty, my sister's husband arrived from the film production company where he then worked in Old Compton Street, and after she'd left I joined a table of journalists I knew and drank some more and talked the kind of inconsequential but amusing bollocks that keeps life both going and bearable. It was on the train home that I started sobbing uncontrollably.

Shortly after this I sat down with my stepmother to talk things over. She wanted to sell the house, which she'd been trying to persuade my father to do for years, because it was both too big and too full. We didn't mention that it was now full of the ghost of my father's death as well, but we probably didn't need to. We discussed our various options, all of which were conditional on both the law's delay and the speed of her cancers, but I told her that however long the latter took (and I said I hoped it would take a long time) I'd do whatever was necessary.

Perhaps because of my experiences with my grandmother, or perhaps because it's just what people do, for years I'd been conscious of the approaching prospect of becoming entirely responsible for my parents. They never gave me any cause to brood on this, and had often been almost cavalier in trying to make me forget about it altogether, in their reluctance to divulge their medical adventures, or let me talk to them about getting some help around the house, or discuss the options for moving into sheltered accommodation. Nonetheless, for a long time I'd had an image in my mind, of me standing on the fulcrum of a see-saw, with my children at one end and my parents at the other.

Had my father been less stubborn or proud, this inevitable process could have crept up on me incrementally, but as soon as he died it happened suddenly, with a jolt.

It wasn't a surprise, and for a long time I'd rehearsed the various options, so I knew that if my stepmother outlived my father, it would all be down to me. My stepmother's thirty-year-long rift with my sister made that inevitable, because I also knew there would be a terrible injustice in involving my sister in caring for the woman who'd tried to freeze her out of our already fractured family, irrespective of how anyone might choose, retrospectively, to apportion the blame. But quite apart from all that, I loved my stepmother, as much for her faults as in spite of them, and there should also, always, be that nagging imp somewhere round your brainstem constantly reminding you to do the right thing and not, in short, be a schmuck.

So that's how we proceeded. To begin with my stepmother stayed in Stanmore with her sister, with me and my sister making frequent visits as we mined into the paperwork. On my birthday, that February, Anna, Fred, Rose, me and the dog all went up to Stanmore on the tube. My stepmother, three days into solitary living, opened the door with a sigh of relief, thanked God that we were there, and we then had another nice day, although my neck muscles tightened and I bit my lower lip when she gave me my birthday present, saying that my father had picked it out specially for me before Christmas. It was a pen holder, on a marble base, but without a pen.

By now my stepmother had tried a few days in Hove at her sister's home, more or less unchanged since her sister's husband had died a couple of years beforehand, and then they'd come back to Stanmore together. Then my step-aunt needed to go home to sort out her own affairs and those of her son and daughter-in-law and their adopted son.

My stepmother had never, ever lived on her own. She'd either lived with her family, or for thirty years in nursing accommodation, or for the thirty years after that with my father. I'd even lingered too long, living with my parents, specifically because she didn't like being in the house on her own overnight. When it became clear that she didn't want to go back to Hove, or stay in Stanmore on her own, the see-saw thumped down on my stepmother's side with a bump.

This is the flip side to the process of emancipation you go through when you reach something like adulthood. What do you do with your parents? I knew that things would have been easier if it had been my father who'd been left on his own, because we'd have been able to have had jovial rows about him being an obdurate old bugger and, probably just for form's sake, there would have been a mock tug of war, as my sister and I tried to do what we thought best for him, and he resisted it. He also had a vast reservoir of inner resources to fall back on, and I imagine he would have pottered along quite happily on his own, until grudgingly accepting our helping hands. My stepmother was different, and my relationship with her was different to the one I'd had with my father: not quite so close, so not quite as permissive of the forgivableness of a harsh if well-intended word. And the awful precedent of my grandmother was constantly in my mind.

For a few days I did a furious amount of internal horse-trading, until, in a sweaty phone call, I asked my stepmother directly where she thought she might want, ultimately, to live. But I'd forgotten that she'd been ground through my grandmother's mill too, and had always said that she'd never impose a geriatric on a family with teenage children. Whether she really meant it or not, she told me that she didn't want to live with us on a permanent basis anyway. She and we were too set in our different ways for such an arrangement to work. So we talked, in a general sort of way, about the new block of sheltered flats down the road from us, recently built on the site of an anomalous Rolls-Royce showroom that had, for years, been lurking off Lewisham High Street, just behind a parade of pound shops, pubs, Indian restaurants and curious bazaars selling a wealth of useless tat. She said that that sounded perfect, that we'd be close but not under each other's feet, and in the meantime, in the very short term, she'd spend a fortnight with us before her sister could come back to Stanmore, and we'd proceed from there. So I drove across London to pick her up, and then drove back home again.

Those two weeks were strangely wonderful. Whether it was conscious or not, my stepmother was conducting her own grief-therapy, in the way she was best equipped to. She told stories, many of which I'd heard before, but which I listened to again with much greater care and appreciation than I'd shown before. She told me other things I'd never heard about at all, and a lot of those stories make up large parts of this book. It was a wonderful example of the therapeutic power of anecdote, but it demonstrated something deeper than that as well: that we constantly seek to take control of our lives, over and over again, by retelling the events that constitute them, literally recreating the life in the retelling, but as our own creation; after all, the real power of the confessional lies less in the forgiveness than in the simple fact of telling. Bearing that in mind, I think she was going through little catharses as well. I remember her talking about her father in ways which suggested she'd just realised what a domestic ogre he'd been, and she told me she'd just remembered how members of his family, on one of their visits to England from Argentina, had described her and her sisters as 'Charlie's little slaves'. She talked about her mother a lot as well, and for the first time I (and possibly she as well) appreciated the extent of her mother's drinking problem. When her mother had died at the nursing home run by nuns, in her room my stepmother and her sisters had discovered drawers and wardrobes crammed with empty sherry bottles. As a teenager, I remember thinking that this was quite a funny story, and in my mind that's how it stayed, and recreating a depressing reality as an amusing anecdote is probably the best method of control there is. But now she told me about how her mother had often been too drunk to drive to visit her patients when she'd been a district nurse, and there was an entirely darker side to my image of the little old lady who liked the occasional tipple.

She also put me right on something I'd believed to be true for years, mostly because that was the way she'd told it to me. Some years previously she'd given us a large wooden-and-wickerwork chair, which had been at her parents' house for decades. We always called it Uncle Norman's chair, because she'd told me that it had belonged to her father's brother Norman, who'd fought in the First World War and been injured and then captured by the Germans, who carried out a field amputation on his shattered leg. According to my stepmother's original story, the operation had been botched, and because a small length of femur protruded from the end of his stump he was unable to wear a prosthesis, and years later would sit in his chair and clean his pipe out on the knob of extending thigh bone. This was a very good story. It was disgusting and slightly Gothic, and because of that it was also quite funny.

But now she told me that Norman was nineteen when he'd been captured and operated on, and that his disability had more or less blighted his life. Moreover, he never cleaned his pipe out like that. I suppose the previous anecdote had helped diminish the tragedy, sanitising it into a new, gruesomely amusing narrative, although now she probably thought that she should put the record straight.

I also think, because she knew she was dying, she was having a last leisurely stroll through the landscape of her memories, looking at some things from a different perspective while she revisited other places and took enormous comfort and reassurance from the fact of their unchanging familiarity. It was a pretty comprehensive tour, and I was now an appreciative audience for her traveller's tales. Which is just as well, because everything now went into fast-forward.

I took her to see oncologists. I talked at length with her new GP (who's our GP, whose level of care and treatment rehabilitated her profession in my mind, after the experiences with the man in Edgware). I discussed it all with the nice and helpful Macmillan nurse, and all of them said, a month or so after my father died, that the prognosis was obviously bad, but we were looking at more like a year than months, and that I should plan accordingly. My stepmother was dead three and a half months after my father.

On her eighty-third birthday, she was back in Stanmore with her sister, but was meant to be coming to stay with us again for a few days, except that on the Saturday morning when I was meant to be picking her up, my step-aunt phoned me early to say I should get over to Stanmore as quickly as I could. My stepmother was in a bad way, and said that in the middle of the night she really thought she was dying. She clearly needed to go into hospital. It took us hours, with me phoning her old GP (who was unavailable), then district nurses and Macmillan nurses, and then finally phoning her consultant at the Royal Free, who told me to bring her in as an accident-and-emergency patient in order to sidestep the bureaucracy that required her to be referred to the hospital by other people or agencies who were, because it was a weekend, all otherwise unavailable. Fluid had built up in the lining of her lungs, whither the cancers had spread from her kidney.

She spent two weeks in the Royal Free, and I'd take the Northern Line up there from London Bridge almost every day and sit at her bed while she talked about the nurses, the ones she liked and the ones, in her opinion, who were rubbish. And she told me about how it wasn't all that easy to tell who was a nurse and who wasn't, as they all wore a variation on the nylon safari suit, and as often as not it wasn't a nurse at all but someone just coming round to ask if she wanted to top up the credit on her TV and telephone. And she told me how everyone seemed to be terribly jolly, and everyone felt useful and appreciated, and I extrapolated from that that a clever manager had come in and empowered everyone, and she told me that beneath it all no one had any idea what was going on, and she told me how she was able to administer the interferon to herself far better than any of the staff. And she told me how they'd wake up other patients in her geriatric oncology ward at four o'clock in the morning to take blood from them, and I was there myself when the consultant came on his rounds and explained that these days they liked to include the patient as part of the team, so that they could play a role in deciding about treatment, so what would she like them to do?

I took Fred with me to see her one Saturday afternoon, and we took the Northern Line up to Belsize Park, just north of Camden Town and south of Hampstead, and as we walked up the hill he kept saying to me, 'What a shithole.'

The next day I had to work, but I phoned her in the evening to ask her how she was feeling, and she said, matter-of-factly and almost breezily, that this was the end, and there wasn't much more to be done. Anna found me a few minutes later, crying over the laundry I was hanging up to dry.

After two weeks they said she could go home (but only after I'd arrived the previous day to take her away, and was told that I had to come back the next day). Her bed had been next to the toilets, so she'd got up each time she needed a pee and walked there unaided, but no one had encouraged her to take any more exercise than that, apart from the little exercises she did herself, using her own initiative, to stave off bedsores or deep-vein thrombosis. But now she couldn't walk more than ten paces without oxygen.

She came back to Lewisham with me, after we'd been back to Stanmore and she'd collected a lot of stuff, including her jewellery and lots of papers and bit and bobs (including photographs and little flimsy pictures of saints she'd been given by friends in Argentina at their first communions), and as I backed out of the short drive, with her oxygen cylinder between her legs she said goodbye to the house with a smile, knowing better than me that she'd never see the place again.

One of the nice things about nice Miss Smith in Form 2 was that she'd read us the Narnia books, and my old Puffin copy of *The Lion, The Witch and the Wardrobe* is the one she gave me, with her signature in it, when I was about seven. That's the copy I read to Fred and Rose when they were little, and I read through the entire sequence of books until I came to *The Last Battle*, which was the only one I hadn't read, or had read to me, when I was a child. I found the beginning rather boring, so after I'd said goodnight to my children I flipped to the end, and read that appalling chapter about how all the children in the books had been dead all along. I was outraged that C.S. Lewis could be so cheap, right at the end of a series of children's books which begins with one of the best scenes in all of literature, where Lucy wanders through the wardrobe, through the stuffy darkness and warm furs, into Narnia, also in darkness save for an old street lamp, but crisp and cold and sheaved in snow. That scene is so good because it could have come out of a movie by Cocteau or Bergman or Buñuel, or been used by early Freudians as a textbook. Now it seemed that the whole thing was nothing more than Enid Blyton meets the Book of Revelation, and the old sod had blown it all because he couldn't resist giving us all a glimpse of his didactic hooves before saying goodbye.

That's too harsh a judgement (like Lewis's own), and his valedictory cack-handedness shouldn't invalidate the entire series, because many of the books remain both magical and haunting. *The Magician's Nephew*, for instance, chronologically the first of the Chronicles of Narnia, has an extraordinary scene where the woman who will become the White Queen travels, via the Wood between the Worlds, to a planet which she then destroys by uttering the Unspeakable Word.

We all need unspeakable words, like we need taboos, so we can break them *in extremis*. I remember when I was in the sixth form at school, and there was a boy in my English set who for some reason or other irritated the hell out of me. He knew this, and exploited it to the hilt, as people do. One day we were in a lesson talking about the handkerchief scene in *Othello*, and just to be annoying he asked the teacher, a nice man called Andy Grant, how we could be sure that it was a handkerchief, and not, for instance, a small tablecloth. I suppose he thought that this was an acceptable level of ribbing the beak, the kind of thing that might endear him to his fellow pupils. I just found it deeply, deeply irritating, so said, 'Of course it's a fucking handkerchief, you stupid fucking wanker.' Grant immediately told me to moderate my language, and also told me to stay behind afterwards. He tried to make me feel ashamed of myself, that I'd somehow let the side down by my sudden descent into the demotic of the gutter. To reinforce his point, he used the standard teacher's tactic of flattering me, saying that I had far too large a vocabulary to sink to using such words, but I politely pointed out that my vocabulary included words to suit every occasion, and on this occasion it needed to be said forcefully that the point of contention between Othello and Desdemona was, indeed, a handkerchief, and the best way to reinforce the seriousness of this unquestionable fact was with my deployment of the defining adjective. Moreover, it was also beyond dispute that my fellow pupil was not only a time-wasting creep, but also one of the biggest fucking wankers who'd ever drawn breath.

I was, of course, being a smart-arse, but I'm sticking to the principle.

One of my stepmother's favourite stories was about me when I was around three years old. My mother and future stepmother had taken me in the back of the car, in a little metal car seat with integral table, to pick my sister up from the rather swanky primary school she was attending in Bushey at the time. Another of the pupils at this place was the daughter of Franklin Engleman, one of the stars of BBC Radio in the 1960s, and standing outside the school gates my mother was showing off one of the foster-babies, in its carrycot in the proto-hatchback boot of the car. At this point my stepmother would adopt the 'refained' voice of what she called the 'posh mamas', to establish the scene in her listeners' minds. According to my stepmother, my sister then skipped out of school, and my mother opened the car door for her and said to me as I scooted my little toy cars round on the little metal table in front of me, 'Look, Martin! It's your sister! What have you got to say to your sister, then?' According to my step-mother, I looked up briefly and said, 'Bugger off!'

Although I don't remember any of this, who in their heart of hearts could blame me?

As I remember it, we were a moderately foul-mouthed family, and the commonest epiphets were 'bloody' and 'bugger'. When she was very small my sister would suddenly yell 'Bug!' behind my mother's back, and my mother would then look round in fury. My sister, of course, would smile sweet innocence, and wait a minute or so before whispering 'ger . . .'. And while the foulness of the language never reached the mesmeric heights of invention displayed by my wife or daughter, I remember, when I was a teenager, my stepmother once muttering 'Buggeroo!' as she took a hot dish out of the oven, and 'buggeration' was a nice neologism we all used for as long as I can remember.

I only remember hearing my stepmother use a variation on the word 'fuck' once. It was during her period of anecdotive therapy after my father had died, and she was telling me a story I hadn't heard before about my Aunt Jean. After my mother died Jean had taken to dropping round, unannounced, and during these visits I'd often lock myself in my room in order to avoid her. In any other circumstances this would have been an act of unforgivable and punishable rudeness, but I got away with it because the circumstances were different, and I suspect that my father wished that he'd been able to do the same thing. My stepmother told me that one day Jean made an announced visit, and went to the churchyard with my stepmother and our dead dentist's widow, to put some flowers on my mother's grave, which she apparently chucked on the tombstone because she didn't want to leave her vase behind. She then took my step-mother and the dentist's widow to the Chinese restaurant in Stanmore and told them that she and the rest of my mother's family had had a meeting and decided that one or other of them had to marry my father for the sake of me and my sister, adding, as my stepmother phrased it, 'if you don't like the fucker you can always have separate rooms'.

When I told Dawne this story, she told me she'd heard it too, from our dead dentist's widow, though needless to say her family had never had a meeting to discuss the identity of my stepmother-to-be.

My father was equally sparing with the word 'fuck' and its variants. I remember him telling me in precise and lengthy detail just what it meant when, aged eight, I'd been dared by my sister to ask him, after we'd seen it, written in letters five feet high, on a wall on some waste ground in Canons Park where we'd been playing that afternoon.

The other time I remember him using it was just before he went on his Far Eastern trip, and we were sitting watching the television, and for reasons I can't now remember my father started singing or, more correctly, reciting the words to a Flanders and Swann song about the months of the year and the appalling weather brought on by each one. I don't know why, but he ended by paraphrasing the last line, 'bloody January again', as 'fucking January again'. I remember we were all slightly shocked, so he probably did it to tease my mother.

As my stepmother spent more and more time in hospitals, either at appointments or in wards, I'd try and debrief myself by talking to Anna, and defuse and diffuse the stress building up in me. I remember launching into a lengthy rant about how much I hated fucking hospitals, not because they smelled of shit but because these production lines of disease and death tried to kid themselves and everyone else that they were nothing of the kind, with their stupid fucking shops and flower stalls and bright floral curtains demarcating the dying, and those endless fucking corridors, their false ceilings buckling at the edges, hung with all those absolutely fucking awful paintings by children, pharmacists, patients and 'friends'. And

I wondered precisely what kind of perverted ghoul would ever like to be thought of as a 'friend' of a hospital? Benefactor, employee, client, nodding acquaintance, enemy or victim I could understand, but a 'friend'?

These days 'fuck' is no longer the ultimate Unspeakable Word, and as I ranted I hadn't quite got to the point where I needed to invoke it.

A few weeks after my father died, Anna had booked us a package deal to Sorrento over Easter, working out early on that by that stage I'd be badly in need of a holiday. I thought that my stepmother would be able to go to her sister's in Hove again, but she caught a respiratory infection and so wasn't feeling strong enough to face the car journey. I wasn't happy about leaving her in the house on her own, and she wouldn't countenance the idea of me hiring an agency nurse to look after her, given her long-held low opinion of such people. But nor did she want us to cancel the holiday. So, after talking to her about it, I booked her in to a BUPA nursing home in Blackheath. I still wasn't happy, but having cased the joint and talked to the staff, it seemed the best option.

We had a wonderful time in Sorrento. I didn't manage to find the hotel where we'd stayed in 1967, but we went up Vesuvius, as my sister and my father and stepmother had in 1971, and I trousered a lump of pumice as a souvenir for my stepmother. And we went to Capri and I found the street where, again in 1967, my sister and I had lost our mother when she'd been window-shopping and we'd wandered on as usual, and where my sister tapped a black-haired woman on the shoulder who'd turned round and then turned out to be a perfect stranger. And we went to Naples on the train, and on our way to the harbour to catch the hydrofoil back to Sorrento, half a mile or so down the seafront from where

I'd been stopped from seeing someone beheaded by a tram, we saw a car lying inexplicably on its roof in the path of a tram on the same tram tracks, surrounded by a huge crowd of disputatious Neapolitans.

But back home, as soon as I visited my stepmother in the nursing home, I felt as if I hadn't been away at all, although the week seemed to have crammed months of accelerating entropy into itself. My stepmother had been in reasonably good spirits, and still fairly mobile when I'd left her. My mother-in-law and sister-in-law had been to visit her, as had her sister and nephew and niece, but a week on from when I'd last seen her she'd undergone a terrible transformation. She was slumped in her chair, her feet horribly swollen, hardly able to speak and her eyes squeezed tightly shut. She told me that she'd asked to be taken into hospital the night before. I looked at her and told her that I should never have thought of putting her in this place. I then spoke to the duty nurse on her floor, who said my stepmother seemed to be very depressed, but didn't want to take part in the group activities and refused to take any antidepressants. I said that her husband had recently died, she'd been forced to abandon her home and she was dying of cancer, and wouldn't they be feeling a bit depressed in the same circumstances? I got a non-committal response, and was told that the doctor attached to the home didn't think her condition warranted hospitalisation.

I took her home the next day, and I remember trying to be jolly in the car as I complained about the car in front of us as I drove across Blackheath, saying it was probably going so slowly because they must have had a living human brain in an open bucket of plasma on the back seat. It was the kind of comment that she'd usually have rolled her eyes at as she tolerated me being silly. When we got home all she could do was sit in an armchair in the dining room, and couldn't eat, or even look up, and that evening, three months to the day since my father died, she was admitted to Lewisham Hospital, where she'd been the matron thirty-one years previously.

We waited in accident and emergency for about three hours before we were eventually seen by a doctor, and waited another two hours before they admitted her to a ward. During this time I tried to make inconsequential conversation, then rubbed her naked back to ease her backache and general pain, and saw her mastectomy scar for the first and last time. At about two thirty in the morning, I asked a nurse when my stepmother would be transferred to a ward, and she told me curtly that I'd already been told this, and it wasn't her job to tell me again.

And so then my stepmother was in Lewisham Hospital, first on a general ward, then in a room with another old woman, and each time they moved her I said, 'She used to be the matron here; she's one of yours.'

And Anna came to see her one evening and she'd been left to sit on a bedpan for three-quarters of an hour.

And I went to see her, and she wanted to be lifted up in the bed because she was in considerable pain, so I went to the nurses' station where at first they ignored me, and then they said someone would come in a minute, and then twenty minutes later a nurse finally came in, looked at me and my stepmother and more or less barked as she said, 'What is it *this* time?'

And I was there when the consultant came to see her, and he asked her what she wanted. Doubled up, her eyes closed, she said, 'I want to get better.'

He said that that wasn't going to happen now, so she had to decide what she wanted to do.

I said that I thought a hospice might be the best place for her, and then he left.

I caught up with him outside, because I wanted to speak to him about how to arrange her transfer and things like that, but I could hardly speak because I was trying to stop myself from crying.

He was an Irishman, with curly, greying red hair and an almost perfectly spherical head.

He looked tired and slightly desperate, and referred me to the Macmillan nurses.

He was unwilling or unable to make eye contact.

By this stage I'd utilised the Unspeakable Word. One evening, almost mad with frustration at my helplessness to prevent the casual callousness she suffered in Lewisham and at the BUPA nursing home, I was pacing up and down the dining room, ranting again, while Anna sat listening to me, indulging me. And then, not really knowing where the term came from, I suddenly yelled, 'The thing is, they're all members of the fucking Cuntocracy!'

I knew what I meant.

I meant that these people – these carers, these nurses and doctors – didn't have to behave like that; they could, with a small effort, have abdicated their frustration or resentment or tiredness or professional disengagement, and all they had to do was just try a little bit harder, because they were only cunts because they actually chose to be cunts. And because cunt is now one of the very few Unspeakable Words left to us, it wrought its magic.

Anna laughed. Everyone I shared my neologism with laughed, including Giles Fraser, a colleague on the *Guardian* who's also the surprisingly foul-mouthed Vicar of Putney.

The point is, you can recruit almost anyone you want to the Cuntocracy, and although the precise membership qual-ifications are fluid, varying from individual case to case, everyone I spoke to seemed instinctively to understand precisely what I meant, and who was eligible for election. (Just to clarify this, I think that we all recognise the unspoken

287

subtlety with which the Inferno of Profanity is divided into different circles, at different depths: the deepest circle is for cunts, and there are others for pricks, arseholes, wankers, shits, tossers and so on. Down deep in the bottom of the pit lurk cunts like John Birt, Peter Mandelson, Rupert Murdoch, Paul Dacre, most other newspaper editors, our immediate bosses at work and so on, and other people occupy the higher levels. Having thought about it at length, I think on balance that Tony Blair inhabits the circle for arseholes.)

Anyway, I spoke the word, and the magic worked, albeit indiscernibly. It's the same in principle as what my father had done when he'd told stories about his colleagues and recreated them as fools and knaves; it's the same process, although less intense, that my stepmother used when she turned her life into a series of anecdotes; it's what I do as a cartoonist, and what everyone does when they tell a joke about something that's happened in their lives, and someone else laughs.

It's almost as if our world is trapped beneath an outer shell, a crazy paving of grinding tectonic plates stiffened into hard geology by the petty and major injuries committed against us mostly by the thoughtlessness of other people.

But once you say the Unspeakable Word, you can at least begin to chip away at the clinker of that outer planet, and start to get back to the more familiar and comfortable reality underneath.

I made a point of not paying the bill for the nursing home until we got probate on my stepmother's estate, months and months and months after she'd died.

Although nobody at Lewisham Hospital bothered to tell me, my stepmother was transferred to St Christopher's Hospice in Sydenham, the first of the hospices set up by Dame Cecily Saunders, and where she died herself just over a year after my stepmother. I went to see her as soon as I found out she'd been transferred, and I apologised once more for the unforgivable treatment she'd suffered at Lewisham. She half opened her eyes and smiled at me as she said, in a whisper, 'Don't worry, dear, Lewisham's always been a dump.'

When I was driving her back to our home in Lewisham from what turned out to be her last appointment with her oncologist at the Royal Free, and he'd told her the cancers had spread and that there really wasn't much hope left, I asked her what she felt about all that. We were just driving past the countercultural clutter and mannered tattiness of Camden Lock, a place I always associate in my mind with summer rain and people in huge shaggy coats, smelling of compost and patchouli oil, sometime around late July in 1971. She looked down at the oxygen cylinder between her knees and said, 'Well, I've had a long and mostly happy life, and you play with the hand you're dealt. Now your father's dead I can't really see the point.'

It seems a harsh and yet wise way of looking at things, and I knew for certain at that point that all she now really wanted to do was to die. After her first breast cancer, when she was sixty-nine, I think she thought she was going to die then, but instead she had another twelve years of reasonably good health, travelled the world, pottered around and saw my children grow. Then, with the second bout of breast cancer, when she had her mastectomy, that could have been it too, but she survived that, and although the cancer in her kidney was the beginning of the end, as it came it wasn't that bad up until right at the very end. We've already seen that she could easily have died when she was twenty, in the Blitz, so maybe all of it was an unexpected bonus.

Earlier, she'd drawn up a genealogy of cancer in her family, and for generations the women in her family had all died, young or old, of cancer. 'Well,' she once said to me, 'thank God I never had children, when you think about it.'

And although she did as she was told by the doctors, with good humour, and took the drugs and injected herself with the interferon and attended the appointments, I think she was only doing it to be polite, or for form's sake. But she ended up confounding all those experts who gave her months and months, rather than a matter of weeks.

My stepmother, for both good and ill, was tough, and so she toughed it out, but by hastening rather than retarding her end in what people glibly now call the 'battle with cancer'. Through a massive and stubborn effort of will, she willed herself to die, almost as if she was using telepathy to speed up the division of the cancerous cells as they colonised and colonised yet further her beckoning body.

If so, the telepathy spread further, and without knowing how I knew when she was going to die to the day, so I made certain arrangements accordingly. I drove her elder sister down to Sydenham from her flat in central London in order to say goodbye the Saturday before she died; I brought Fred and Rose over to see her at the beginning of the week she died. It was the May Day bank holiday, and we'd just gone for a walk in Crystal Palace in the pouring rain to look at the Victorian dinosaurs, and I told her it was a bank holiday and it was raining, and I remember she raised her eyebrows in her familiar way and rolled her eyes, and although she was hardly able to speak, we knew she was saying 'bloody typical' in a way we all recognised. And I went to see her on Thursday, and I knew that it would be the last time, and I leaned over her, after I'd sat and held her hand for an hour or so, and whispered in her ear 'Goodbye, Jos. I love you very much. Thank you for being my mother, and thank you for being so proud of me.'

She died at around six o'clock the following morning.

It was what she wanted. More to the point, and from my point of view, it was the way I wanted it to be, once she'd been moved to the hospice. Here they practised what my stepmother would often describe as 'what I call nursing'. They took time with the patients, and they took care, and they filled the wards with flowers and peace and calm and, without needing to state it, clearly articulated that they were offering all the scraps of dignity on offer in an antechamber to Death which, unlike most other hospitals, isn't ashamed to admit that that's what it is.

They phoned me at around ten to seven that Friday morning, and although I knew what the phone call was going to be, I remember rushing to the phone outside Rose's bedroom saying 'Oh no, oh no' over and over to myself. Then I drove over to Sydenham, past the Horniman Museum and skirting round Crystal Palace Park, and walked into the light, bright 1960s building, and walked into the ward and pulled back the curtains round her bed, pressing my hands into my mouth like I had when I saw my father's corpse, the tears pricking in my eyes, saying 'Oh Jos, oh Jos' as I looked at her, the lines beginning to smooth away from her face as her bodily fluids began to settle and rigor mortis started to set in, and I went and kissed her forehead and said goodbye again, noticing the little orchid they'd placed on her pillow, and I also noticed the half-smile on her sallow face.

Stuff

I don't expect to see my parents again, except in my dreams.

After my stepmother died, I received dozens of letters from her friends, people she'd know as children in Argentina, or whom she'd trained with to be nurses when they were teenagers, or whom she'd trained, or who'd met her when she was a patient in hospital herself, or she'd met with my father on holiday, or people she'd just gone up to somewhere and spoken to in Spanish. Many of them wrote, kindly and comfortingly, to say that they knew she was now in heaven and reunited with my father.

To be honest, I doubt it.

When I was getting her out of the BUPA nursing home, she was taken down by a nurse in the lift in a wheelchair, while I took her bags down via the stairs. When we got home and she was sitting hunched up in the armchair, although she had her eyes squeezed tight shut and could speak in barely more than a croaking whisper, she clearly felt compelled to tell us what the nurse had said to her in the lift. He'd asked her if she prayed to Almighty God, and she told us that she'd replied that sometimes she did, and he then told her to pray very hard, because He was now her only hope.

At various points in my life I've been enjoined to do the same thing, to a lesser or greater degree, by at least one paedophile, lots of schoolboys, some students, gibbering indigents on street corners, people I've met at parties, several schizophrenics and, on a less one-to-one basis, by bishops, priests, vicars, nuns, authors, poets, politicians and terrorists.

And I remember the precise moment I stopped being a confused adolescent agnostic, vaguely seeking after truth. Although I couldn't tell you the date, I know that it was lunchtime, in the spring of 1977, and I was sitting in the senior common room at school having another conversation, which wasn't quite an argument, with the Christians who were my contemporaries. And I remember the head boy, an earnest and muscular young conformist called Phil Taylor, telling me that irrespective of how you behaved or lived, if you didn't accept Jesus into your heart, then you couldn't go to heaven. I don't know why on earth I should have taken his word for it, but I remember undergoing an almost physical moment of epiphany as I finally understood that I wanted absolutely nothing to do with any God who was so conceited, insecure and paranoid that the bugger needed my affirmation or anyone else's in order to feel good enough about himself so he'd hand over the keys to his stupid kingdom. From that moment on I've been a hardline and unforgiving atheist, and I've been hardening ever since.

There is, of course, just a chance that I'm wrong, and when I die it won't be a purely physiological phenomenon which makes me imagine I'm being drawn towards the light, and thereafter I'll find myself surrounded by the incorporeal remnants of everyone I've ever known. If so, I can't think of anything worse.

The promise of life after death is the ultimate pig in a poke. It's also highly unlikely, if you think about it, and I also think it's grossly impertinent. But most of all it's a cheap shot, exploiting everyone's greatest vulnerability, not only our fear of extinction, but also our collective yearning for something to make sense of our unimportant little lives. I sometimes think that that yearning is the greatest curse our evolution into our presumption to rationality has lumbered us with, even if in practice, for most people, it simply provides them with something else to fill their thoughts with during the empty days. But that underlying itch, compelling us to need to explain it all, in order to justify it, is as pervasive as it is corrosive.

I remember the day my father died, when we finally got home from Stanmore, and I started crying again, thinking about my father's clock collection. I said to Anna how it was all just a waste, all the time he'd taken collecting and fixing and gloating over all his clocks, but she told me I was looking at things the wrong way round, and I should see my father's life up to the point when it ended, and not judge it after it had ended.

She was quite right, but I remember her telling me after her father died that she felt so empty and miserable she'd walk down the street hoping a building would fall on her. I felt the same, in the late summer of the year after my father and stepmother died. I knew I was being irrational, but I couldn't stop myself from thinking how their lives had been an utter waste of time because, in the end, they'd died. But I was still looking at things the wrong way round, and part of me was being crushed by the assumption that there must be some final, eschatological audit, some end point when it does all get justified and so there'll be some point to it all. Some people might say that that was God whispering to me through the ether, telling me that we all have that ultimate end point, long after we're dead. I prefer to recognise it as grief, and therefore as a specifically human response to an inescapable component of human life, motivated by the same instinctive factors that make us love, hate, remember, imagine and, it's worth adding, not throw our babies away when they cry all night long.

I once read somewhere that a blister caused by extreme cold is physically identical to one caused by extreme heat. I've also heard that the hormones released by tears have the same effect as the ones you release when you laugh. And, in a strange way, I almost enjoyed grieving for my parents. The physical sensation of the tears welling behind my eyeballs and the stinging in my mucous membrane wasn't entirely unpleasant, and it's not uncommon to want to recapture the feeling of such deep emotion, if only because of the physical intensity of its depth.

I got very cross when I heard that they were trying to drug my stepmother out of what they diagnosed as depression when she was grieving and dying in the BUPA nursing home. Apart from anything else, she wouldn't take the antidepressants because they made her vomit, but earlier, each time she'd been in hospital or seen a Macmillan nurse or a social worker, she'd been asked if she wanted counselling. Each time she'd politely declined the offer, and would later tell me about it in her stuff-and-nonsense voice.

It's beyond question that many good, kind people do their very best to help other sad people feel happier, but I remember one night coming back from the pub to the slum I lived in as a student to find two rather thin and weedy young men I didn't know sitting, their arms folded on the backs of their chairs, staring smilingly into each other's eyes. We had a lot of people passing through our home most of the time, and their presence didn't bother me that much, but I asked one of my fellow tenants what these two were doing. He said they were co-counselling, and when I asked what that was, he explained that it was a new therapeutic method whereby two people shared all their fears and worries and anxieties until they felt happy about everything. I'd thought they were in love, but it seems that instead they just weren't anxious about anything any more. I remember asking my friend what the point was of always feeling happy about everything that happened to you. I'd always thought that evolution had equipped us with a spectrum of emotions to help us cope with situations as they arise, and we utilise them accordingly. I asked if these two would just smile and feel happy if their families got murdered or their clothes were eaten by rats or they accidentally stuck a joss stick in their eye. He said that the point was that they wouldn't feel bad about themselves, in the way that bad feelings about bad things make you feel.

Maybe my stepmother's response was a generational thing, or maybe it was professional: as she'd say herself, in her line of work you had to get used to bad things happening, and she'd seen a lot of bad things. But maybe it was a recognition that it's almost insanely utopian to expect everyone to be happy all the time, when there's no particularly good reason why they should be. Then again, along with demanding an explanation, an expectation of perfectibility is another of those peculiarly human traits that we're cursed with.

Long after I was adopted, and the Abortion Act had drastically reduced the number of children up for or available for adoption, yet more kind, well-intentioned people started policing potential adopters with an eye to perfection. Many of these children had been removed from fatally imperfect parents, so I suppose it's understandable that people acting on their behalf did their very best to overcompensate, and left the children languishing in care homes because their prospective parents were too old, too fat, too white or too black. It's possible that when I was adopted, social workers with the gift of foresight might have denied my adoptive parents' attempt to adopt me because, within a decade, my mother would be too dead, and beyond everything else I should have been protected from the possibility of unhappiness.

The Nazis wanted a perfect society in which everybody, inevitably, would be happy, and so set about the systematic annihilation of anyone who'd make the survivors feel unhappy. The Soviet Union was the same. I'm even suspicious about that line in the Declaration of Independence about the pursuit of happiness, because when you chase something it tends to run away. There's also an assumption that happiness is the default setting for human beings, and if you deviate from constant happiness then that deviance is both pathological and, of course, treatable, with the option, ultimately, of putting the mildly discontented out of their comparative misery. That seems a pretty one-dimensional view of things to me, although it's now a widely held one. It's probably promulgated to make us think we'll get happy if we go shopping.

Not that I'm advocating unhappiness. I remember a lot of moments of unalloyed bliss, like when I started going out with Anna and I felt that all I needed to do was kick gently on the pavement and I'd be able to leap twenty or thirty feet in the air. And I felt the same when the children were born. Without getting too pretentious about it, there have been other moments of bliss which, if I was sufficiently gullible, I might even describe as spiritual, like when I once woke up in a friend's parents' spare room when I was about seventeen or eighteen, pulled aside the curtain and, wiping away the veil of condensation on the windowpane, saw a seagull performing neat ellipses in the damp, dull morning sky. Just the memory of that makes me feel joyous, as does the memory of walking between hedgerows in late spring towards my then girlfriend's house in south Buckinghamshire, prior to us going out to a field for a snog.

Although when I arrived at her house, and despite the fact that I'd been going out with his daughter for about two months, as her father answered the door he looked at me in a puzzled way and said, 'Yes? What can I do for you?'

I'm as much of a sucker for a nice sunset as anyone else, but I've experienced most other emotions too, all the way down the scale.

But you need the shadows as well as the light to see things in their proper perspective.

And if we're talking about an organism as complicated as a human being having a default setting, you might just as well say that the default setting is cancer, that inbuilt obsolescence that's designed to stop us living for ever and thus imprisoning our genes. All the rest is just a passing disease that the cancer finally manages to kick off when you die.

The second wave of grief for my parents passed, at around the same time as I started writing this book, and you're at liberty to make of that what you will. But it also passed because I finally recognised a dimension to the grief I hadn't factored in before. I was dwelling too long on what I imagined was the futility of life, but it was also coming up to a year since my sister and I sold our parents' house. Once more, Anna focused my thoughts when she said that the house she'd grown up in was almost like an extra parent to her, and she couldn't quite face the thought of ever even walking past it again, even a decade and a half after her mother sold it. (It's now lived in by the broadcaster John Humphreys. I met him once and said that he lived in the house my wife had grown up in, and I was going to say what she thought every time she heard him on the radio when he interrupted and finished the sentence for me: 'Yeah, I know! "'E's the cunt who lives in my fuckin' 'owse!"')

The house is one of the few of my main protagonists that I've neglected to name. It had an odd name, with an odd provenance. When my father bought it in 1958 from a Mr Wilson, it was called 'Mayook', a stupid and meaningless name which was still visible on the old wooden gates my father had removed shortly after he took possession of the place, which then rotted at the base of the middle oak tree for another twenty years or so, next to the remnants of the old upright piano we'd acquired when I was six or seven and had spent a joyous weekend smashing to pieces in our sitting room.

Instead of 'Mayook' my parents chose 'Waitemata', which was suggested by the New Zealand dentist who lived in the flat adjacent to theirs before they moved to Stanmore. I think my father liked it because he was told that it was the name of a popular New Zealand lager, without necessarily knowing that the lager had, in its turn, been named after a famous bay on the South Island of New Zealand. Apparently it's the Maori for 'sparkling water'. Then again, given the fact that there was no sparkling water to been seen for miles, he may have liked it because it was guaranteed to lead to decades of confusion.

For years I couldn't spell it, and I remember when I was eleven or twelve, and was filling in a form that required my address, I had to go out over and over again to the front of the house to see how its name was spelt, each time forgetting once I got back inside the house. At any rate, throughout my association with the house I've had to spell out the letters of its name even more often than I had to spell my surname. Other confusions were less predictable. When she married my father, my stepmother heard from several of her friends that when they saw the name of the house and compared it with my father's alternative name, Ossie, they assumed, not unreasonably, that my stepmother had married some kind of Antipodean. However, it's pure coincidence that probably one of my father's closest living blood relatives, Don Rowson, has ended up in New Zealand.

'Waitemata' isn't a very beautiful house, and my father buggered it about for decades to make it even less alluring. He added the extension at the back, then widened the garage at the front, throwing its symmetry completely out of kilter. Part of the reason for widening the garage was in order to accommodate an inspection pit – I suspect in order for me to service the cars. However, after a few months we found out that the pit had filled up with water, as the builders must have nicked a pipe during construction. I remember suggesting to my father that it could be a miraculous spring, and advised him to open a religious shrine. Beyond the garage, he trashed the front garden, replacing the lawn with shrubs and compost heaps, and for years the last of the Austin A40s, having failed its MOT, sat rusting beneath the oak trees. On the other side of the garage, the garden fence with our next-door neighbour had long since been replaced with an ugly wicker thing erected by the neighbour after my father had accidentally burned down the original fence and refused to replace it, on the basis that he preferred open-plan front gardens, on the American model. As a result the neighbour and my father feuded for decades, until my stepmother, unsolicited, voluntarily started to look after him during his final illness. To add to the general ambience, I remember one day my father and I found an old sack of cement that had set solid in the dampness of the garage, so we dumped it at the base of one of the oak trees in the front garden, leaned a panel of rusting corrugated iron against it, decided as a joke that it was an artistic installation and called it 'The Unknown Political Prisoner *En Famille*'.

As my father didn't like drawing the curtains, on several occasions people rang the doorbell and were surprised to find anyone in, as they thought the place had been abandoned, curtainless and with cars dumped willy-nilly off the road.

Even so, the front of the house wasn't without its charms. When they filled in the ditches and replaced the street lighting in the road, my father bought one of the old, converted gas lamps off the council for a fiver and it stood, slightly askance from a true perpendicular, like a little evocation of Narnia, and birds would regularly nest beneath its pyramidal top.

He buggered the inside about too, in ways I've already described, so for the last twenty years or so that I knew the place, it was significantly different from the house I'd grown up in. Nonetheless, and despite the fact that I'd had several homes since, after my parents died it was still the predicating home: still my extra, enormous parent, with a few exasperating or embarrassing ways about it, but still with an unquantifiable extra dimension which continued, unchanged and unchangeable, right up to the end. My stepmother recognised this extra dimension too, and the last day she was there with me, after we'd collected all the tiny totemic things she wanted to salvage, as I was backing out of the drive she'd said, with a wistful smile, 'Goodbye, Waitemata.'

Together the house and garden contained smells unchanged since I was tiny, smells I still catch occasionally when I rummage through something I took away from the house, either in the vast oak cupboard my father's grandfather knocked together from cannibalised bits of furniture round a piece of wood he'd found, bearing the legend 'Obediah Pahrington, in the Year of Our Lord 1709', or in a sachet of old photographs, or in my stepmother's handbag, still not quite emptied of its contents since the day she died.

The smell of my stepmother's perfume lingered in our spare room for months after she died, although it's only in my memory that I can smell my father, and his barely notice-able odour of fishpaste.

By the time my father died, the chaotic cornucopia of stuff had been brought under slightly more control than it had displayed in the early 1970s, and the house never really got to be like my grandmother's house, but I was told by another of my stepmother's cousins, who visited my parents from her home in Geneva the year before they died, that when she'd asked my father if he'd considered moving, he crumpled his eyebrows and said it was all now just too much.

In Philip K. Dick's dystopian science-fiction novel *Do Androids Dream of Electric Sheep?*, in the aftermath of a terrible war which has resulted in the almost complete disappearance of all non-robotic animals, human cities are slowly being inun-dated by what their inhabitants called 'kipple'. These are the bits and bobs of everyday life, the dingbats and doofahs people take for granted and then discard, but which are now creeping ever forward and encroaching like shifting sand dunes of crap. I think that's probably how my father viewed the contents of Waitemata, although he did his best to shore up against the encroachment.

For years he'd been offloading stuff on to me and, to a lesser extent, my sister. I remember when Anna and I moved into our first house together, he and my stepmother turned up to look at the house, but with their car, a four-wheeler fibreglass Reliant Kitten my father had bought because it couldn't rust away like the old A40, crammed with crap. This included about sixty or seventy wire coat hangers and the old gas fire with the magical little door into another world. When I asked him why on earth he was dumping all this stuff on me, he said he thought the fact that we had a cellar meant that was a better place for the junk than his house, and he was probably right. When we moved a few years later, I deliberately left the gas fire down in the cellar as a little offering to the household gods.

But even this slow policy of redistribution did little, in the end, to diminish the volume of stuff left in the house, and particularly in the loft. If, after my parents had died, my sister and I had simply moved Waitemata's entire contents to a warehouse or something, and then called in a forensics team, I can't imagine what conclusions they would have come to. There were obvious things, like chairs and tables and beds, and then there were the hundreds of tools, thousands of nuts and bolts and screws and nails, as well as around 130 clocks, most of them early electric ones, some of them in several bits. There were my stepmother's clothes, and almost as many of my father's, with a surprisingly large number of jackets, shirts and ties, occupying all the drawer and wardrobe space in my old bedroom. Then there were magazines, all carefully catalogued in cardboard box files, covering subjects including virology, microbiology, horology, model engineering and the various enterprises of the large number of companies he and my stepmother owned shares in. So there were also hundreds of share certificates, as well as utility bills and other official correspondence. Forgetting the linen, the dozens and dozens of tea towels, the kitchen utensils, the cupboards full of Pyrex, the souvenir mugs of King's College Hospital my stepmother would buy each year when she went to the annual King's Nurses' Reunion, the pads of Post-it notes, the cardboard drawers full of elastic bands, plastic bags, books of stamps, stationery, pencils, rubbers, calendars, bookmarks, batteries and so on, there was also the weird stuff, like the bottles of horse blood.

In addition to the box of human bones in the loft, up there there were also old board games from the 1930s, old textbooks from the 1950s, teach-yourself-French gramophone records, centrifuges, demijohns, wine- and beer-making kits, doll's house furniture, old gravy jars, broken clockwork kitchen timers, lacrosse sticks, golf clubs, reflex hammers, tin boxes full of the components of a lead toy garden, limbless lead soldiers, bags of teddy bears, bits of the old model railway and some of the old cardboard 00-scale houses he'd made on holiday, TV sets, mysterious electronic equipment, my father's scientific papers, a full run of the first year of *Penthouse* plus about thirty copies of *Forum* from the late sixties and early seventies (I'd known that they were up there for years), old suitcases (from which my father had thoughtlessly steamed off all the old luggage labels from the fifties and sixties), old Christmas decorations, rolls of garish retro wallpapers from around 1975, dozens of Matchbox toy cars, their packets purposefully unopened and wrapped in plastic, several dozen old milk bottles, a case for microscope slides (but no microscope), lampshades, lamps, ancient waffle irons, garden irrigators, cardboard clock kits, some empty whisky bottles, a fireman's axe, an old Quality Street tin containing the remnants of my grandfather's treasured coin collection, bags of my father's curling photographs, a reel-to-reel tape recorder, hundreds more tools, corrosive liquids, some old oil paintings I'd never finished when I was about sixteen, a decorating table, parts of an intercom system, a huge old model boat, a beautiful pre-First World War German toy fort, my Great-Uncle Jak's tram, rolls of polystyrene for purposes of insulation, but never used, ranks of dexion shelving, a broken Meccano clock, some of the glass scientific instruments my father had made when he used, briefly, to attend glass-blowing evening classes, my stepmother's old dolls, half restored at the antique-restoration classes they attended together but never finished because their teacher ran off with one of the other students, photographic developing trays, lengths of lead piping, wood, steel and other metals, curtain rails, a disembodied cathode ray tube, binoculars, several telescopes, a full run of *Practical Wireless* from 1956 to 1962, a strongbox containing, among other things, my father's will, which my sister eventually found six months after he died, a little wooden box full of wire-and-cotton-wool Easter chicks, a clockwork drunk I'd been bought at Glasgow airport when I was five or six, some silver-ware awarded in Ashton-under-Lyne for gardening to people whose names were a mystery to me, a sonically powered toy spaceship I remember my father bringing home one day when I was about ten, which he'd bought in Leather Lane and never gave to me, some execrable examples of my grandmother's taste in ghastly kitsch, a gargantuan electric typewriter, some rather nice veneered wooden jewel boxes, what we assumed was a tank for electrolysis, an empty plastic cider barrel, a blue ceramic wall-mounted seahorse flower vase I remember being bought in Capri in 1967, coils of wire and hosepipes, a bulky 1970s stereo system on which I'd first listened to *Wish You Were Here* by Pink Floyd, some older gramophones, including a broken, hornless wind-up one for 78s and several dozen packets of surgical catgut expropriated from the London Hospital and with an expiry date in 1962.

In my father's house there were many mansions, most of them full to overflowing. As far as the hypothetical forensics team is concerned, they could have detected several crimes, including petty pilfering in the case of the catgut and the horse blood, which I finally found out is the perfect medium for growing viral cultures, though what my father thought he was going to do with it at home I've no real idea. He once told me that he'd taken the fireman's axe after its original owner had been killed during the war, and the old Quality Street tin of coins was evidence of something which isn't exactly a crime, but isn't entirely laudable either. As we sorted out the house, I found several notebooks cataloguing my grandfather's coin collection, but when Anna and I started valuing what was left for purposes of probate, we soon realised that my father must have flogged all the coins that were worth anything years before, and then dumped the rest in the tin, put them up in the loft and forgotten about them.

But perhaps I'm being over-fastidious about filial piety, and my father was just facing up to the fact that it's always best to live for the here and now. I remember how he'd say, in his typical way, that he didn't see the bloody point in cleaning the car's back window because he wasn't interested in seeing where he'd already been.

It was only after his mother died and he inherited her money that my father could start getting really serious about his clock collection and begin the process of building it up into something quite extraordinary, from which he derived immense pleasure and considerable pride. After some initial interest from the Science Museum (who eventually said they were very interested in several of the pieces, but didn't have the budget to acquire them), we sold the clocks through Christie's, which is almost what he would have wanted, although neither my sister nor I had the time or expertise to trickle them out on to the market over years and years, as he'd really wanted us to. There was one he was particularly proud of, the patent model for an early Synchronome electric clock, which he'd bought for about six hundred quid and which he kept away from the rest of the collection, in the spare bedroom, in case any other clock enthusiast came round and found out that he had it. I think he would have been pleased that it sold for over a thousand pounds more than the estimated price.

When I first saw the Christie's catalogue for the sale, full of photographs of all those clocks, removed from the domestic context I'd known them in for so many years, I felt the pricking at the back of my eyeballs again. His clocks, lots 1–111, were in a section all of their own, prefaced by a little biography I'd written of my father which was illustrated by a photograph of him in his academic robes. My sister and I divided the money between us, and I used some of it to fix various of the clocks I'd kept, and another part of it to buy a clock myself, an unsold lot from the same auction. It's a Soviet ship's chronometer, one of those chunky round silver-coloured wall-mounted things, with 'CCCP' in the middle of the dial. It's clockwork, and the best thing of all about it is that it has a twenty-four-hour dial, so while the big hand sweeps round the minutes of the hour as usual, the little hand moves at half its normal speed, marking off twenty-four hours instead of twelve. This means it's almost impossible to tell the time from it, because half past ten in the morning looks like half past five, and so on. It's in our kitchen now, and it keeps good time, and I like to think that it's a nice little monument not only to my father's enthusiasm, but also to his sense of the ridiculous and the now obvious unlikelihood that the Soviet Union would ever have invaded Western Europe, not least of all because they'd never have been able to synchronise their watches.

A few of the clocks didn't sell, and my sister and I went to Christie's warehouse in Nine Elms to pick them up. In the shadows by one of the service doors there was a stuffed American bison, about nine feet long and seven feet high, likewise unsold at a recent auction. It was only with an immense effort of self-control that I didn't buy it on the spot.

It took us months and months to clear the house, and we didn't do too much while my stepmother was still alive, even though she'd abandoned the place several months before she died. Occasionally my sister and I would go there to try and sort things out, and we started off quite well. My sister managed to sell our father's ludicrous 1976 Reliant Kitten easily enough, despite the fact that neither of us could get it into reverse gear, but there are pockets of enthusiasm for almost everything out there if you only look. She sold it to someone who was clearly relishing the prospect of fixing it more than the embarrassment of driving it. We got the clocks into storage early on as well, and the man from Christie's had a friend who was setting up a clock workshop, who took almost all the tools, my father's clock books, the catgut, the centrifuge and the copies of *Forum* (which he said were for his accountant). Later, a couple of men who run a memorabilia store in Greenwich Market bought a job lot of the rolls of old wallpaper, some light fittings, some Venetian glass horses' heads which had remained unopened since my parents had bought them on another scientific junket in 1974, some lino, the stereo, all except two of my father's ties, which I kept, and a rather beautiful retro lilo pump from the early 1960s, illustrated with an idealised painting of a beach scene, the colour slightly too bright, the people slightly too perfect. Someone else took some medical textbooks, the old slide drawer and a sinister-looking culture we found at the back of a cupboard, and a few days before we finally sold Waitemata a hospice in Kenton took away a lot of the kitchen equipment and most of the furniture, including the truly horrible coffee table, its round glass top covering an enormous and functioning clock dial.

And yet, with each of these erosions, the emptying house still seemed horribly full and hauntingly unchanged, even after it became spookily silent once all the familiar ticks and clonks had left along with the clocks. Notelets written on in either of my parents' handwriting were still stuck up by the phone, a pile of box files would still contain other notes my father had made on how to wire a clock or programme his mobile phone, along with all the other tiny things, and each time I went there on my own a terrible kind of inertia would set in and I'd find it almost impossible to sort anything at all, and

I'd ring my sister just so she could tell me to get out before the doom and gloom set in too deeply.

One of our problems, being dutiful children as well as executors, was what to do with the little things my father had treasured, and had brought into the house with his usual twin mantras, that 'It'll come in useful to someone one day' and that 'It's bound to be worth something to someone one day'. When I heard him say the second of these I'd often reply that the stars would have cooled, the earth finally tipped off its axis and humans evolved beyond recognition by the time that happened, but posthumously I couldn't bring myself to be so flip and contemptuous about his excitement. But it was almost inevitable that all the Matchbox toy cars, sold as 'collectibles' and unopened so as not to lose their value, would be worth nothing, because they were governed by the universal if oxymoronic law which states that if you collect something because it's collectible, because thousands of other people are doing the same it therefore ceases to be collectible, because only the things which no one collects are truly collectible.

This law didn't quite apply to the collection of milk bottles, all twenty-five of them carefully wrapped in tissue paper. They had weirdly beautiful logos of arcane design printed on their sides, and as my father had always insisted that they must be worth something to somebody, and as it was my duty to his estate to get as much for them as possible, I got on the Internet and quickly found Milk Bottle News, a website designed for lovers of the milk bottle, and emailed the man who runs it. He was so excited that he phoned me up, asking for more details, so I spent a whole morning in the emptying house carefully cataloguing the bottles ('diagonal sans-serif farm logo, with scrolls; tableau of cows beneath a fingerpost reading "To Health Via Milk"; slight chip on rim') and then emailed him the results. He replied that I'd been very thorough, but to be honest they were all a bit late for him, but someone would probably pay me about a pound a bottle. I resisted my first temptation to leave them on the doorstep, and we now use some of them as flower vases.

Then there were the photographs, bags and bags full of them stuffed in cupboards, quite apart from all the albums filled with pictures of their trips to Greenland or up the Yellow River or at Niagara Falls or in Mexico or standing in front of the national monument in Tirana, towards the end of Enver Hoxha's reign of terror. A lot of these were of people I didn't know, many of whom were now almost certainly dead. Nonetheless, and despite the fact that a part of me thinks that if you throw away a photograph (just like if you throw away a book) somewhere someone's soul will die, I had to throw away most of them. I decided which ones to keep mostly on aesthetic grounds, like the picture of my stepmother when she'd worked briefly as an assistant matron at a geriatric hospital in Dulwich in the late 1960s, surrounded by old dears and codgers sitting looking grumpy or confused and wearing Easter bonnets. There was another photo of my stepmother when she'd been a ward sister, and it's of an old hospital ward, taken in black and white, with a Christmas tree and nativity scene just discernible at the back of the room. The picture is taken from the other end of the ward, with the rows of beds lined up against the two walls, stretching away to give the perspective. In each bed a young woman is smiling to the camera and holding a baby. I also found a photograph of my father, taken when he must have been around fifteen or sixteen. I think it was taken in Interlaken in Switzerland, and it shows my father standing with his parents, all of them on skis, their fists round the end of ski poles. Between my father and his father there stands a man dressed up as a polar bear, also on skis. My grandfather looks prosperous and sternly authoritative, while my father looks embarrassed and bored.

In the end, Dawne's son Paul took away everything that no one else could possibly want. It took him and his employees in his waste-management firm a day and a half to clear Waitemata, and in the end they dumped two tons of the acquired detritus of several lifetimes, the old umbrellas, beds, fridges, hosepipes, rickety tables, dexion shelves, fondue sets, old paperbacks, knitting patterns, RSPB bookmarks and Whiskas cat calendars, lengths of dowelling and carrier bags, blankets and bell jars, photograph albums and old scientific papers and stupid trays embossed with a vile floral pattern. It was looking at that going into yet another bin bag that actually triggered the tears, exposing the heartbreak I was feeling.

But what can you do? I didn't have Osborne House at my disposal, and legally cremating my father and my stepmother inside and along with the house wasn't an option. And anyway, you can't memorialise the people you love who've died just by fetishising the material acquisitions they made when they were alive. I kept reminding myself, as the house got emptier and emptier until it reached the condition it was in when I dreamed about the dik-dik, that our memories of the dead should serve as their memorial, and that's the way each of us is granted a small stretch of immortality, until there's no one left alive to remember us.

Months earlier, just after my father had died, I discovered some of the things he'd obviously thought worth keeping, rather than just acquiring and hoarding. It was when we still couldn't find his will, and I was searching through his desk. He'd sorted through it himself not long beforehand, which was when he found the journal he thought his father had kept at the end of the First World War and which he'd given me the day we went together into Northwick Park. I didn't get round to reading it for about a year and a half, and it turned out that it had been written by his grandfather, visiting my father's father in northern France in early 1919. It contains extraordinary testimony about the aftermath of war, describing villages and towns completely destroyed, Chinese coolies clearing away all the old weapons and artillery for salvage, German prisoners of war digging up the corpses of French soldiers for reburial elsewhere, as well as a stroll my grandfather and great-grandfather had across no-man's-land at Passchendaele, and it's clear that my father never read it himself.

He'd offloaded that on to me, just in case I was interested, because he obviously wasn't. But he'd kept a lot of other stuff he must have valued, and which I've kept too. He'd kept his grandfather's cards, embossed with his name; he kept all his diplomas and certificates, along with group photographs of himself at school, university, on Sir Geoffrey Keynes's team at Bart's, at the Public Health Laboratory Service and other places besides. He'd also kept his father's diplomas and certificates, and his wives': these included my mother and stepmother's nursing qualifications as well as my mother's swimming certificate which she was awarded in her thirties (I remember her going to the swimming lessons) and my stepmother's O-level certificate, for getting an A grade in Spanish after going to evening classes the same year I took my O levels.

He'd also kept his references, including the letter from 1959 from his boss at the Public Health Laboratory, declining his offer to rescind his resignation, saying that he seemed to be better suited temperamentally to research, and addressing him, at the beginning of the letter, as 'Dear Rowson'. There was another letter, about viruses, written in 1962 by a South African he'd met in transit at Kiev airport.

There was other stuff, including slide rules, log tables, elegantly labelled old boxes of staples and paper clips, German banknotes from the time of the Great Inflation, two old flint-lock pistols, several long anal thermometers and three copies of *The Times*. One contained my mother's death notice, so was the same edition my teacher had read when I thought he was showing off; another contained my grandmother's death notice; the third included a letter written to the editor by a group of eminent scientists, protesting at the way my father's Institute was being closed down and how he, referred to as someone with an international reputation, was being forced into early retirement. There was also my mother's old address book, and several address books of my father's, clearly from the 1940s and 50s, containing the addresses and phone numbers of a surprisingly large number of pubs. There was also a box containing a photograph album of my parents' wedding in 1954, with pictures of my father looking amused and embarrassed in the picture where his mother-in-law is holding his hand, as well as a contact sheet of photos of my sister as a baby, and a pile of letters my father had received after my mother died.

These included letters from friends, acquaintances, head teachers, colleagues, the doctors who'd been treating my mother at the London Hospital, letters from my mother's family regretting the rift in the family and saying how they'd always remember my mother as they'd known her in the old days. There was also a letter from the mother of my best friend at the time, a boy called Clive Brazier whom I haven't seen since we met again five years after going to different secondary schools, when we were about seventeen or eighteen, and succeeded in thoroughly alienating each other with our respective adolescent poses. As I sat there reading through these, I started to cry again. And then I found an old leather writing case, with his initials embossed on the front, by the handle. My spirits improved, because I thought I'd found where he'd left his will, but instead I found some far more interesting things.

Apart from his and my stepmother's passports and some old bank books, in one of the case's internal pockets there was an envelope containing birth certificates for my father, my mother, my stepmother and my great-aunt; my grandparents' and parents' and great-aunt's marriage certificates; my grandmother's and mother's and great-aunt's death certificates, as well as Christopher's birth and death certificates. There were also documents relating to my adoption and my sister's, which might have given me a shock if my parents hadn't been wise enough to operate a policy of full disclosure from early on. There was also his wartime identity card and, folded up very small, a sheet of lined paper on which were written, in my father's familiar sloping handwriting, four poems. It's pretty clear that he wrote them down after my mother died, and as I can find no trace of them anywhere else and they contain some of my father's typical spelling mistakes, I think he must have written them himself, although I may be wrong.

Here they are, in the way he wrote them out.

The willows moved in a silent dance
To the tune of death
In the autumn breath
And the end came on with a furtive glance.
The river lay there waiting the man
She knew must come for she alone was young
Being borne of death were time began
And the end came on as his song was sung.
Next time there may be no choice for me
So I turned from the scene & the welcoming smile
To look what there was in the world to see
And there I found what I felt behind
But I lost what I had & after a while
The end came on with nothing beyond.

The night and day were wholly spent
In building from a memory
A woman so perfect she could not be.

314

Time and distance with each moment
Made every fault a perfect thing;
A [nd?] every flaw a master touch
Creating beauty far too much
For any poet to sing.

The future can destroy the past,
And if it does there ends my dream,
But if it should withstand the blast
She's far to [*sic*] perfect it would seem.
My pedistal [*sic*] girl is lost to me
By the height of her shrine and the depth of the sea

Christopher, how nice to be Christopher
whose voice alone they know
and only she knows more.
His voice is enough for them,
but the cat by the fire &
she know more of him, who
alone in the desert [the alternative word 'waste' is written
   below] can stand
the Sun & not leave his bones
to mark the trail they
travelled together.

One half reaches the brink of death
And the other stays behind;
One half goes with the turning world
And the other stays behind.
Failure and partial failure
With never a change of course.
There's never a death & never a birth
But life & life, & life alone.

I found these poems between my father's death and his funeral, so I copied them out in my best copperplate and put them in an envelope along with a letter I wrote to my dead father. A lot of the letter was taken up with a lengthy apology for doing something as senseless as writing to a dead person, when he and I both knew that there's no such thing as life after death; I then thanked him and told him I loved him and said, in the unlikely event that some trace of him remained in the other-worldly beyond, I'd appreciate some sign or other reminding me where he'd put his will. By the time I finished, I could hardly see the words I was writing.

My sister put the envelope in his coffin when she went to see his body, which the jobsworth undertakers had been too impatient to let her do the day he'd died. To allow for that, we'd gone to the expense of having him embalmed, like Lenin, an outlay he would have deeply resented. My sister told me that he was barely recognisable.

I've never asked my sister what my father was wearing in his coffin, and I don't know what my stepmother was wearing in hers either, a few months later. But I remember being told that my mother wore her wedding dress, and I remember being shown the little blue teddy bear that my father put in the coffin beside her, and I remember the slightly startled expression in its button eyes and on its loose thread mouth. It was cremated with her, and presumably its ashes still mingle with hers.

I also found two letters and a telegram. All dated from the 1940s. One of the letters was a long, rambling description of a trip to Dublin undertaken by my father's old university friend whom I met at his funeral. I showed it to him later, and he said he found it deeply gauche and rather embarrassing. The other one was from a young woman called Robin, and was gossipy in tone, talking about the shortcomings of people I assume were their mutual friends, and hints at an easy intimacy between the writer and the recipient. I have absolutely no idea who Robin was.

The telegram is unsigned, and was sent from Cambridge to my father's digs when he was a junior doctor. All it says is 'THE WISE MAN BELIEVES IN COPULATION WITHOUT POPULATION'.

We sent notice of my father's death to everyone in my step-mother's address book, which was the one they both used. I did the same after my stepmother died. However, in the inter-vening period she mentioned several times that each Christmas my father received a card from someone whom I'll call Sandy, whom my stepmother didn't know, and whose address she didn't have. She was anxious, in order to keep everything in order, that this person should know about my father dying, but I couldn't find an address book with any name like that in it.

Only months later, long after they were both dead and I was sorting again through my father's desk, did I find the right book, with the right name, the original surname crossed out and altered, with several addresses, all of them except the last one also crossed out. By this time I thought I'd worked out who Sandy was: I thought she'd been one of my father's research students from the 1970s, so I wrote to her, telling her my news and saying who I'd guessed she was. I also enclosed a copy of the address I'd read out at my father's funeral.

She wrote back, thanking me for my letter, and disabusing me as to who she was. She wrote that she'd known my father in London in the late 1940s, that they'd gone out together for a while and that she'd almost married him, but wrote that it was her fault that she hadn't. She wrote that they stayed in touch, so she knew about him marrying my mother, and

Christopher's death, and how our parents had adopted my sister and me, and she also knew about my mother's death. And she wrote that my father had come to see her the night before he married my stepmother and had said that she was going to look after us all.

Other people's lives are like unfinished jigsaws, with a variable number of pieces missing. Usually the missing pieces don't matter, and you can get a clear view of what the puzzle's meant to be from what you've got, so there's no real point grovelling round on the floor looking for them. I can't see the point of speculating on my father's behalf about what might have been, or even dwelling too long on the implications of that telegram, if only because there's now no way of knowing whether it was just a joke, a warning, ironic congratulations or deathly commiserations about some unknowable and almost certainly fictional tragedy that ended in a back-street abortionist's or possibly another adoption agency.

Although we found the will, we didn't find the human skull he promised me, or the microscope my sister had always coveted, or his ARP warden's helmet, or any bankrolls of roubles or stashes of Soviet gold, or troves of other stuff that probably wouldn't have meant much anyway.

In the summer of the year after they'd died, and after we'd sold Waitemata, we had my father and stepmother's ashes interred in Stanmore churchyard. It was a very hot July day, the culmination of a lengthy email exchange I'd had with the local vicar, Alison Christian. I'd smiled when I first learned what her name was, and for some reason or other it made me think of a modern Anglican pack of Happy Families, with Reverend Christian the Vicar, Mr Christian the Vicar's husband, and so on. She'd told me during this exchange that they didn't allow the scattering of ashes in the churchyard, although my stepmother, aware of the fact that with the addition of my father to my mother and Christopher the grave would be full, had specifically requested that her ashes be scattered nearby. But Rev. Christian had found a compromise, and said that there was room for my stepmother's ashes to be poured into the plot, even if there was no room for her casket. We'd parked up the road in Green Lane, just opposite Waitemata, which I noticed with some pleasure the property speculator neighbour had still failed to sell on.

All around were the sites of my childhood recklessness, the gardens we'd trespassed in, bordered by the fences we'd scrambled over, the fields we'd rolled down with the ditches and gullies we'd collapsed in, and nearby the ponds whose wafer-thin ice we'd deliberately walked across, before sloshing home in the gathering dusk, our sodden socks slipping down into the squelching muck at the bottom of our wellies. And just down the road was the sweetshop where, around 1970, I'd brushed past a grubby urchin who'd actually shouted 'Bluebottle!' at a policeman on the other side of the road, just like something out of an Ealing Comedy. The sweetshop was now the estate agent's which was signally failing to sell my parents' house.

In the churchyard, the old seventeenth-century church, abandoned to ruination when they built the new one in the 1830s, stood as stark testimony to the way things had changed. When I was a child it was an ivy-clad ruin, with a rather inadequate sign nailed halfway up one of its dilapidated red-brick walls warning passers-by that it was a dangerous structure. That, of course, hadn't stopped us constantly trying to get in, and I think that once we even succeeded. But English Heritage or someone had long since taken charge, shored up its crumbling walls and made it safe, stripped away all the ivy and nettles around its fallen towers and the bulk of the ancient family tombs inside, and the mud and muck and squashed grass had been replaced by neat and tidy heritage gravel, thoughtfully strewn over safety-conscious hard core.

Just beyond the western boundary of the churchyard, past some tilting Victorian gravestones, the thin litter of fallen yew leaves mixed in with the rubbishy podsol of dry earth, flecks of mud and scraps of stick and the loose stacks of grass cuttings, was what had been the old RAF base when I was a child. Along with Bentley Priory up towards Bushey, they'd fought the Battle of Britain from here, and later on had played a part in the possibility of Apocalypse which, distantly but constantly, had dogged my parents almost all their adult lives up until the end of the Cold War.

That was the world, under permanent threat of nuclear annihilation, that I'd been born into, and although we all know that the Past can be the most seductive siren imaginable, I find it hard to get too elegiac about it. Everyone tends to look back at their childhood and willingly allow themselves to be sucked into a comforting bog of nostalgia, where all the colours are slightly brighter and life more innocent, but maybe my generation should balance *Listen With Mother*, Sooty and Sweep, jamboree bags and three old pence for a bottle of pop against the constant likelihood of being carbonised down to radioactive dust in an instant.

The two churches had been built on the prediction of another apocalypse which we're still waiting for, and if you think about it, in its civilised mutation the human species can't get enough of the promise of apocalypses. My parents had lived through the threat and reality of war, the threat but unreality of another war, and in its wake all those subsequent little apocalypses, from environmental catastrophe to Aids to global warming, all of them there just to make us feel bad about ourselves. I suppose a general fear of universal catastrophe is just another way we cope with the prospect of death, comforting ourselves that it's going to happen to everyone else and they're going to die too, preferably at the same time, so we don't have to go alone into the dark unknown. On that hot sunny day, with its snide, unstated insinuation that the sunshine on the dappled lawns, kissing the lichen on the grave-stones, was also melting the polar ice caps, there was also the temptation to think that at least my parents had been spared whatever new fresh hell history had to offer, but I think that that's a generalisation beyond the personal that goes too far. There's no reason whatsoever to view each individual life in the context of human history, but just in terms of itself, and we shouldn't live our lives as just a spectator sport. Anyway, the RAF base was now an estate of ticky-tacky houses and flats for commuters with their bus-sized cars.

I went and introduced myself to Rev. Christian, a nice, friendly and kind woman, and she introduced me to Clifford, the sexton, who was nominally in charge of the actual busi-ness of committal, but who Rev. Christian told me in a whis-pered aside wasn't at all well, so her husband had actually excavated the grave and would fill it in again, but I should give Clifford the £20 tip anyway. And then I joined our little party, made up of Anna, Fred, Rose, my sister, her husband and their two sons, my step-aunt and her son and daughter. Some of us started crying, although I didn't, and I think this was because I'd spent so long with my sister in the house clearing it out, and the house had become so caught up with my memories of my parents and my childhood, that I'd already wrung the last of the grief out of me. This was a month or so before the second wave of grief hit me.

Rev. Christian conducted a little service before asking us all if we wanted to say something, and I remember Anna sniffing back her tears, her mouth downturned, as she said how kind and generous my parents had always been, while

Rose clung to her side. I said something about how funny my father was, and how I was conscious that, somehow or other, they were still both almost palpably among us, and the others said stuff too, though I can't now remember what it was.

Then poor, sick, old Clifford, his robes of office flapping slightly in the gentlest of breezes, placed my father's casket in the grave and then poured out my stepmother's ashes next to it, although the slight breeze carried part of her off on to his shoes and the cuffs of his trousers, so at least partially we fulfilled her wishes to be scattered.

But before then, with the best of intentions, Rev. Christian had departed from the strict form of words in the prayer book and began to say that we shouldn't see this as an end, but just as a staging post to eternal life. I bridled slightly as she continued, asking us all to think of our earthly lives as being like a tadpole before it becomes a frog, or a bulb before it flowers into a daffodil, or a caterpillar before it breaks out of its cocoon to be transformed into a beautiful butterfly.

Although I couldn't stop myself from thinking about sandwiches transfiguring into turds.

I had a strange dream the night before I married Anna. I was in the little terraced house we'd just bought in New Cross, although it was strangely if subtly different, as things often are in dreams. I'd just come in through the front door, and found to my horror that everyone I'd ever known was there for a party, the idiots I'd been at school with when I was five, and when I was ten, and when I was fifteen, and everyone else as well, and as I pushed my way through the melee, they'd each turn round, a glass in their hand, demanding rather petulantly to know why I hadn't invited them to my wedding. I remember that in the dream I kept smiling and offering limp excuses about numbers and how I couldn't be expected to ask everyone, as I tried to sidle, apologetically, back through the house. I finally managed to reach the kitchen at the back of the house, where my future mother-in-law was standing on her own and looking severe. In the dream she told me to make sure that I'd washed my testicles thoroughly before I got married to her daughter.

I'm too young to remember the Lady Chatterley Trial, with its comforting assertion of the potency of the Unspeakable Word, but I'm old enough to remember the Beatles' first LP. I remember when *The Likely Lads* first appeared on TV, and I'm also aware of the paradigmic shifts going on all around me between that series and *Whatever Happened to the Likely Lads?* seven years later, quite apart from the fact that my mother died almost exactly halfway between the two. There have been even greater changes since then and now, when both series are likely to turn up, in the middle of the night, on UK Gold.

I said earlier that everyone reaches the imago stage, when they're fully formed, at different times. My mother was probably at her best as a little girl in America during the war, although she carried on being at her best, in her own way, and maybe would have got better had she lived. For my stepmother, it's clear that Argentina and the war marked her transformation into her imago phase, and she stayed like that, not changing much for the next sixty or so years. I'm not sure when it happened to my father. I think maybe it was a slow process of unending metamorphosis that carried on throughout his life. But who can say?

And who can say that Christopher and Naomi didn't achieve their own imago, in the tiny amount of time they had? Each life justifies itself, however long or short it is, not in any wider universal or theological sense, but just because it is: neither a good thing nor a bad thing; just a thing.

I tend to think of my parents within the context they lived in the 1960s and 70s, not because those were the decades that defined them, but because that was when they played their part in defining me.

Recently, like the Soviet Union, the 1970s has been dismissed as a decade of unalloyed awfulness, starting with the Three-Day Week and power cuts and ending with the Winter of Discontent, when, according to a famous and convenient political myth, the dead lay unburied. I was almost twenty at the time, and I have no memory whatsoever of corpses rotting in the streets, like some scene from the Thirty Years War (or all the forgotten wars we've been having far more recently). And my memory of the power cuts of the early seventies is a memory of quiet excitement at adventures with candlelight and another instance of my father's practical inventiveness. I remember watching *The Benny Hill Show* on one of our old black-and-white portable TVs which my father had wired up to a car battery, and how the picture started to narrow from left and right as the battery ran down, until it falteringly, vertically occupied the central three inches of the screen.

I don't take that as a metaphor for anything.

A year or so ago I saw a newspaper report that suggested that the people of England were happiest in the summer of 1976. The managerialists and devotees of the free market, who tacitly insist that we can only be happy when we're shopping and when we have an infinite choice of things we don't need, must have been surprised if not shocked by that finding. After all, we had 25 per cent inflation, the unions were running the country (although I still don't see why they shouldn't have), we were in the middle of a drought, you couldn't buy anything which didn't fall to pieces in your hands and the place was filthy. Then again, it was also the middle of a decade which started with Bowie and Bolan and Pink Floyd, and ended with the Sex Pistols, along with the Muppets and Tom Baker as Dr Who, so what's not to like? And another of my blissful memories is of coming home from my rail trip round Europe in the summer of 1978, dirty and tired and lumbered with a rucksack I very nearly threw into the Channel during my midnight crossing, and I remember going through Dover and sitting on the train through Kent, its fields shrouded in thick smoke, punctuated by streaks of flame along the ground as the stubble burned, and I remember a feeling of elation at being back in grubby, grumpy old England.

But maybe memories are too fractured and fragmented to be reliable indicators of anything, just like dreams. Or, for that matter, like life. In the end, you're born, you live, you fill the empty days as best you can, and then you die. And that's it. But however bleak that may sound to you, it's not so bad, and whatever anyone may tell you, it's infinitely preferable to the alternative.

And in fact it's not bleak at all, because we constantly recreate our lives and the lives of other people by telling stories about them, and the dreams and the memories intermingle as the myths begin to spin round all of us, weaving themselves into a warm, cosy, protective blanket.

I like to think about my parents' lives, all the people they knew and the times they lived through, the babies my mother and stepmother delivered into life and the babies my mother fostered when their tiny lives proved to be a burden to other people, and the other people whose lives may or may not have been saved, by their actions or by my father's research, with or without the unwitting contribution of my pet mice, and about the thin, thin threads connecting all those strangers back to my parents, which inevitably snag for an instant on me on their way. And I like to think about all the stories, known, unknown and unknowable, wrapped around them.

And I like to think about my parents and how they spread their blankets over me.

And I then like to think about how, in a small way, I'm their little victory of nurture over nature.

Actually, I just like to think about my parents.

Here's a last memory of my father. When I was around fourteen or fifteen, one Sunday afternoon some of my stepmother's more distant relations had come round to lunch, and I'd excused myself from the company, saying that I had homework to do, although really I was sneaking upstairs to watch *Casablanca* on the little black-and-white portable TV in my bedroom. My father had always liked Humphrey Bogart; he'd nearly named me after him, and his old university friend whom I'd met at his funeral told me that they'd go and see Bogart movies over and over again, whenever they were on in Cambridge, in the brown gloom of the mid-1940s. Perhaps my father recognised their mythic potency; perhaps he understood that their grainy exaggerations of the realities of human existence served in their small way to make that existence either more bearable or, more likely, enjoyable. Perhaps he just liked them, and that was it. But as I was lying on my bed, about ten minutes into the film, my father came into my room and lay down on the bed beside me and we watched the film together.

Although it's another Bogart film, *The Maltese Falcon*, that sums things up best. After Mary Astor has been led away by the cops, the DA turns to Bogart's character Sam Spade and asks him what the falcon is anyway. Bogart replies, deadpan, but with a hint of contemptuous regret, 'The stuff that dreams are made of.'

All in all, I'm rather pleased they got the quotation wrong.